Pearson Revise

Pearson Edexcel GCSE

German

Revision Workbook

Series Consultant: Harry Smith
Author: Heather Murphy

Audio for Speaking and Listening at your fingertips

Scan the green audio QR codes to immediately launch high-quality recordings of native speakers. These are exam-style tracks for realistic assessment practice and can particularly help you with:

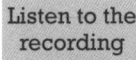

- **Listening: Dictation task practice**
  Listen three times for exam-style practice.
- **Speaking: Read aloud practice**
  Targeted pronunciation practice of sounds helps build your confidence.
- **Speaking: Role play practice**
  Hear the teacher part and speak your answers in the pauses.

Transcripts for all audio files can be accessed here.

Support for longer writing tasks

Space is provided in this Workbook but sometimes you'll need to use your own paper too. Full sample student responses are given in the answer section so that you can self-assess. Remember that there is more than one correct answer for this type of question.

Practice papers

Help to check that you are exam-ready with a full set of practice papers containing exam-style questions for Speaking, Listening, Reading and Writing, for both Foundation and Higher tier.

Higher and Foundation tiers

Questions which only apply to Higher Tier are marked with an

Difficulty scale

The icon next to each exam-style question tells you how difficult it is.

Some questions cover a range of difficulties.

Also available:

The Revision Guide helps you revise vocabulary and grammar with a manageable topic-by-topic approach. Worked example questions and pages on each exam paper will build your skills ready for assessment, and digital resources such as quick quizzes, vocab checks, videos and flashcards are all included!

Pearson Edexcel publishes the only official Sample Assessment Material on its website. The questions in this Workbook have been designed to familiarise you with the type of tasks you may meet in the exam, and are tailored to help you to practise specific skills. Remember that the actual assessments may not look like this.

Contents

My people
1 Physical descriptions
2 Character and personality
3 My family
4 Friends
5 Relationships
6 Dealing with problems
7 Daily routine
8 Clothing and fashion
9 Identity
10 Celebrations
11 When I was younger
12 My life in the future

Health
13 Food and drink
14 Meals at home
15 Shopping for food
16 Eating out
17 A healthy diet
18 Sport
19 Advantages of sport
20 Physical wellbeing
21 Mental wellbeing
22 Feeling unwell
23 Avoiding health risks

Free time
24 Sports stars
25 Hobbies and interests
26 Music and dance
27 Arranging to go out
28 Reading
29 Television
30 Film and cinema

Media and technology
31 Mobile technology
32 Social media
33 Internet
34 Computer games
35 Pros and cons of technology
36 Films on the internet

Local environment
37 My home
38 My town
39 Facilities in town
40 Finding the way
41 Shops and shopping
42 At the market
43 Transport
44 Buying tickets for travel
45 Places of interest near me

Environment
46 The environment
47 Environmental problems
48 The dangers of pollution
49 The natural world
50 Individual actions for the environment
51 How to recycle

My school
52 My school
53 School subjects
54 My teachers
55 The school day
56 School uniform
57 School rules
58 School clubs
59 School trips
60 Homework
61 Stress at school
62 Preparing for exams
63 My ideal school

My future
64 Plans for next year
65 Future studies
66 Future career
67 Pros and cons of some jobs
68 My dream job
69 Gap year
70 Equality and helping others

Tourism
71 Holiday activities
72 Camping
73 Holiday accommodation
74 Other holiday accommodation
75 Making a complaint
76 Pros and cons of travelling
77 Plans for next summer
78 Past holidays
79 Holiday problems
80 Lost property
81 Places to visit
82 Holiday jobs
83 Buying gifts and souvenirs
84 Weather
85 Tourism and the environment

About the exams
86 Practice for Paper 1: Speaking
87 Practice for Paper 1: Speaking
88 Practice for Paper 2: Listening
89 Practice for Paper 2: Listening
90 Practice for Paper 3: Reading
91 Practice for Paper 3: Reading
92 Practice for Paper 4: Writing
93 Practice for Paper 4: Writing

Grammar
94 Gender and plurals
95 Indefinite articles and possessives
96 Nominative and accusative cases
97 Other cases and prepositions
98 Prepositions with the accusative or dative
99 *Dieser*, *jener* and *jeder*
100 Adjective endings
101 Comparative and superlative adjectives
102 Personal pronouns
103 Word order 1
104 Conjunctions
105 Word order 2
106 The present tense
107 Reflexive and separable verbs
108 Irregular verb tables 1
109 Irregular verb tables 2
110 Using irregular verbs in different tenses
111 *Sein* and *haben*
112 Modal verbs in the present tense
113 The perfect tense with *haben*
114 The perfect tense with *sein*
115 The imperfect tense
116 The future tense
117 The conditional

Practice papers
118 Paper 1: Speaking (Foundation)
119 Paper 2: Listening (Foundation)
122 Paper 3: Reading (Foundation)
127 Paper 4: Writing (Foundation)
129 Paper 1: Speaking (Higher)
130 Paper 2: Listening (Higher)
133 Paper 3: Reading (Higher)
138 Paper 4: Writing (Higher)

139 Answers

A small bit of small print
Pearson Edexcel publishes Sample Assessment Material and the Specification on its website. This is the official content and this book should be used in conjunction with it. The questions in this Workbook have been written to help you practise every topic in the book. Remember: the real exam questions may not look like this.

1-to-1 page match with the German Revision Guide ISBN 9781292471679

Had a go ☐ Nearly there ☐ Nailed it! ☐   **My people**

Physical descriptions

Describing friends and family members

1 Alina, Felix and Sascha are describing a friend or family member.

   What do they say?

   Listen to the recording and complete the sentences by putting a cross [×] in the correct box for each question.

(a) Alina's dad is …

☐	**A** tall and slim.
☐	**B** tall and slightly fat.
☐	**C** tall and sporty.

(b) He has …

☐	**A** short black hair.
☐	**B** short grey hair.
☐	**C** short dark brown hair.

(c) Felix's friend is …

☐	**A** smaller than Felix.
☐	**B** thinner than Felix.
☐	**C** taller than Felix.

(d) He has …

☐	**A** dark blue eyes.
☐	**B** brown eyes.
☐	**C** light blue eyes.

(e) Sascha's sister has …

☐	**A** long blonde hair.
☐	**B** a small nose.
☐	**C** green eyes.

> In the Listening exam, use the 5 minutes' preparation time to make a quick note of a few of the key words you might expect to hear. For Q1(a) here, you might note *kleiner / dünner / größer*, so you know what to listen out for.

(5 marks)

> Listen to the recording three times and try doing the following:
> First time: make quick notes.
> Second time: write your answers.
> Third time: check your answers.
> This is one suggestion. Practise and find out the method that works best for you.

Translation

2 Translate the following five sentences **into German**.

   (a) I am sixteen years old and quite tall.

   ....

   (b) I have short blonde hair.

   ....

   (c) My friend has a round face and blue eyes.

   ....

   (d) My brothers are smaller than me.

   ....

   (e) She is beautiful and looks sporty.

   ....

> For Q2(a), you need the *ich* form of the verb *sein*, and for (b), the *ich* form of the verb *haben*. For (c), you'll need an *er / sie / es* form to match *mein Freund* (he) / *meine Freundin* (she).

(10 marks)

1

My people   Had a go ☐   Nearly there ☐   Nailed it! ☐

Character and personality

Writing about yourself

1 Write something about yourself for a survey.

You **must** include the following points:
- what sort of person you are
- what a good friend of yours is like
- how your teachers describe you.

> Remember that in an exam, this question will require a future time frame for bullet point 3. That's not the case here, as you need to focus on character and personality vocabulary and can use the present tense throughout.

Write your answer **in German**. You should aim to write between 40 and 50 words.

....
....
....
....
....

(14 marks)

Read aloud

2 Your new German exchange partner, Chris, has sent you a description of herself.

Read out the text below, then listen to the audio in the Answers section to check your pronunciation.

> Ich denke, dass ich meistens sehr freundlich bin, und ich versuche, zu anderen Leuten immer nett zu sein.
> In der Schule bin ich fleißig, weil ich einige Fächer nicht einfach finde.
> Zu Hause bin ich nicht so gestresst und kann meine Freizeit genießen.
> Meine Eltern finden mich ehrlich und vertrauen mir total.

(8 marks)

> Sounds to take note of here:
> - v – sounds like a soft 'f'
> - z – has a crisp 'ts' sound
> - ei – sounds like the English word 'I'
> - ä – sounds like 'a' and 'e' combined
> - -e – final 'e' is a sounded syllable
> - st – sounds like 'sht'
> - a – can be long or short; in *dass* it's short, but in *total* it's long.
> Listen to the recording to practise these sounds.

Track 2

Listen to the recording

Now play the recording of two questions related to what you have read.

You are expected to say a few words or a short phrase / sentence in response to each question. One-word answers will not be sufficient to gain full marks.

(4 marks)

Had a go ☐ **Nearly there** ☐ **Nailed it!** ☐

My people

My family

My family

1 Read part of Jana's homework project on the subject of family.

> Ich habe eine relativ kleine Familie. Meine Eltern wohnen nicht mehr zusammen, und wir sind vier zu Hause. Es gibt meinen Bruder Ben, meine Mutter, Linda und mich. Wir haben auch eine kleine Katze. Wir sind meistens glücklich zusammen, weil Ben und ich viel gemeinsam haben. Wir sind beide sehr aktiv und sportlich und verbringen viel Zeit zusammen. Unsere Mutter hat lange Arbeitsstunden in einem Geschäft und hat nicht genug Zeit für uns, aber sie liebt uns sehr.

Complete the sentences below.

Put a cross [×] in the correct box for each question.

(a) Jana's family is …
- ☐ **A** quite small.
- ☐ **B** unhappy.
- ☐ **C** quite big.

(b) Jana has …
- ☐ **A** no pets.
- ☐ **B** a cat.
- ☐ **C** a rabbit.

(c) Jana and her brother …
- ☐ **A** don't like sport.
- ☐ **B** have the same interests.
- ☐ **C** don't spend much time together.

(d) Jana's mum …
- ☐ **A** is unemployed.
- ☐ **B** works from home.
- ☐ **C** works long hours.

(4 marks)

Describing a family

2 Describe **ONE** of these pictures. Your description must cover:
- people
- location
- activity. **(8 marks)**

> Start by saying which people you can see in the picture you have chosen. How old are they? What relation might they be to each other? What do they look like? What are they wearing?
>
> Then say where they are. If the picture is taken outside, you can comment on the weather too.
>
> Also comment on what the people are doing.

Picture 1

See this photo in colour

Picture 2

See this photo in colour

Listen to the recording

When you have finished your description, scan the QR code to listen to two questions relating to your chosen picture. Pause the recording between each question to allow yourself time to answer. You are expected to say a few words or a short phrase / sentence in response to each question. One-word answers will not be sufficient to gain full marks.

(4 marks)

3

My people

Had a go ☐ Nearly there ☐ Nailed it! ☐

Friends

Writing about friends

1 Write a response to a survey about friends.

You **must** include the following points:
- details about a good friend or friends
- why friendships are important to you
- what you plan to do with your friends next weekend.

Write your answer **in German**. You should aim to write between 40 and 50 words.

> Opinions are always better if you can explain them using *denn* or *weil*.

> Note that the third bullet point asks for a response in the future time frame. Do this **either** with the normal future tense: *Ich werde mit Freunden ins Kino gehen. Wir werden Tennis spielen.* **Or** simply use a present tense with a future time marker (e.g. *morgen, am Samstag, nächstes Wochenende*): *Am Sonntag gehen wir einkaufen.*

....
....
....
....
....
....
....
....
....
.... **(14 marks)**

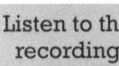

Role play

2 **Setting:** A talk on school radio

Scenario:
- You are talking on school radio about friends.
- Scan the QR code for the teacher's voice. Pause the recording between each prompt to allow yourself time to answer.
- The teacher will play the part of the interviewer and will speak first.
- Your teacher will ask questions **in German** and you must answer **in German**.
- You are expected to say a few words or a short phrase / sentence in response to each prompt. One-word answers will not be sufficient to gain full marks.

> **Task:**
> 1 Say something about your friends.
> 2 Describe your best friend.
> 3 Ask the interviewer about his / her friends.
> 4 Say why friends are important to you.
> 5 Ask the interviewer a question about activities with friends.

(10 marks)

4

Had a go ☐   Nearly there ☐   Nailed it! ☐   **My people**

Relationships

Problems with family

1 Read Robin's blog on a youth problem forum.

> Mit meiner Familie verstehe ich mich im Moment gar nicht gut, und ich finde es sehr schwierig, mit meinen Eltern zu reden. Sie wollen nicht zuhören, wenn ich versuche, mit ihnen ehrlich zu sein. Das Problem? Ich bin ihr Sohn und ich bin schwul. Ich habe auch einen netten Freund, den ich liebe, und das können sie nicht akzeptieren. Natürlich möchte ich ein besseres Verhältnis zu meinen Eltern haben, aber das scheint unmöglich zu sein.

Answer the following questions **in English**. You do not need to write in full sentences.

(a) Describe Robin's current relationship with his parents. (**2** details)

.... **(2 marks)**

(b) What happens when he tries to be honest with them?

.... **(1 mark)**

(c) What does Robin say is the problem? (**2** details)

.... **(2 marks)**

(d) What can't his parents accept? (**2** details)

.... **(2 marks)**

(e) What would Robin like to have?

.... **(1 mark)**

> Look at any indications provided about how much information you should give. For Q1(c), there are two aspects to the problem and you should mention them both for 2 marks.

Translation

2 Translate the following sentences **into English**.

(a) Ich habe viele nette Freunde.

....

(b) Ein guter Freund von mir ist sehr intelligent und fleißig.

....

(c) Ich mag ihn, weil er immer Zeit für mich hat.

....

(d) Wir machen jeden Tag unsere Hausaufgaben zusammen.

....

(e) Gestern haben wir Computerspiele gespielt.

.... **(10 marks)**

> Words you might overlook here are *nette, sehr, immer, unsere* – this is because the sentence would still make sense without them, but it would not be fully translated.
>
> Time markers can give you further clues to the tense, so pay attention to them – in sentence (e) *Gestern* (yesterday) clearly has to be followed by a past tense verb.

My people

Had a go ☐   Nearly there ☐   Nailed it! ☐

Dealing with problems

Picture task

See this photo in colour

You can often use *Es gibt* (there is / are) or *Ich sehe* (I can see) to get started.

Remember that you can describe the appearance of the people, their clothes, where they are and what they are doing.

1 Describe the photo. Write four short sentences **in German**.

   .... **(2 marks)**

   .... **(2 marks)**

   .... **(2 marks)**

   .... **(2 marks)**

Describing relationship problems

2 Describe **ONE** of these pictures.

   Your description must cover:
   - people
   - location
   - activity.   **(8 marks)**

Picture 1

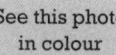

See this photo in colour

Picture 2

See this photo in colour

Choose the picture you think gives you more to say, not the one you like best.

Once you have chosen, make some bullet point notes to use as a rough guide, but don't be tempted to write a script and read it out.

Good picture starting points are:
- How many people, male or female, young or old, who they might be
- What they look like, what they are wearing, whether they are happy or sad
- Where they are, indoors or outdoors, in a particular room, in town, in a cinema, etc.
- What they are doing, eating, playing, talking about or laughing about. Are they swimming, working, arguing … ?

Remember that in the exam you will be describing pictures which are in colour, so it's good to practise this.

Listen to the recording

When you have finished your description, scan the QR code to listen to two questions relating to your chosen picture. Pause the recording between each question to allow yourself time to answer. You are expected to say a few words or a short phrase / sentence in response to each question. One-word answers will not be sufficient to gain full marks.   **(4 marks)**

Had a go ☐ Nearly there ☐ Nailed it! ☐

My people

Daily routine

My typical day

1. Write to a German friend about a typical day.

   You **must** include the following points:
   - your weekday morning routine
   - your breakfast
   - how you got to school yesterday
   - what you will do this weekend.

   Write your answer **in German**. You should aim to write between 80 and 90 words.

   > It's fine to answer some points in more detail than others, as long as you cover all the points.
   >
   > Keep an eye on the word count. You can exceed the recommended number of words, but it's best to focus on quality and accuracy rather than quantity.

   ....
   ....
   ....
   ....
   ....
   ....
   ....
   ....
   ....
   ....
   ....

   (18 marks)

Read aloud

2. Yusuf, your friend, has sent you some information about his daily life.

   Read out the text below, then listen to the audio in the Answers section to check your pronunciation.

   > Ich stehe immer spät auf.
   > Ich ziehe mich schnell an.
   > Zum Frühstück esse ich zwei Brötchen und Obst.
   > Um Viertel vor sieben muss ich das Haus verlassen.
   > Dann fahre ich mit dem Rad zur Schule.

   (8 marks)

   > Listen to these sounds to help you get the pronunciation right:
   > - *st* – say 'sht'
   > - *ä* – imagine an 'a' with an 'e' sound after it
   > - *ü* – combines 'u' and 'e', try pursing your lips and saying 'u'
   > - *z* – say 'ts'
   > - *v* – say a soft 'f'
   > - final *-d* in *Rad* – say it like a 't'
   > - final *-e* in *Schule* – pronounce the 'e' as a separate syllable.

   Track 7

Listen to the recording

Now play the recording of two questions related to what you have read.

You are expected to say a few words or a short phrase / sentence in response to each question. One-word answers will not be sufficient to gain full marks.

(4 marks)

My people

Had a go ☐ Nearly there ☐ Nailed it! ☐

Clothing and fashion

Picture task

See this photo in colour

1 Describe the photo. Write four short sentences **in German**.

   ……………………………………………………………………………………………………… . (2 marks)
   ……………………………………………………………………………………………………… . (2 marks)
   ……………………………………………………………………………………………………… . (2 marks)
   ……………………………………………………………………………………………………… . (2 marks)

Dictation

2 You are going to hear someone talking about clothes.

Sentences 1–2: write down the missing words in the gaps provided.
In each gap, you will write one word **in German**.

Example: Mein <u>Pulli</u> ist <u>warm</u> und <u>modisch</u>.

1 Sind ………………… neuen ………………… ………………… ?

2 Es ist mir ………………… ………………… , auf Modetrends zu ………………… .

Sentences 3–6: write down the full sentences that you hear in the spaces provided, **in German**.

Example: <u>Ich möchte ein neues weißes Hemd kaufen.</u>

3 ……………………………………………………………………………………………… .
4 ……………………………………………………………………………………………… .
5 ……………………………………………………………………………………………… .
6 ……………………………………………………………………………………………… . (10 marks)

Here are some key sounds to listen out for:
- final -*e* – this is a sounded syllable (*dein**e***)
- *qu* – sounds like 'kv' (*bequem*)
- final -*ig* – sounds more like *ich* (*wichtig*)
- *v* – sounds like 'f' (*Vater*).
- *ä* – sounds like an 'a' combined with an 'e' (*trägt*)

Listen to the recording to practise these sounds.

Track 10

Had a go ☐ **Nearly there** ☐ **Nailed it!** ☐

My people

Identity

Describing people, places and activities

1   Describe **ONE** of these pictures. Your description must cover:

  • people
  • location
  • activity.

(8 marks)

Start by saying something about the people you can see in the image you have chosen. You could also comment on their mood if the picture makes it clear.

When you have finished your description, scan the QR code to listen to two questions relating to your chosen picture. Pause the recording between each question to allow yourself time to answer. You are expected to say a few words or a short phrase / sentence in response to each question. One-word answers will not be sufficient to gain full marks.

(4 marks)

Writing about friends and identity

2   Write to a German friend about yourself and your friends.

You **must** include the following points:

  • what is important to you in life
  • what you like to do with friends
  • an occasion when you have helped a friend
  • what you will do this weekend.

Write your answer **in German**. You should aim to write between 80 and 90 words.

....

....

....

....

....

....

....

....

....

....

(18 marks)

My people Had a go ☐ Nearly there ☐ Nailed it! ☐

Celebrations

Picture task

See this photo in colour

> Remember to describe the people, where they are and what they are doing.
>
> It's a good idea to stick to the present tense.

1 Describe the photo. Write four short sentences **in German**.

   .... **(2 marks)**
   .... **(2 marks)**
   .... **(2 marks)**
   .... **(2 marks)**

Translation

2 Translate the paragraph **into German**.

> In my family we always celebrate a birthday. We do that in order to spend time together and have fun. My older brother has his birthday in April. Last year we went to a campsite for the weekend. Next year I would like to have a big party at home.

> Watch out for verbs in different tenses. There are present and perfect tenses here and also a conditional, so don't forget the very handy *ich möchte* … with an infinitive at the end.
>
> There is also an example of the *um … zu* structure, so check how that is used and don't forget that *zu* + infinitive go to the end of the clause / sentence.

   ....
   ....
   ....
   ....
   .... **(10 marks)**

Had a go ☐ Nearly there ☐ Nailed it! ☐

My people

When I was younger

Read aloud

1 Mika, your friend, has written to you about his childhood.

Read out the text below, then listen to the audio in the Answers section to check your pronunciation.

Remember: you can annotate the read aloud text to remind you of key pronunciation rules.

> Als ich ein Kind war, wohnte ich in einem Dorf.
> Ich liebte Fußball und spielte jeden Tag.
> Ich ging gerne mit meinen Eltern schwimmen.
> Meine Schule war sehr klein.
> Die Lehrer waren immer nett und freundlich.

You could mark in pencil where the natural breath pauses are, to help you read steadily rather than rushing through the text.

Sounds to take note of here:
- -d – sounds like 't'
- w – sounds like 'v'
- ie – sounds like the English 'ee'
- j – sounds like 'y'
- schw – sounds like 'shv'
- ei – sounds like the English 'I'.

Listen to the recording to practise these sounds.

Track 12

Listen to the recording

Now play the recording of two questions related to what you have read.

You are expected to say a few words or a short phrase / sentence in response to each question. One-word answers will not be sufficient to gain full marks. **(4 marks)**

Activities during childhood

2 Describe **ONE** of these pictures. Your description must cover:
- people
- location
- activity. **(8 marks)**

Picture 1

See this photo in colour

To deal with location, say where the people are – inside or outside, in a park, at home, in school etc.

Listen to the recording

When you have finished your description, scan the QR code to listen to two questions relating to your chosen picture. Pause the recording between each question to allow yourself time to answer. You are expected to say a few words or a short phrase / sentence in response to each question. One-word answers will not be sufficient to gain full marks. **(4 marks)**

Picture 2

See this photo in colour

11

My people | Had a go ☐ Nearly there ☐ Nailed it! ☐

My life in the future

Dictation

1 You are going to hear someone talking about their future hopes and plans.

Sentences 1–3: write down the missing words in the gaps provided. In each gap, you will write one word **in German**.

Example: Ich möchte kein Studium machen.

1 Meine .... sind ....

2 Ich .... es in England nicht ....

3 Das Wetter .... ist so ....

Sentences 4–6: write down the full sentences that you hear in the spaces provided, **in German**.

Example: Ich will lieber arbeiten.

4 ....

5 ....

6 .... **(10 marks)**

> Here are some key sounds to listen out for:
> - *ä* – sounds like a combination of 'a' and 'e'
> - *ch* – sounds like 'ck'
> - *j* – sounds like 'y'
> - *ö* – sounds like 'er'
> - final *-d* – at the end of a word sounds like 't'.
>
> Listen to the recording to practise these sounds.
>
> Track 16

My life now and future plans

2 Write a blog about your life now and your future plans.

You **must** include the following points:
- a typical day in your life now
- what is good and not so good about your life
- something you have done recently which you enjoyed
- how you would like your future life to be.

Write your answer **in German**. You should aim to write between 130 and 150 words.

> You can cover some points in more detail than others, so develop the ones where you have most to say. Here, bullet point 1 is one where you may be able to write in more detail than for others. But be sure to write something about all the bullet points given.

....

....

....

....

....

....

....

> You can continue your answer on your own paper if you run out of space here. In the exam, you will have more space than this.

(22 marks)

Had a go ☐   **Nearly there** ☐   **Nailed it!** ☐   Health

Food and drink

Going grocery shopping

1 Noah and his boyfriend, Tim, are planning a meal for Sunday.

   Complete the gap in each sentence using a word from the box below.

   There are more words than gaps.

ice cream	fruit	meat
vegetables	fish	cake
chocolate	meal	coffee

> You can see from the box and the questions that each answer is some type of food!
>
> When you listen for the first time, try to jot down each food item you hear to help you work out the answers.

(a) Noah checks that Tim has bought ……………………………… . **(1 mark)**

(b) They still need to buy ………………… this afternoon. **(1 mark)**

(c) Noah asks whether they need anything else for the ………………… . **(1 mark)**

(d) Tim suggests they should buy ………………… and ………………… . **(2 marks)**

Foods I like and don't like

2 Listen to Ben talking about food. What do you learn?

   Complete the sentences by putting a cross [×] in the correct box for each question.

   (a) Ben is …

☐	**A** a food fanatic.
☐	**B** a keen cook.
☐	**C** not very interested in food.

   (1 mark)

   (b) Ben enjoys eating …

☐	**A** sausages.
☐	**B** fruit.
☐	**C** cake.

   (1 mark)

   (c) Yesterday they ate …

☐	**A** escalopes and salad.
☐	**B** fish and chips.
☐	**C** escalopes and chips.

   (1 mark)

> The questions give you some ideas about the food-related words you will hear. Before the recording starts, it's a good idea to take a moment to think what these words would be in German, to help you identify them once the recording starts.

Health

Had a go ☐ Nearly there ☐ Nailed it! ☐

Meals at home

Target grade 1-5

Translation

1 Translate the following sentences **into English**.

(a) Ich esse nicht gern Gemüse.

....

(b) Morgens trinke ich heiße Schokolade, die sehr lecker ist.

....

(c) Mein Vater kocht jeden Tag das Abendessen.

....

(d) Gestern haben wir Wurst mit Pommes gegessen.

....

(e) Wenn ich Hunger habe, esse ich gerne Pommes.

.... **(10 marks)**

Target grade 5-9

Read aloud

2 Mia, your friend, has sent you some information about what she eats at home.

Read out the text below.

> Ich bin Vegetarierin und esse deshalb kein Fleisch und keinen Fisch.
> Ich esse jeden Morgen ein gutes Frühstück, denn das gibt mir Energie.
> Meiner Meinung nach ist das die wichtigste Mahlzeit des Tages, und ich gehe nie aus dem Haus, bevor ich gegessen habe.
> Mein Lieblingsessen ist ein Schokoladenkuchen, den meine Mutti macht.

(8 marks)

Sounds to take note of here:
- *g* – a hard sound, so not like the English 'j'
- *ei* – sounds like the English word 'I'
- *j* – sounds like 'y'
- short *e* – as in *denn*
- *z* – sounds like 'ts'
- *v* – a soft 'f' sound.

Listen to the recording to practise these sounds.

Track 19

Now play the recording of two questions related to what you have read.

You are expected to say a few words or a short phrase / sentence in response to each question. One-word answers will not be sufficient to gain full marks. **(4 marks)**

Had a go ☐ **Nearly there** ☐ **Nailed it!** ☐

Health

Shopping for food

Listen to the recording

Role play

1 **Setting:** In a village shop in Austria

Scenario:
- You are in a village shop in Austria.
- Scan the QR code for the teacher's voice. Pause the recording between each prompt to allow yourself time to answer.
- The teacher will play the part of the shopkeeper and will speak first.
- Your teacher will ask questions **in German** and you must answer **in German**.
- You are expected to say a few words or a short phrase / sentence in response to each prompt. One-word answers will not be sufficient to gain full marks.

Task:
1 Greet the shopkeeper and say you would like some milk.
2 Say you need some bread.
3 Say you would also like some eggs.
4 Say how many eggs you would like.
5 Ask a question about their opening times.

> For one task at Foundation tier you will need to ask a question – practise how to do this.

(10 marks)

> Remember: in German, you often don't need a word for 'some …', e.g. *Ich möchte Eier* – 'I'd like *some* eggs'.

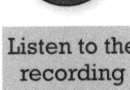

Listen to the recording

Role play

2 **Setting:** In a grocery shop in Germany

Scenario:
- You are in a grocery shop in Germany.
- Scan the QR code for the teacher's voice. Pause the recording between each prompt to allow yourself time to answer.
- The teacher will play the part of the shopkeeper and will speak first.
- Your teacher will ask questions **in German** and you must answer **in German**.
- You are expected to say a few words or a short phrase / sentence in response to each prompt. One-word answers will not be sufficient to gain full marks.

Task:
1 Say what you would like to buy.
2 Say you also need some coffee.
3 Ask whether there is a bakery nearby.
4 Say thank you and that's all you need.
5 Ask where you can buy fruit.

> Remember: in German, you often don't need a word for 'some … ', e.g. *Ich möchte Kaffee* – 'I'd like *some* coffee'.

(10 marks)

> For two tasks at Higher tier you will need to ask a question – practise how to do this.

| Health | Had a go ☐ Nearly there ☐ Nailed it! ☐ |

Eating out

Role play

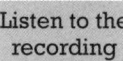

Listen to the recording

1 **Setting:** In a restaurant

Scenario:
- You are in a restaurant.
- Scan the QR code for the teacher's voice. Pause the recording between each prompt to allow yourself time to answer.
- The teacher will play the part of the waiter / waitress and will speak first.
- Your teacher will ask questions **in German** and you must answer **in German**.
- You are expected to say a few words or a short phrase / sentence in response to each prompt. One-word answers will not be sufficient to gain full marks.

> Remember that this is a formal and transactional situation, so you will be addressed in the formal *Sie* form. You can answer in the *Sie* or *du* form, but don't change between the two.
>
> Don't develop your answers in great detail – just give the essential information required by the task as clearly as you can.

Task:
1 Say you want a table for two people.
2 Say that you would like to see the menu.
3 Order two items to eat.
4 Say what you would like to drink.
5 Ask whether they have Wi-Fi.

(10 marks)

Role play

Listen to the recording

2 **Setting:** In a restaurant

Scenario:
- You are in a restaurant.
- Scan the QR code for the teacher's voice. Pause the recording between each prompt to allow yourself time to answer.
- The teacher will play the part of the waitress / waiter and will speak first.
- Your teacher will ask questions **in German** and you must answer **in German**.
- You are expected to say a few words or a short phrase / sentence in response to each prompt. One-word answers will not be sufficient to gain full marks.

Task:
1 Say how many people you would like a table for.
2 Say where you would like to sit.
3 Ask a question about the menu.
4 Say what you would like to eat and drink.
5 Ask a question about missing cutlery.

> Don't forget that you can use *Darf ich … ?* as a polite way of saying 'May I / Could I … ?'

(10 marks)

Had a go ☐ Nearly there ☐ Nailed it! ☐   **Health**

A healthy diet

Healthy eating

1 Read these 10 rules about healthy eating for young people.

> **Iss dich gesund!**
> Alle Jugendliche brauchen verschiedene Arten von Essen*, um gesund zu sein.
> Hier sind unsere Top-Regeln:
> Regel 1:   Täglich Obst essen. Das vermeidet das Hungergefühl.
> Regel 2:   So oft wie möglich frisches Gemüse essen, um mehr Energie zu haben.
> Regel 3:   Ab und zu Fisch oder Fleisch essen, um die Muskeln zu stärken.
> Regel 4:   Regelmäßig Käse und andere Milchprodukte essen. Die sind gut für die Knochen.
> Regel 5:   Genug Wasser trinken, um den ganzen Körper zu schützen.
> Regel 6:   Selten Kuchen und Schokolade essen, denn zu viel kann Krankheiten verursachen.
> Regel 7:   Langsam und ruhig essen, um eine Mahlzeit richtig zu genießen.
> Regel 8:   Sehr oft etwas Grünes essen – das ist gut für das Herz.
> Regel 9:   Jeden Tag mit einem guten Frühstück anfangen – der beste Start in den Tag!
> Regel 10: Nicht zu oft Fastfood essen – das kann dick machen.

* *Arten von Essen* – types of food

Answer the following questions **in English**. You do not need to write in full sentences.

(a) Why should you eat fruit daily? ....

(b) According to the text, why are fresh vegetables good for you? ....

(c) How often should you eat meat or fish? ....

(d) What should you consume in order to have strong bones? ....

(e) What can you do to protect your whole body? ....

(f) What does rule 7 recommend? ....

(g) What types of food improve heart health? ....

(h) What does rule 9 advise? ....

(8 marks)

Translation

2 Translate the following paragraph **into English**.

> Ich esse normalerweise gesund, obwohl ich manchmal Pommes genieße. Sie sind lecker, wenn man Hunger hat. Das Frühstück ist für mich die wichtigste Mahlzeit des Tages, denn das gibt mir die Energie, die ich für den ganzen Morgen brauche. Gestern habe ich Eier mit Brot gegessen und morgen werde ich viel Obst vorbereiten.

....
....
....
....
....

(10 marks)

Health

Had a go ☐   Nearly there ☐   Nailed it! ☐

Sport

Picture task

See this photo in colour

To respond to this question, always begin with the people you see in the picture. You could say how many people there are, whether they are male or female, how old they are, what they look like, what they are wearing etc.

1 Describe the photo. Write four short sentences **in German**.

.... **(2 marks)**

.... **(2 marks)**

.... **(2 marks)**

.... **(2 marks)**

Listen to the recording

Describing activities

2 Describe **ONE** of these pictures. Your description must cover:

- people
- location
- activity. **(8 marks)**

When you have finished your description, scan the QR code to listen to two questions relating to your chosen picture. Pause the recording between each question to allow yourself time to answer. You are expected to say a few words or a short phrase / sentence in response to each question. One-word answers will not be sufficient to gain full marks.

(4 marks)

Picture 1

See this photo in colour

Picture 2

See this photo in colour

18

Had a go ☐ Nearly there ☐ Nailed it! ☐

Health

Advantages of sport

Translation

1 Translate the following sentences **into English**.

(a) Ich bewege mich oft.

....

(b) Jeden Morgen gehe ich laufen.

....

(c) Sport ist gesund und macht auch viel Spaß.

....

(d) Gestern haben mein Bruder und ich Handball gespielt.

....

(e) Wenn ich schwimmen gehe, bin ich nicht mehr so gestresst.

.... **(10 marks)**

> If you see *gestern / letzte Woche*, the verb is likely to be in a past tense.
> When you see *wenn*, look to the end of the **clause** for the verb.

Read aloud

2 Your friend Lea has sent you some information about her lifestyle.

Read out the text below, then listen to the audio in the Answers section to check your pronunciation.

> Ich treibe regelmäßig und sehr gerne Sport, vor allem Tennis und Handball.
> Wenn ich mich genug bewege, fühle ich mich immer besser und bin glücklicher.
> Ich hoffe, ich werde ein längeres Leben haben, weil ich aktiv bin.
> Ich würde sagen, Sport hilft mir, die negativen Wirkungen von Stress zu vermeiden.

(8 marks)

> Pay attention to these sounds:
> - *ei* in *treibe / weil* – sounds like the English word 'I'
> - *Sp* in *Sport* – sounds like 'shp'
> - *St* in *Stress* – sounds like 'sht'
> - *w* in *wenn / weil / werde / Wirkungen* – sounds like 'v'
> - *ä* in *regelmäßig / längeres* – sounds like a combination of 'a' and 'e', a bit like the first part of the English word 'air'
> - *ü* in *glücklicher / würde* – sounds like 'u' and 'e' with your lips pursed
> - final *-e* in *treibe / gerne / werde*, etc. – pronounced as a separate syllable.
> Listen to the recording to practise these sounds.

Track 26

Listen to the recording

Now play the recording of two questions related to what you have read.

You are expected to say a few words or a short phrase / sentence in response to each question. One-word answers will not be sufficient to gain full marks. **(4 marks)**

19

Health

Had a go ☐ Nearly there ☐ Nailed it! ☐

Physical wellbeing

Translation

1 Translate the following sentences **into English**.

(a) Ich schlafe immer gut.

....

(b) Mein Freund und ich spielen gern Fußball.

....

(c) Wenn ich Zeit habe, gehe ich morgens laufen.

....

(d) Letztes Wochenende bin ich mit meinem Stiefbruder schwimmen gegangen.

....

(e) Ich möchte später Tennis spielen.

.... **(10 marks)**

> Check the verb first – be aware of the person and the tense.
>
> Check carefully to ensure you don't miss any small words like *gern* or *morgens*.

Role play

2 **Setting:** At a fitness centre

Scenario:

- You are at a fitness centre.
- Scan the QR code for the teacher's voice. Pause the recording between each prompt to allow yourself time to answer.
- The teacher will play the part of the receptionist and will speak first.
- Your teacher will ask questions **in German** and you must answer **in German**.
- You are expected to say a few words or a short phrase / sentence in response to each prompt. One-word answers will not be sufficient to gain full marks.

Listen to the recording

> Remember that this is a transactional situation, so you may be addressed in the formal *Sie* form.
>
> To be polite, it's usual to use *bitte*.

Task:
1 Say what activity you would like to do.
2 Say what time you would like to book for.
3 Say how many people it is for.
4 Ask what time the centre closes today.
5 Ask a question about the price.

....
....
....
....
.... **(10 marks)**

> During the preparation time, make bullet point notes of what you need to say to respond to each task.

Had a go ☐ Nearly there ☐ Nailed it! ☐

Health

Mental wellbeing

Dictation

1 You are going to hear someone talking about maintaining good mental health.

Sentences 1–3: write down the missing words in the gaps provided. In each gap, you will write one word **in German**.

Example: Es gibt <u>Druck</u> in der <u>Schule</u>.

1 Ich .... oft ....

2 Für .... sind gute Freunde ....

3 Bewegung und .... sind mir ....

Sentences 4–6: write down the full sentences that you hear in the spaces provided, **in German**.

Example: <u>Ich spreche über Probleme.</u>

4 ....

5 ....

6 .... **(10 marks)**

Listen to this audio to practise these German sounds.
- *ch* – is a soft throaty sound
- *-e* – at the end of a word is a separate syllable
- *w* – sounds like 'v'
- *ö* – sounds like 'er'
- *-ig* – at the end of the word is a soft throaty sound like the German *ch* above.

Track 30

Translation

2 Translate the paragraph **into German**.

> I sometimes feel stressed because there is a lot of pressure at school. If I am worried, I talk to my teacher. That always helps. In my opinion, it is important to do exercise, to spend time with friends and to talk about problems. It's a bad idea to suffer alone.

....

....

....

....

.... **(10 marks)**

Watch out for these structures and, if you've forgotten them, check how they work in German:
- reflexive verbs
- *weil* – word order
- *wenn* – word order
- strong verbs
- inversion
- *zu* + infinitive clauses.

Health

Had a go ☐ Nearly there ☐ Nailed it! ☐

Feeling unwell

Picture task

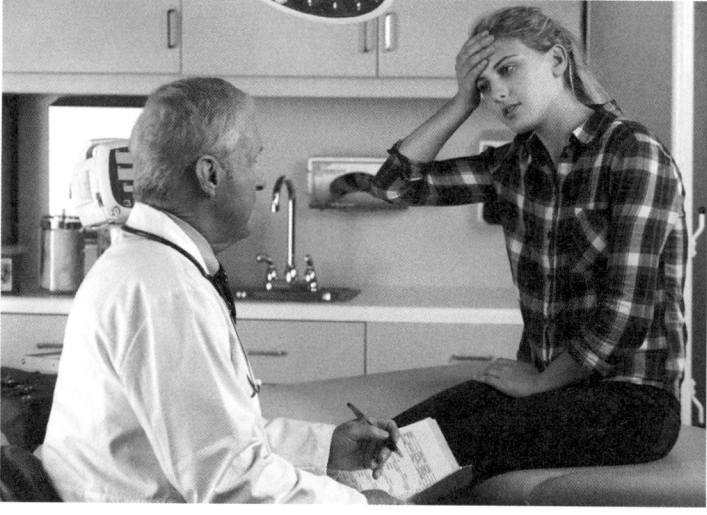

See this photo in colour

Remember to mention:
- the people (gender, age, clothes, appearance)
- the situation / place
- what they are doing
- anything else you observe.

1 Describe the photo. Write four short sentences **in German**.

.... (2 marks)

.... (2 marks)

.... (2 marks)

.... (2 marks)

Role play

2 **Setting:** At a doctor's surgery

Scenario:
- You are at the doctor's surgery.
- Scan the QR code for the teacher's voice. Pause the recording between each prompt to allow yourself time to answer.
- The teacher will play the part of the doctor and will speak first.
- Your teacher will ask questions **in German** and you must answer **in German**.
- You are expected to say a few words or a short phrase / sentence in response to each prompt. One-word answers will not be sufficient to gain full marks.

Remember that the teacher will speak to you in the formal *Sie* form.

Task:
1 Say what the problem is.
2 Say how long you have been unwell.
3 Ask a question about what you should do.
4 Say what you plan to do this afternoon.
5 Ask a question about how long the illness will last.

Take care with task 2 – you'll need to use *seit*.

During the preparation time in the exam, think about the correct question words to use and make some notes for reference.

....

....

....

....

.... (10 marks)

Had a go ☐ Nearly there ☐ Nailed it! ☐

Health

Avoiding health risks

Picture task

See this photo in colour

Just remember:
- Who? What? Where?
- Who is in the picture? Describe their appearance, mood and clothes.
- What are they doing? Are they dancing, laughing, talking etc.?
- Where are they? Indoors or outdoors, at home, in a club etc.?

1 Describe the photo. Write four short sentences **in German**.

.... (2 marks)

.... (2 marks)

.... (2 marks)

.... (2 marks)

Staying healthy

2 Write to a German friend about health issues.

You **must** include the following points:
- what you do to be healthy
- what you think about smoking
- what you have done recently for your fitness
- how you will celebrate the end of the exams.

Some of your responses may be more detailed than others, and that's OK.

Make sure you respond in the right tense. For this question, there will always be two present tense points, one in the past and one in the future.

Write your answer **in German**. You should aim to write between 80 and 90 words.

....

....

....

....

....

....

....

....

.... (18 marks)

Free time

Had a go ☐ Nearly there ☐ Nailed it! ☐

Sports stars

A famous Paralympian

1 Read this text about Verena Bentele, a former German Paralympian.

> Verena war im Februar 1982 in Bayern geboren und ist ihr ganzes Leben blind gewesen. Sie interessierte sich immer für Sport, vor allem für Wintersport. Sie hat ihre ersten Medaillen* 1998 gewonnen und hat dann 2009 einen schweren Unfall gehabt. Im folgenden Jahr hat sie ihr bestes Jahr gehabt, wo sie bei den Winterspielen fünf Goldmedaillen gewonnen hat.

Pay special attention to the years and try to work out what happened when.

*Medaille – medal

Complete the sentences below.

Put a cross [×] in the correct box for each question.

(a) Verena was blind …

☐	**A** from age 2.
☐	**B** from birth.
☐	**C** from age 18.

(b) Verena's main interest was in …

☐	**A** winter sports.
☐	**B** athletics.
☐	**C** running.

(c) She won her first medals in …

☐	**A** 1998.
☐	**B** 1989.
☐	**C** 2009.

(d) In 2009 she …

☐	**A** won five medals.
☐	**B** had an accident.
☐	**C** had her best year.

(4 marks)

Medaille (medal) has been explained, so you should be able to have a good guess at the compound noun *Goldmedaille* (*Gold + Medaille* – 'gold medal').

Playing competitive sports

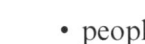

2 Describe **ONE** of these pictures. Your description must cover:
- people
- location
- activity.

(8 marks)

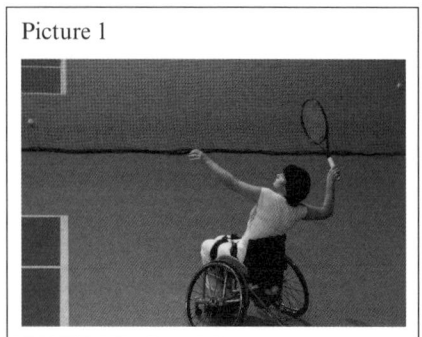

Picture 1

See this photo in colour

Picture 2

See this photo in colour

Listen to the recording

When you have finished your description, scan the QR code to listen to two questions relating to your chosen picture. Pause the recording between each question to allow yourself time to answer. You are expected to say a few words or a short phrase / sentence in response to each question. One-word answers will not be sufficient to gain full marks.

(4 marks)

Had a go ☐   Nearly there ☐   Nailed it! ☐   **Free time**

Hobbies and interests

Recreational activities

1   Describe **ONE** of these pictures. Your description must cover:

   • people
   • location
   • activity.   **(8 marks)**

When you have finished your description, scan the QR code to listen to two questions relating to your chosen picture. Pause the recording between each question to allow yourself time to answer. You are expected to say a few words or a short phrase / sentence in response to each question. One-word answers will not be sufficient to gain full marks.   **(4 marks)**

Remember: people – location – activity!

Picture 1      See this photo in colour

Picture 2      See this photo in colour

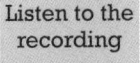

A survey about hobbies

2   Read this report on popular hobbies among adults in Germany last year.

> Gartenarbeit war im letzten Jahr für 23% der Deutschen das beliebteste Hobby. 26% der Bevölkerung gingen in ihrer Freizeit gern einkaufen. 20% der Befragten* fotografierten gern. Die beliebteste sportliche Aktivität war der Besuch im Fitness-Studio – damit verbrachten etwa 10,9% ihre Freizeit. Andere Freizeitaktivitäten, die man erwähnte, waren zum Essen ausgehen, Kinobesuche und auch traditionelle *Gesellschaftsspiele*, wo man mit Freunden oder Familie bequem um den Tisch sitzt, um einen lustigen Abend zu verbringen.

* *Befragten* – people surveyed

(a) Answer the following questions **in English**. You do not need to write in full sentences.

   (i)   What was the preferred hobby for 23% of Germans?

   .... **(1 mark)**

   (ii) What percentage of people enjoyed shopping?

   .... **(1 mark)**

   (iii) What sort of sports activity was the most popular?

   .... **(1 mark)**

(b) Which of these is the best translation of the word *Gesellschaftsspiele*?

   Put a cross [×] in the correct box.

☐	**A**	ball games
☐	**B**	board games
☐	**C**	computer games

25

Free time

Had a go ☐   Nearly there ☐   Nailed it! ☐

Music and dance

Describing a music event

Picture 1

See this photo in colour

Picture 2

See this photo in colour

1 Describe **ONE** of these pictures. Your description must cover:
   - people
   - location
   - activity. **(8 marks)**

> People – what do they look like and what are they wearing?
> Place – where are they?
> Activity – what are they doing?

When you have finished your description, scan the QR code to listen to two questions relating to your chosen picture. Pause the recording between each question to allow yourself time to answer. You are expected to say a few words or a short phrase / sentence in response to each question. One-word answers will not be sufficient to gain full marks. **(4 marks)**

Music preferences

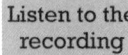

2 Listen to Mika talking about music.

What does he say?

Listen to the recording and complete the sentences by putting a cross [×] in the correct box for each question.

(a) Mika …

☐	**A** likes different types of music.
☐	**B** prefers classical music.
☐	**C** only likes rock music.

(b) He thinks rap music …

☐	**A** is meaningless.
☐	**B** is too loud.
☐	**C** has a message.

(c) He used to listen to …

☐	**A** pop.
☐	**B** rock.
☐	**C** musicals.

(d) In the future he would like to …

☐	**A** learn to dance.
☐	**B** be a singer.
☐	**C** manage a band.

(4 marks)

> You'll notice here that two questions are not in the present tense, so listen for an imperfect tense verb for question (c) and a future time frame for question (d).

Had a go ☐   Nearly there ☐   Nailed it! ☐   **Free time**

Arranging to go out

Making plans for the weekend

1 Leonie and Max are talking about weekend plans.

What do they say?

Listen to the recording and complete the sentences by putting a cross [×] in the correct box for each question.

(a) On Saturday Max wants to …

☐ **A** go for a walk.
☐ **B** go shopping.
☐ **C** go cycling.

(b) He wants to buy …

☐ **A** clothes.
☐ **B** books.
☐ **C** trainers.

(c) Leonie says she wants to …

☐ **A** get up early.
☐ **B** have breakfast.
☐ **C** lie in.

(d) They plan to meet …

☐ **A** at the marketplace.
☐ **B** at the shopping centre.
☐ **C** at a café.

(e) Later they will …

☐ **A** have lunch.
☐ **B** have ice cream.
☐ **C** have coffee.

(5 marks)

Dictation

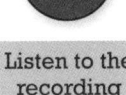

2 You are going to hear someone talking about social arrangements.

Sentences 1–2: write down the missing words in the gaps provided. In each gap, you will write one word **in German**.

Example: Ich <u>gehe</u> sehr oft am <u>Wochenende</u> aus.

1 Ich .... einen .... Freund.

2 Wir haben .... zu .... auf der .... kennengelernt.

Sentences 3–6: write down the full sentences that you hear in the spaces provided, **in German**.

Example: <u>Samstags gehen wir normalerweise zusammen tanzen.</u>

3 ....

4 ....

5 ....

6 .... **(10 marks)**

> Don't panic when the recording starts. Try doing the following to see if it works for you:
> - Listen first for gist and use the first time you listen to note down some words you hear in the right places.
> - During and straight after the second time you listen, try to fill in the gaps and write the sentences.
> - Check your work as you listen for the third time and note anything you need to think about when the recording has finished.

27

Free time

Had a go ☐   Nearly there ☐   Nailed it! ☐

Reading

My reading habits

1 Write a response to a survey about your reading habits.

You **must** include the following points:
- how often you read books
- what sort of books you like / dislike
- what you plan to read next.

Write your answer **in German**. You should aim to write between 40 and 50 words.

> You need to respond to every bullet point, so don't miss one out.

> Express opinions, especially for bullet point 2.

> Remember that bullet point 3 is in the future time frame. You can either use the future tense or use a future time expression with a present tense verb or with *wollen* (to want to).

....
....
....
....
....
....
....
....
....

(14 marks)

Translation

2 Translate the paragraph **into German**.

> I like reading and I always have a book with me. When I was younger, I read all the Harry Potter books. Now I prefer to read detective stories. At the moment, I am reading a new novel called *The Rules*. The main character is a boy who loves computers.

> Don't be confused by 'I am reading'. This is just another way of saying 'I read', so use the normal present tense in German.

> You can translate the book title *The Rules* as *Die Regeln*.

....
....
....
....
....
....
....
....
....

(10 marks)

Had a go ☐   Nearly there ☐   Nailed it! ☐   **Free time**

Television

Read aloud

Sounds to watch out for here:
- *j* – sounds like 'y' in English
- *ei* – sounds like the English word 'I'
- *ö* – sounds like 'er'
- *z* – sounds like 'ts'
- *ch* – a throaty sound, as in *ich*

1 Elif, your friend, has sent you some information about her television viewing.

Read out the text below.

> Ich sehe jeden Tag fern.
> Meine Lieblingssendung ist eine Komödie.
> Die ganze Familie macht eine Pause, um diese Serie anzusehen.
> Gestern habe ich einen Dokumentarfilm über Pferde gesehen.
> Heute Abend will ich die Nachrichten sehen.

(8 marks)

Now play the recording of two questions related to what you have read.

You are expected to say a few words or a short phrase / sentence in response to each question. One-word answers will not be sufficient to gain full marks.

(4 marks)

Role play

2 **Setting:** An interview on television viewing

Scenario:
- You are being interviewed about television viewing.
- Scan the QR code for the teacher's voice. Pause the recording between each prompt to allow yourself time to answer.
- The teacher will play the part of the interviewer and will speak first.
- Your teacher will ask questions **in German** and you must answer **in German**.
- You are expected to say a few words or a short phrase / sentence in response to each prompt. One-word answers will not be sufficient to gain full marks.

> **Task:**
> 1 Say how often you watch television.
> 2 Say what sort of programmes you like.
> 3 Ask the interviewer to repeat the question.
> 4 Say what you think of violence in TV programmes.
> 5 Ask the interviewer about their viewing habits.

> Use the preparation time in the exam to make a few bullet point notes about each task. Your notes will be a great support and prompt during the exam.

....
....
....
....
....

(10 marks)

Free time

Had a go ☐   Nearly there ☐   Nailed it! ☐

Film and cinema

Role play

1 **Setting:** At a cinema

   Scenario:

   - You are at a cinema.
   - Scan the QR code for the teacher's voice. Pause the recording between each prompt to allow yourself time to answer.
   - The teacher will play the part of the cinema employee and will speak first.
   - Your teacher will ask questions **in German** and you must answer **in German**.
   - You are expected to say a few words or a short phrase / sentence in response to each prompt. One-word answers will not be sufficient to gain full marks.

   > **Task:**
   > 1 Say what sort of film you want to see.
   > 2 Say what time you would like to book for.
   > 3 Say how many tickets you want to book.
   > 4 Say what you think of the cinema.
   > 5 Ask a question about the price.

   > Use some of your preparation time to write some bullet point notes for each task. Use your notes as a prompt during the exam.

(10 marks)

Translation

2 Translate the following paragraph **into English**.

   > Ich gehe selten ins Kino, weil die Karten heute so teuer sind, aber ich finde es immer eine gute Erfahrung, wenn ich mit Freunden einen Film sehe. Die besten Filme sind meiner Meinung nach Actionfilme, weil alles sehr schnell passiert und es immer spannend ist. Letzten Monat habe ich einen deutschen Krimi gesehen.

   > Look at every word and don't overlook the small but important ones like *so, sehr, immer* etc.

....
....
....
....
....
....
....
....
....

(10 marks)

Had a go ☐   Nearly there ☐   Nailed it! ☐   **Media and technology**

Mobile technology

Target grade 4-5

My mobile phone

> Read carefully through the text, making a quick note of the meaning of words you immediately recognise.

1   Read Yusuf's blog about mobile phones.

> Mein Handy ist für mich absolut nötig – aus vier Gründen. Grund eins – ohne Handy weiß ich nicht, was in der Welt passiert. Grund zwei – ohne das GPS-System kann ich meinen Weg durch die Stadt nicht finden. Grund drei – ohne Handy bekomme ich keine Nachrichten von Freunden und – Grund vier – ich kann keine lustigen Fotos sehen.

Complete the tables **in English**. You do not need to write in full sentences.

(a) **First** reason he finds his phone essential

....

(1 mark)

(b) **Second** reason he finds his phone essential

....

(1 mark)

(c) **Third** reason he finds his phone essential

....

(1 mark)

(d) **Fourth** reason he finds his phone essential

....

(1 mark)

Target grade 5-9

Dictation

2   You are going to hear someone talking about mobile technology.

Sentences 1–2: write down the missing words in the gaps provided. In each gap, you will write one word **in German**.

Example: Ich <u>schicke</u> jeden <u>Tag</u> E-Mails an meine <u>Bekannten</u>.

1 Ich .... die .... toll und ....

2 Ich kann .... von meinen ....

Sentences 3–6: write down the full sentences that you hear in the spaces provided, **in German**.

Example: <u>Man kann ausländische Filme herunterladen.</u>

3 ....

4 ....

5 ....

6 ....   (10 marks)

Listen to the recording

> Listen to this audio to practise these German sounds.
> - *g* – a hard sound, as at the start of the English word 'green'
> - *ie* – sounds like the English 'ee'
> - *ä* – sounds like a combined 'a' and 'e' sound (a little like 'ay')
> - *ch* – a soft throaty sound
> - *w* – sounds like 'v'.
>
> Track 42

31

Media and technology

Had a go ☐ Nearly there ☐ Nailed it! ☐

Social media

Pros and cons of social media

1. Write a response to a survey about social media.

   You **must** include the following points:
   - how you use social media
   - what you see as the pros and cons of social media
   - how you will use social media this evening.

   Write your answer **in German**. You should aim to write between 40 and 50 words.

   > Make sure that you respond to each bullet point and that what you write is relevant to the task. Remember to express your opinion in bullet points 1 and 2 and to use a future time frame to respond to bullet point 3.

   ....

   ....

   ....

   ....

   ....

   ....

   ....

   (14 marks)

Pros and cons of social media

2. Write a blog about social media use.

   You **must** include the following points:
   - why you find social media useful
   - the negative aspects of social media
   - how you have used social media recently
   - how you will stay safe online in the future.

   > Answer all the bullet points in the right tense – two require the present, one the past and one the future. To aim high, try to develop and extend your ideas by adding further detail and make your opinions convincing by explaining them, using *denn* or *weil*.

   Write your answer **in German**. You should aim to write between 130 and 150 words.

   > Write in paragraphs with one paragraph per bullet point. This makes it clear to read as well as helping you not to omit any vital content.

   ....

   ....

   ....

   ....

   ....

   ....

   ....

   ....

   ....

   > In the exam you will have more space to write your answer. Here you can continue your answer on your own paper if necessary.

   (22 marks)

Had a go ☐ **Nearly there** ☐ **Nailed it!** ☐

Media and technology

Internet

Spending time online

1 Describe **ONE** of these pictures. Your description must cover:
- people
- location
- activity. **(8 marks)**

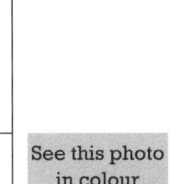

Picture 1

Picture 2

> You should say something about the people shown in the picture – their age, gender, appearance and clothing. If their feelings are apparent, you can also comment on this.
>
> You should then comment on where they are – indoors or outdoors. If indoors, in what sort of place; if outdoors, you can refer to the weather conditions.

> You should also refer to what the people are doing – using appropriate present tense verbs. For picture 1, the verbs *lesen*, *arbeiten* and *lernen* will be useful, and for picture 2 *sehen*, *ansehen* or *anschauen* could be used.

When you have finished your description, scan the QR code to listen to two questions relating to your chosen picture. Pause the recording between each question to allow yourself time to answer. You are expected to say a few words or a short phrase / sentence in response to each question. One-word answers will not be sufficient to gain full marks. **(4 marks)**

Translation

2 Translate the following sentences **into English**.

(a) Ich finde das Internet nötig.

....

(b) Zu Hause haben wir einen neuen Computer.

....

(c) Meine Eltern denken, ich verbringe zu viel Zeit online.

....

(d) Gestern habe ich einen Film heruntergeladen.

....

(e) Wenn ich Zeit habe, spiele ich gern Videospiele.

.... **(10 marks)**

> Look at the tense of the verb. Most here are in the present tense, but one is not.

Media and technology

Had a go ☐ Nearly there ☐ Nailed it! ☐

Computer games

Playing computer games

1 Write to a Swiss friend about computer games.

You **must** include the following points:
- what you like about computer games
- what the negative aspects of gaming are
- which game(s) you have played recently
- which game you would like to try next.

Write your answer **in German**. You should aim to write between 80 and 90 words.

> On a real Writing paper, this would be one of two options. Choose the option that you know most vocabulary and phrases for. You can invent your likes, dislikes and experiences – the important thing is that you aim to use the German you know correctly.

....
....
....
....
....
....
....
....
....

(18 marks)

Role play

2 **Setting:** In a games shop

Scenario:
- You are in a games shop.
- Scan the QR code for the teacher's voice. Pause the recording between each prompt to allow yourself time to answer.
- The teacher will play the part of the shop assistant and will speak first.
- Your teacher will ask questions **in German** and you must answer **in German**.
- You are expected to say a few words or a short phrase / sentence in response to each prompt. One-word answers will not be sufficient to gain full marks.

> **Task:**
> 1 Say what sort of game you are looking for.
> 2 Say which games you usually play.
> 3 Ask a question about a new version of a game.
> 4 Say which game you will buy.
> 5 Ask a question about the price.

> Remember that your teacher will speak to you in the formal *Sie* form, but you can use either the *Sie* or *du* form to ask questions.

(10 marks)

> If you are not an expert on computer games, use vocabulary you know to say something plausible, e.g. *Ich mag Spiele über Fußball* or *Ich liebe Actionspiele*. There is no need to be able to name actual games.

Had a go ☐ **Nearly there** ☐ **Nailed it!** ☐

Media and technology

Pros and cons of technology

Picture task

See this photo in colour

1. Describe the photo. Write four short sentences **in German**.

   .... **(2 marks)**
   .... **(2 marks)**
   .... **(2 marks)**
   .... **(2 marks)**

   > You can begin your sentences with *Es gibt …* (There is / are …) or *Ich sehe …* (I can see …) or *Auf dem Foto gibt es …* (In the photo there is / are …).

Pros and cons of technology

2. Write a blog about technology and young people.

   You **must** include the following points:
   - how you use technology
   - the pros and cons of technology for young people
   - how you have used the internet recently
   - how you think technology will improve your life in future.

   Write your answer **in German**. You should aim to write between 130 and 150 words.

   > Remember to:
   > - say something about each bullet
   > - express and explain opinions
   > - develop in some detail the points where you have more to say
   > - write your response in paragraphs
   > - check that you have responded in the correct tense for bullet points 3 and 4.

   ....
   ....
   ....

   > Continue your answer on your own paper if necessary.

   ....
   ....
   ....
   ....
   .... **(22 marks)**

Media and technology

Had a go ☐   Nearly there ☐   Nailed it! ☐

Films on the internet

Streaming films

1 Mila is talking about streaming films.

What does she say?

Listen to the recording and complete the sentences by putting a cross [×] in the correct box for each question.

(a) Mila thinks that television is …

☐	A	boring.
☐	B	old-fashioned.
☐	C	relaxing.

(b) An advantage of streaming is that …

☐	A	you have more choice.
☐	B	you don't have to pay.
☐	C	you can see the latest films.

(c) She likes watching films in her …

☐	A	living room.
☐	B	dining room.
☐	C	bedroom.

(d) She pauses the film to …

☐	A	answer the phone.
☐	B	have a snack.
☐	C	walk her dog.

(4 marks)

Using technology

2 Translate the following paragraph **into English**.

> Im einundzwanzigsten Jahrhundert brauchen wir kein traditionelles Fernsehen mehr, da das sehr altmodisch ist. Heute haben wir das Internet und die Möglichkeit, alle Arten von Sendungen anzuschauen. Mit Netflix kann man sehen, was man will und auch die Uhrzeit wählen. Gestern habe ich mir einen interessanten Dokumentarfilm über Hochschulbildung angesehen.

> Make pencil notes as you read through the text for the first time, to capture the words you know.
>
> Then try to translate a chunk of language at a time – stop at commas and full stops, as they mark a natural break.
>
> If there are words you don't know, try to work them out and have a go, rather than leaving a gap.

> *Hochschulbildung* is a challenge here, so break it down: what does *hoch* mean? What does *Bildung* mean? What is a *Hochschule*?

....

....

....

....

....

....

....

(10 marks)

Had a go ☐ **Nearly there** ☐ **Nailed it!** ☐

Local environment

My home

Translation

1 Translate the following five sentences **into German**.

(a) My house is quite modern.

....

(b) There is a large kitchen.

....

(c) I like my bedroom because it is comfortable.

....

(d) In the evening we often watch a film.

....

(e) Last weekend we worked in the garden.

.... **(10 marks)**

> Check the verbs. One is not in the present tense.

> Watch out for dative case here – remember that it is used to describe the position / location of something, so after prepositions like *in*.

Dictation

2 You are going to hear someone talking about their home.

Sentences 1–2: write down the missing words in the gaps provided. In each gap, you will write one word **in German**.

Example: Meine <u>Familie</u> lebt in einer <u>Wohnung</u>.

1 Ich .... in einem kleinen .... in der ....

2 .... Haus hat einen .... und einen ....

Sentences 3–6: write down the full sentences that you hear in the spaces provided, **in German**.

Example: <u>Ich mag meinen Wohnort, weil er sauber ist.</u>

3 ....

4 ....

5 ....

6 .... **(10 marks)**

Sounds to watch out for here:
- *st* – sounds like 'sht'
- *ch* – throaty sound, as in *ich*
- final *-ig* – also sounds like *ich*
- *qu* – sounds like 'kv'
- *ö* – sounds like 'er'
- *äu* – combination that sounds like 'oy'
- final *-d* – as in *Gegend*, sounds like 't'
- *v* – sounds like 'f'.

Listen to the recording to practise these sounds.

Track 47

Local environment

Had a go ☐ Nearly there ☐ Nailed it! ☐

My town

Picture task

See this photo in colour

Remember to mention the people, place and activity.

The weather would be a good thing to mention here too.

1   Describe the photo. Write four short sentences in **German**.

   .... **(2 marks)**
   .... **(2 marks)**
   .... **(2 marks)**
   .... **(2 marks)**

Remember that you can start your sentences with *Es gibt …* (There is / are …) or *Ich sehe …* (I can see …).

Where I live

2   Felix is talking about his town.

   What does he say?

   Listen to the recording and put a cross [×] in each one of the **three** correct boxes.

Listen to the recording

Felix's town …

☐	**A**	is a cultural centre.
☐	**B**	has a lot of industry.
☐	**C**	has seven famous bridges.
☐	**D**	has a riverside market every day.
☐	**E**	has a successful concert hall.
☐	**F**	has a very modern art gallery.

There's a lot of information here, so it's a great idea to make rough notes as you listen, to help you capture the detail of what is said.

(3 marks)

Check which adjective describes which noun! Is it the music centre which is historic or the art gallery?

Check the time references – how often does the market take place?

Had a go ☐   **Nearly there** ☐   **Nailed it!** ☐   **Local environment**

Facilities in town

Describing what a town offers

1 Describe **ONE** of these pictures. Your description must cover:
- people
- location
- activity. **(8 marks)**

Picture 1

See this photo in colour

Picture 2

See this photo in colour

> There's a lot to say here. Some suggestions for picture 1:
> - It's outside in a street, the people are on foot and it looks like summer.
> - There are lots of people – describe what one or two are wearing.
> - People are walking, chatting, shopping and carrying bags.
>
> And for picture 2:
> - There are four young people, two girls and two boys.
> - They are shopping.
> - The girls are carrying bags.

> Don't over-develop your responses here. A simple sentence will be enough, so aim to give a short, relevant and clear response.

When you have finished your description, scan the corresponding QR code to listen to two questions relating to your chosen picture (Track 49 for Foundation questions and Track 50 for Higher questions). Pause the recording between each question to allow yourself time to answer. You are expected to say a few words or a short phrase / sentence in response to each question. One-word answers will not be sufficient to gain full marks. **(4 marks)**

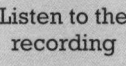

Dictation

2 You are going to hear someone talking about their town.

Sentences 1–3: Write down the missing words in the gaps provided. In each gap, you will write one word **in German**.

Example: Ich <u>wohne</u> in einer kleinen historischen <u>Stadt</u>.

1 Ich .... gern ....

2 Für junge .... gibt es viele ....

3 Wir .... eine tolle ....

> Sounds to listen out for here:
> - w – sounds like 'v'
> - ü – sounds like 'u' and 'e' combined
> - j – sounds like 'y'
> - eu – sounds like 'oy'
> - ie – sounds like 'ee'
> - sp – sounds like 'shp'
> - ä – sounds like 'a' and 'e' combined
> - st – sounds like 'sht'.

Sentences 4–6: Write down the full sentences that you hear in the spaces provided, **in German**.

Example: <u>In meiner Stadt gibt es viel zu sehen.</u>

4 ....

5 ....

6 ....   **(10 marks)**

Local environment

Had a go ☐ Nearly there ☐ Nailed it! ☐

Finding the way

Listen to the recording

Role play

1 **Setting:** Looking for a restaurant in town

Scenario:

- You are on holiday and looking for somewhere to eat.
- Scan the QR code for the teacher's voice. Pause the recording between each prompt to allow yourself time to answer.
- The teacher will play the part of the passer-by and will speak first.
- Your teacher will ask questions **in German** and you must answer **in German**.
- You are expected to say a few words or a short phrase / sentence in response to each prompt. One-word answers will not be sufficient to gain full marks.

> There will normally only be **one** question task in a Foundation tier role play, but here you have to ask **two** questions.

Task:
1 Say what you are looking for.
2 Ask how to get there.
3 Say how long you are staying.
4 Give your opinion of the town.
5 Ask a question about the distance to the restaurant / café.

> Think about how to form the questions during the preparation time in the exam.

(10 marks)

Listen to the recording

Role play

2 **Setting:** On holiday in Austria

Scenario:

- You are on holiday in Austria and looking for a campsite.
- Scan the QR code for the teacher's voice. Pause the recording between each prompt to allow yourself time to answer.
- The teacher will play the part of the passer-by and will speak first.
- Your teacher will ask questions **in German** and you must answer **in German**.
- You are expected to say a few words or a short phrase / sentence in response to each prompt. One-word answers will not be sufficient to gain full marks.

Task:
1 Say what you are looking for.
2 Say how long you are staying in the area.
3 Ask a question about getting to the campsite.
4 Say what you will be doing tomorrow.
5 Ask a question about buying food nearby.

(10 marks)

Had a go ☐   **Nearly there** ☐   **Nailed it!** ☐

> Local environment

Shops and shopping

Shopping for clothes

1 Describe this picture. Your description must cover:
   - people
   - location
   - activity. **(8 marks)**

See this photo in colour

> Say something about the person you can see in the picture – age, gender, appearance, mood and clothes can all be mentioned.
>
> Say something about the location of the picture – here, say something like 'she is in a clothes shop in town'.
>
> Finally, say what the person is doing – here, you could say 'she is shopping / looking for a new sweater / buying new clothes'.

Listen to the recording

When you have finished your description, scan the QR code to listen to two questions relating to your picture. Pause the recording between each question to allow yourself time to answer.
You are expected to say a few words or a short phrase / sentence in response to each question. One-word answers will not be sufficient to gain full marks. **(4 marks)**

At the bookstore

2 Describe this picture. Your description must cover:
   - people
   - location
   - activity. **(8 marks)**

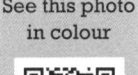
See this photo in colour

> Put together *Buch* and *Laden* to make *Buchladen* (m) to describe this location.

> Practise using colour adjectives in these examples to describe things like hair and clothing.

Listen to the recording

When you have finished your description, scan the QR code to listen to two questions relating to your picture. Pause the recording between each question to allow yourself time to answer.
You are expected to say a few words or a short phrase / sentence in response to each question. One-word answers will not be sufficient to gain full marks. **(4 marks)**

Local environment

Had a go ☐   Nearly there ☐   Nailed it! ☐

At the market

Role play

1 **Setting:** At the market

   Scenario:

   - You are at the market buying something to wear.
   - Scan the QR code for the teacher's voice. Pause the recording between each prompt to allow yourself time to answer.
   - The teacher will play the part of the stallholder and will speak first.
   - Your teacher will ask questions **in German** and you must answer **in German**.
   - You are expected to say a few words or a short phrase / sentence in response to each prompt. One-word answers will not be sufficient to gain full marks.

> Use the preparation time to plan your response to each task.
> - Here, you need to buy an item of clothing, so choose a word you're familiar with.
> - For the size, just say 'large' or 'small'.
> - Think about which colour words you know.

Task:
1 Say what item of clothing you would like to buy.
2 Say what size you would like.
3 Say which colour you like.
4 Give your opinion of the item of clothing.
5 Ask a question about the price.

> Each of your responses should include a verb. So for task 2, say *Ich möchte* and then the size.

(10 marks)

Role play

2 **Setting:** At the market

   Scenario:

   - You are at the market buying some flowers as a present.
   - Scan the QR code for the teacher's voice. Pause the recording between each prompt to allow yourself time to answer.
   - The teacher will play the part of the stallholder and will speak first.
   - Your teacher will ask questions **in German** and you must answer **in German**.
   - You are expected to say a few words or a short phrase / sentence in response to each prompt. One-word answers will not be sufficient to gain full marks.

Task:
1 Say that you would like to buy some flowers.
2 Say who the flowers are for.
3 Ask what colours the stallholder has.
4 Give your opinion of the flowers.
5 Ask whether the stallholder has some larger flowers.

> Make sure every response includes a verb. So don't just say *Blumen, bitte ...* or *Welche Farben?* as this only partly fulfils the task and won't get full marks.

(10 marks)

> Write brief notes in German in the right order using bullet points. This will allow you to glance at your notes and know what you need to say next.

Had a go ☐ Nearly there ☐ Nailed it! ☐   **Local environment**

Transport

Getting around

1. Write to someone you know about transport and how you get around.

   You **must** include the following points:
   - how you get to school
   - your opinion about good and less good ways of getting around
   - where you went recently and how you travelled
   - whether you will drive a car in the future.

   Write your answer **in German**. You should aim to write between 80 and 90 words.

   > Check the tense of the task before you start writing. It's a good idea to note down on the exam paper which task is in which tense.

   > There will always be **three** different time frames in this type of question (past, present and future, including the conditional form), which appear on both the Higher and Foundation tier papers.

   ....
   ....
   ....
   ....
   ....
   ....
   ....
   ....

   (18 marks)

Translation

2. Translate the following paragraph **into English**.

   > Die öffentlichen Verkehrsmittel in meiner Gegend sind wirklich schlecht, weil ich in einem Dorf auf dem Land wohne. Es gibt wenige Busse, und wir müssen oft das Auto benutzen, denn es gibt keine Alternative. Gestern hat mein Bruder mich zur Schule gefahren. Es regnete stark, und ich konnte nicht mit dem Rad fahren.

   ....
   ....
   ....
   ....
   ....

   (10 marks)

   > Check through your finished translation to make sure it sounds like usual English. If it doesn't, you may need to think about rephrasing. An example here is *es regnete stark*, which literally means 'it was raining strongly'. Ask yourself how you would express this idea – you could write 'it was raining hard / heavily' or 'it was pouring down / with rain'.

Local environment

Had a go ☐ Nearly there ☐ Nailed it! ☐

Buying tickets for travel

Buying tickets

Listen to the recording

1 Hanna is at a train station.

What does she mention?

> There are some numbers involved in the conversation – both times and prices.

Listen to the recording and complete the sentences by putting a cross [×] in the correct box for each question.

(a) Hanna wants to go to …

☐	A	Munich.
☐	B	Berlin.
☐	C	Cologne.

(b) She wants to travel …

☐	A	this evening.
☐	B	this afternoon.
☐	C	tomorrow morning.

(c) She will arrive at her destination at …

☐	A	8 am.
☐	B	8 pm.
☐	C	11 pm.

(d) She wants …

☐	A	a single ticket.
☐	B	a return ticket.
☐	C	a seat reservation.

(e) Her ticket costs …

☐	A	93 euros.
☐	B	30 euros.
☐	C	39 euros.

> Remember that for travel purposes the 24-hour clock is used; so, for example, *19:00 Uhr* is 7:00 pm.

(5 marks)

Role play

Listen to the recording

2 **Setting:** At a train station

Scenario:

- You are at a train station, buying a ticket.
- Scan the QR code for the teacher's voice. Pause the recording between each prompt to allow yourself time to answer.
- The teacher will play the part of the assistant and will speak first.
- Your teacher will ask questions **in German** and you must answer **in German**.
- You are expected to say a few words or a short phrase / sentence in response to each prompt. One-word answers will not be sufficient to gain full marks.

Task:
1 Say where you want to travel to.
2 Say which day you want to travel.
3 Ask a question about a train in the afternoon.
4 Say what time you would like to depart.
5 Ask when the train arrives.

> Think about how to formulate the two questions you need to ask.

(10 marks)

> Keep all your responses short, clear and focused on the task. You are not expected to develop your responses in this part of the test.

Had a go ☐ **Nearly there** ☐ **Nailed it!** ☐   Local environment

Places of interest near me

Describing places of interest

1 Describe this picture. Your description must cover:
   - people
   - location
   - activity.   **(8 marks)**

See this photo in colour

> Remember the key guidelines: Who? Where? What?
> - Who is in the picture? Mention their gender, age, appearance, clothes.
> - Where are they? If they are outside, mention the weather too. This is actually a picture of London, but all you need to say is something like 'it's a city ... there are old buildings.'
> - What are they doing?

Listen to the recording

When you have finished your description, scan the QR code to listen to two questions relating to your picture. Pause the recording between each question to allow yourself time to answer.
You are expected to say a few words or a short phrase / sentence in response to each question.
One-word answers will not be sufficient to gain full marks.   **(4 marks)**

Describing places of interest

2 Write to someone you know about places of interest.

You **must** include the following points:
   - a place of interest near where you live
   - whether your area is good for tourists
   - a place of interest you have visited in the past
   - a place you would like to visit in the future.

> Make sure that your response is in the appropriate time frame, so past tense for point 3 and future for point 4.

Write your answer **in German**. You should aim to write between 80 and 90 words.

....
....
....
....
....
....
....
....
.... **(18 marks)**

45

Environment

Had a go ☐ Nearly there ☐ Nailed it! ☐

The environment

Role play

1 **Setting:** Local radio interview

   Scenario:
   - You are speaking on local radio about the environment where you live.
   - Scan the QR code for the teacher's voice. Pause the recording between each prompt to allow yourself time to answer.
   - The teacher will play the part of the interviewer and will speak first.
   - Your teacher will ask questions **in German** and you must answer **in German**.
   - You are expected to say a few words or a short phrase / sentence in response to each prompt. One-word answers will not be sufficient to gain full marks.

   Task:
   1 Say what you think about the environment where you live.
   2 Say what you think the main problem is.
   3 Ask the interviewer to repeat the question.
   4 Say what you plan to do in the future to protect the environment.
   5 Ask the interviewer a question about what they do to be environmentally friendly.

   (10 marks)

Dictation

2 You are going to hear someone talking about the environment where they live.

   Sentences 1–3: write down the missing words in the gaps provided. In each gap, you will write one word **in German**.

   Example: Wir fahren zu oft mit dem Auto.

   1 Die .... ist nicht ....

   2 .... ist ein großes ....

   3 Es gibt .... in dem ....

   Sentences 4–6: write down the full sentences that you hear in the spaces provided, **in German**.

   Example: Wir sollen Energie sparen.

   4 ....

   5 ....

   6 ....   **(10 marks)**

> Sounds to listen out for here:
> - *st* – sounds like 'sht'
> - *au* – sounds like 'ow'
> - *v* – sounds like 'f'
> - *o* – a long sound in some words, e.g. *groß*
> - *e* – a long sound in some words, e.g. *Problem*
> - *w* – sounds like 'v'
> - *a* – a long sound in some words, e.g. *Glas*.
>
> Listen to the recording to practise these sounds.
>
> Track 63

Had a go ☐ Nearly there ☐ Nailed it! ☐

Environment

Environmental problems

Target grade 1-5

Read aloud

1 Your friend Samira has sent you some thoughts on the environment.

Read out the text below.

> Es gibt heute viele Umweltprobleme.
> Die Temperaturen werden immer höher.
> Die Meere sind schmutzig.
> Wir sollen unsere Erde besser schützen.
> In der Zukunft wird es vielleicht nicht genug Wasser geben.

(8 marks)

> Sounds to watch out for here:
> - *v* – sounds like a soft 'f'
> - *w* – sounds like 'v'
> - *ö* – sounds like a combination of 'o' and 'e'
> - *-e* – remember that an *-e* at the end is pronounced as a separate syllable
> - *ü* – sounds like a combination of 'u' and 'e'
> - *z* – sounds like 'ts'
> - *-d* – a final *-d* sounds like 't'.

Listen to the recording

Now play the recording of two questions related to what you have read.

You are expected to say a few words or a short phrase / sentence in response to each question. One-word answers will not be sufficient to gain full marks. **(4 marks)**

Target grade 5-9

Describing the environment

2 Describe this picture. Your description must cover:
- people
- location
- activity.   **(8 marks)**

See this photo in colour

> This is an unusual picture to describe.
> - It has two parts which are very different, so perhaps try to say something about the right-hand side and then the left-hand side.
> - You could use *auf der rechten Seite* and *auf der linken Seite* …
> - There is also a person for you to say something about – a man, walking across a field, wearing trousers and a T-shirt.
> - Feel free to include colour adjectives in your description, even though the picture here is black and white. This will be good practice for the exam pictures, which will be in colour.

Listen to the recording

When you have finished your description, scan the corresponding QR code to listen to two questions relating to your picture. Pause the recording between each question to allow yourself time to answer. You are expected to say a few words or a short phrase / sentence in response to each question. One-word answers will not be sufficient to gain full marks. **(4 marks)**

Environment

Had a go ☐ Nearly there ☐ Nailed it! ☐

The dangers of pollution

Dictation

1 You are going to hear someone talking about the environment.

Sentences 1–3: write down the missing words in the gaps provided. In each gap, you will write one word **in German**.

Example: Wir <u>müssen</u> mehr für die Umwelt <u>machen</u>.

1 Wir .... Energie ....

2 Ich .... mich jeden ....

3 Das .... nicht so viel ....

Sentences 4–6: write down the full sentences that you hear in the spaces provided, **in German**.

Example: <u>Ich versuche, wenig Strom zu benutzen.</u>

4 ....

5 ....

6 .... **(10 marks)**

> Sounds to listen out for here:
> - ö – sounds like 'o' and 'e' combined
> - sp – sounds like 'shp'
> - v – sound like 'f'
> - w – sounds like 'v'
> - -e – final -e is a sounded syllable
> - sch – sounds like 'sh'.

Describing an environmental activity

2 Describe this picture. Your description must cover:
- people
- location
- activity.

(8 marks)

See this photo in colour

> Start with the people – their appearance, clothing and mood.
>
> Then say something about the place – as it's an outdoor shot, you could mention the weather.

> Then describe what they are doing. Don't panic if you don't know some vocabulary – instead find things you *can* say. They are collecting / finding / looking for plastic / rubbish. They are making the park clean. They are helping the environment. They are putting plastic in a bag.

When you have finished your description, scan the QR code to listen to two questions relating to your picture. Pause the recording between each question to allow yourself time to answer. You are expected to say a few words or a short phrase / sentence in response to each question. One-word answers will not be sufficient to gain full marks. **(4 marks)**

Had a go ☐   Nearly there ☐   Nailed it! ☐

Environment

The natural world

Translation

1 Translate the following sentences **into English**.

> Check which tense the verb is in – one will not be in the present tense.

(a) Ich wohne in einem Dorf auf dem Land.

....

(b) Die frische Luft ist gesund.

....

(c) In meiner Gegend gibt es viele Bäume.

....

(d) Letztes Wochenende sind wir in dem Wald wandern gegangen.

....

(e) Es gefällt mir, hier zu leben.

.... **(10 marks)**

My home town

Listen to the recording

2 Paul is describing the area where he lives.

What does he say?

> Take care with sentence (e) as it uses the verb *gefallen*. Remember that this means 'to please' and is used to say what you like.

Complete the gap in each sentence using a word or phrase from the box below.
There are more words / phrases than gaps.

```
lake         sea          river
pollution    industry     airport
concerts     animals      castles
forests      cycle paths  fields
deep         dangerous    safe
```

> Remember that the questions reflect the order in which the information appears in the recording.

(a) Paul's home town is between the .... and the mountains.   **(1 mark)**

(b) Paul is glad that there is no ....   **(1 mark)**

(c) In the summer, tourists come to see ....   **(1 mark)**

(d) Outside the town there are ....   **(1 mark)**

(e) The river is .... for swimming.   **(1 mark)**

> Before listening to the recording for the first time, note down German versions of the English words given in the box. This helps you narrow down the options and discount what is **not** mentioned in the recording. So, for the first line in the box, you might note *See / Meer / Fluss* and then notice that *Fluss* is not mentioned until almost the end of the recording, and that *See* is not mentioned at all.

> There will also be distractors – words that are mentioned but which are not the required answer – so you need to listen closely for more specific detail: *(nicht viel) Verschmutzung* is an example here.

49

Environment

Had a go ☐ Nearly there ☐ Nailed it! ☐

Individual actions for the environment

Being environmentally friendly

1 Write a response to a survey about environmental problems.

You **must** include the following points:

- what you think about environmental problems
- why you think it is important to protect the environment
- what you will do in the future to be more environmentally friendly.

Write your answer **in German**. You should aim to write between 40 and 50 words.

> Remember that the third point on this question is in the **future** tense, so use a verb form which reflects this.

....
....
....
....
.... **(14 marks)**

Read aloud

2 Mia, your friend, has sent you some comments about the environment.

Read out the text below, then listen to the audio in the Answers section to check your pronunciation.

> Ich habe große Angst um unsere Umwelt.
>
> Ich denke, wir haben die Welt mit Verschmutzung kaputt gemacht.
>
> Das schlimmste Problem heute ist der Klimawandel, denn wir sehen jetzt oft Wetterveränderungen.
>
> Wir brauchen bessere Gesetze, um die Erde und das Meer zu schützen, und ich hoffe, dass es nicht schon zu spät ist.

(8 marks)

> Sounds to watch out for here:
> - w – sounds like 'v'
> - j – sounds like 'y'
> - z – sounds like 'ts'
> - ü – sounds like a combination of 'u' and 'e'
> - ä – sounds like a combination of 'a' and 'e'.
>
> Listen to the recording to practise these sounds.

Track 70

Listen to the recording

Now play the recording of two questions related to what you have read.

You are expected to say a few words or a short phrase / sentence in response to each question. One-word answers will not be sufficient to gain full marks.

(4 marks)

Had a go ☐ Nearly there ☐ Nailed it! ☐

Environment

How to recycle

Picture task

See this photo in colour

> Mention the people in the photo first – their age, clothing and appearance.
>
> Mention where they are – outside, in the garden or at home.

1 Describe the photo. Write four short sentences **in German**.

.... **(2 marks)**

.... **(2 marks)**

.... **(2 marks)**

.... **(2 marks)**

> You can begin your sentences with *Es gibt* ... or *Ich sehe* ... This gives you a strong starting point for each response.

Translation

2 Translate the paragraph **into German**.

> I am interested in the environment and want to protect it. So I always sort the rubbish at home and put paper in the blue sack* and plastic in the yellow sack. It is not difficult and everyone should do it. If you sort the things, you can recycle them.

* sack – *Sack* (m)

> Remember: you need a reflexive verb to say 'I am interested in'.
>
> How would you say 'so'? You can use *deshalb* which means 'because of this' or 'that's why'.
>
> Remember the rule about modal verbs like *sollen* sending the infinitive to the end of the sentence.

....

....

....

....

....

....

.... **(10 marks)**

My school

Had a go ☐ Nearly there ☐ Nailed it! ☐

My school

Picture task

See this photo in colour

Remember the key content:
- Who can you see?
- Where are they?
- What are they doing?
- You can start each response with *Es gibt …* (There is / are …) or *Ich sehe …* (I can see …).

1 Describe the photo. Write four short sentences **in German**.

.... **(2 marks)**

.... **(2 marks)**

.... **(2 marks)**

.... **(2 marks)**

Describing children leaving the school

2 Describe this picture. Your description must cover:
- people
- location
- activity.

Mention **who** is in the picture, **where** they are and **what** they are doing!

(8 marks)

See this photo in colour

Listen to the recording

When you have finished your description, scan the QR code to listen to two questions relating to your picture. Pause the recording between each question to allow yourself time to answer. You are expected to say a few words or a short phrase / sentence in response to each question. One-word answers will not be sufficient to gain full marks.   **(4 marks)**

52

Had a go ☐ Nearly there ☐ Nailed it! ☐   **My school**

School subjects

Role play

1 **Setting:** A school interview

Scenario:

- You are being interviewed for a place in a new school.
- Scan the QR code for the teacher's voice. Pause the recording between each prompt to allow yourself time to answer.
- The teacher will play the part of the teacher in the new school and will speak first.
- Your teacher will ask questions **in German** and you must answer **in German**.
- You are expected to say a few words or a short phrase / sentence in response to each prompt. One-word answers will not be sufficient to gain full marks.

Task:
1 Say why you want to come to this school.
2 Say what your best subjects are.
3 Ask a question about sport in the new school.
4 Say what homework you will do this evening.
5 Ask a question about class sizes.

> Keep your responses short, concise and clear – long detailed answers are not needed in this task.

(10 marks)

How do you like your school?

2 Read these forum posts.

> **Robin:** Ich finde alle meine Stunden ganz gut, aber einige Fächer sind besser als andere. Mathe ist mein bestes Fach, aber ich bin schwach in Kunst.
>
> **Malik:** Meine Lieblingsfächer sind Naturwissenschaften und Kunst, aber Englisch finde ich langweilig, und die Hausaufgaben sind zu schwierig!
>
> **Jana:** Ich muss sagen, ich arbeite nicht viel. Ich sollte fleißiger sein! Ich mag den Sportunterricht, denn das macht Spaß, und Englisch und Geschichte sind auch nicht schlecht. Aber warum muss ich jeden Tag Mathe lernen?

Who says what? Choose the correct answers.

Put a cross [×] in the correct column for each question.

	Who …	Robin	Malik	Jana
(a)	… loves science subjects?			
(b)	… thinks there are too many maths lessons?			
(c)	… finds English homework difficult?			
(d)	… is not very hardworking?			
(e)	… enjoys all their lessons?			
(f)	… is not good at art?			

(6 marks)

> For each person, note the subject mentioned and their opinion of it. This will help you choose the right person.

53

My school

Had a go ☐ Nearly there ☐ Nailed it! ☐

My teachers

What I think of my teachers

1 Write a blog about teachers and teaching.

You **must** include the following points:
- what your teachers are like this year
- the characteristics of a good and a bad teacher
- a good lesson you have had recently
- whether you would like to be a teacher in the future.

Write your answer **in German**. You should aim to write between 130 and 150 words.

> Note which tense is required for each bullet point, and ensure you use the right one in your response.

> Aim to express opinions and explain them, particularly in bullet point 2.

> Try to develop your ideas in some detail and aim to use some complex structures, such as:
> - *um ... zu*
> - *dass* – word order
> - *weil* – word order
> - relative clauses
> - inversion – verb in second place
> - *obwohl* – word order
> - the passive
> - the conditional (a good one for bullet point 4).

....

....

....

....

.... **(22 marks)**

Read aloud

2 Mohamed, your friend, has sent you some information about his teachers.

Read out the text below, then listen to the audio in the Answers section to check your pronunciation.

> Ich habe einige tolle Lehrer.
> Meine Englischlehrerin ist sehr freundlich.
> Ich mag den Unterricht in meiner Schule.
> In Kunst bin ich stark und ich finde das Fach nicht schwierig.
> Ein guter Lehrer soll den Schülern helfen.

(8 marks)

> Sounds to watch out for here:
> - final *-e* – sound the syllable
> - final *-ich* – a soft sound in the throat (not 'ick'!)
> - *rr* – try to roll the *r* sound at the back of your throat
> - *st* – sounds like 'sht'
> - final *-ig* – sounds like 'ich' (see above)
> - *ü* – like a 'u' and 'e' combined, with pursed lips.
>
> Listen to the recording to practise these sounds.

Track 74

Listen to the recording

Now play the recording of two questions related to what you have read.

You are expected to say a few words or a short phrase / sentence in response to each question. One-word answers will not be sufficient to gain full marks. **(4 marks)**

Had a go ☐ **Nearly there** ☐ **Nailed it!** ☐

My school

The school day

Writing about my school day

1. Write to a Swiss friend about your school day.

   You **must** include the following points:
   - what lessons you have when
   - your opinion of the school day
   - what you did at break yesterday
   - what you will do in school tomorrow.

   Write your answer **in German**. You should aim to write between 80 and 90 words.

> For bullet point 1, say something about your timetable, which lessons you have on which day or how often you have a subject in the week. Or you could mention your favourite day and say why.

> For bullet point 2, express a couple of opinions and explain them. For example, is the school day too long? Is break too short? Does school start too early?

....
....
....
....
....
....
....
....

(18 marks)

My weekly lesson schedule

2. Elias is talking about his timetable.

   What does he mention?

   Listen to the recording and complete the gaps in the timetable using a subject from the box below.

   There are more subjects than gaps.

> Listen to the recording three times and try the following:
> First time: make quick notes.
> Second time: try to write in your answers.
> Third time: check your answers.

Listen to the recording

Science	German	Art
History	Sport	Music
English	Maths	

	MONDAY	TUESDAY	WEDNESDAY
1	MATHS	ENGLISH	(e)....................
2	(a)....................	(b)....................	MATHS
3	HISTORY	MATHS	SCIENCE
BREAK			
4	ENGLISH	(c)....................	GERMAN
LUNCH			
5	SPORT	GERMAN	ART
6	SPORT	(d)....................	ART

(5 marks)

55

My school

Had a go ☐   Nearly there ☐   Nailed it! ☐

School uniform

Clothes I wear

1 Write to a German friend about school uniform.

You **must** include the following points:
- what you wear at school
- the pros and cons of school uniform
- what you wore for a recent sports lesson
- what you will wear this evening.

Write your answer **in German**. You should aim to write between 80 and 90 words.

> Express and explain opinions – especially in bullet point 2.

> Remember that bullet points 3 and 4 are not in the present tense. You need to use the appropriate time frame to be credited for your responses to these points.

....
....
....
....
....
....
....
....
....
....

(18 marks)

Translation

2 Translate the following five sentences **into German**.

(a) I do not like the uniform.
....

(b) We wear a black jacket and a white shirt.
....

(c) The boys must wear a grey tie.
....

(d) You are only allowed to wear black shoes.
....

(e) Yesterday I bought red socks.
....

(10 marks)

> Check the subject of each sentence and make sure you use a verb to match it.

> Ask yourself whether 'You' in sentence (d) should be translated as *du* or *man*.

> Sentence (e) should include a past tense.

Had a go ☐ Nearly there ☐ Nailed it! ☐

My school

School rules

Role play

1 **Setting:** Survey on school rules

Scenario:

Don't overextend your responses in this task.

Short, relevant and clear comments are best.

- You are taking part in a survey on school rules and are talking to a researcher.
- Scan the QR code for the teacher's voice. Pause the recording between each prompt to allow yourself time to answer.
- The teacher will play the part of the researcher and will speak first.
- Your teacher will ask questions **in German** and you must answer **in German**.
- You are expected to say a few words or a short phrase / sentence in response to each prompt. One-word answers will not be sufficient to gain full marks.

Task:
1 Say what you think about school rules in general.
2 Say which rule you think is good.
3 Say something about a rule you don't like.
4 Say what you think about the school uniform.
5 Ask whether the researcher has any more questions.

Make notes during the preparation time on what you intend to say in the exam.

Take particular care when planning the question tasks.

(10 marks)

Role play

2 **Setting:** Survey on school rules

Scenario:

Don't overextend your responses in this task.

Short, relevant and clear comments are best.

- You are taking part in a survey on school rules and are talking to a researcher.
- Scan the QR code for the teacher's voice. Pause the recording between each prompt to allow yourself time to answer.
- The teacher will play the part of the researcher and will speak first.
- Your teacher will ask questions **in German** and you must answer **in German**.
- You are expected to say a few words or a short phrase / sentence in response to each prompt. One-word answers will not be sufficient to gain full marks.

Task:
1 Say why you think school rules are important.
2 Say which rule is the most important.
3 Ask if the researcher will be speaking to many pupils.
4 Say which rule you don't like.
5 Ask whether the researcher has any more questions.

Make notes during the preparation time of what you intend to say in the exam.

Take particular care when planning the question tasks.

(10 marks)

My school | Had a go ☐ Nearly there ☐ Nailed it! ☐

School clubs

Picture task

See this photo in colour

> Use *Es gibt* … (there is / are …) to get you started.
>
> You can also use *Ich sehe* … (I can see …).

1 Describe the photo. Write four short sentences **in German**.

.... (2 marks)

.... (2 marks)

.... (2 marks)

.... (2 marks)

Role play

2 **Setting:** In the school office

Scenario:

- You are talking to a teacher about after-school activities.
- Scan the QR code for the teacher's voice. Pause the recording between each prompt to allow yourself time to answer.
- The teacher will play the part of the teacher and will speak first.
- Your teacher will ask questions **in German** and you must answer **in German**.
- You are expected to say a few words or a short phrase / sentence in response to each prompt. One-word answers will not be sufficient to gain full marks.

Task:
1 Say why you think after-school clubs are important.
2 Say what sort of clubs you want in your school.
3 Ask a question about when new clubs will start.
4 Say what activity you will do today after school.
5 Ask a question about a film club.

> Think carefully about how to formulate the questions.

> Avoid lengthy answers – short, relevant and clear answers are important here.

(10 marks)

Had a go ☐ Nearly there ☐ Nailed it! ☐

My school

School trips

Translation

1 Translate the following sentences **into English**.

> Check the subject of the sentence and look at the verb – this gives you a starting point.

(a) Ich mag Schulreisen.

....

(b) Manchmal gehen wir an die Küste.

....

(c) Es macht Spaß, weil wir alle zusammen sind.

....

(d) Letztes Jahr sind wir nach London gefahren.

....

(e) Meine Freundin will nach Deutschland fahren.

.... **(10 marks)**

> Check which tense the verb is in – one will not be in the present tense.
> Now look at the nouns and see how they fit with the verbs.
> Then look at which words are left; think what they mean – if you're not sure, make an intelligent guess rather than leave a gap.

> Make sure you account for every word in your translation – don't miss out small but vital words like *gern*, *weil*, *alle*.

Read aloud

2 Your friend Sofie has sent you some information about school trips.

Read out the text below, then listen to the audio in the Answers section to check your pronunciation.

> Ich werde nächsten Sommer nach England fahren.
> Mein Lehrer hat einen Austausch mit einer kleinen Schule organisiert.
> Wir werden im Juli nach London fliegen und werden acht Tage bei unseren Austauschpartnern verbringen.
> Ich freue mich so sehr darauf, mein Englisch nochmal zu üben und etwas über die Kultur zu lernen.

(8 marks)

> Sounds to watch out for here:
> - *ä* – sounds like a combination of 'a' and 'e'
> - final *-d* – sounds like 't'
> - *w* – sounds like 'v'
> - *ich* – sounds soft and throaty, not 'ick'
> - *ü* – sounds like a combination of 'u' and 'e', with pursed lips.
>
> Listen to the recording to practise these sounds.

Track 79

Listen to the recording

Now play the recording of two questions related to what you have read.

You are expected to say a few words or a short phrase / sentence in response to each question. One-word answers will not be sufficient to gain full marks. **(4 marks)**

59

My school Had a go ☐ Nearly there ☐ Nailed it! ☐

Homework

Pros and cons of homework

1. Write a response to a survey about homework.

   You **must** include the following points:
   - how much time you spend on homework
   - the pros and cons of homework
   - what homework you will do this evening.

   Write your answer **in German**. You should aim to write between 40 and 50 words.

> Make sure you address all three bullet points, although you don't need to cover them in equal detail.

> Note that bullet point 3 needs a response in the future time frame.

....
....
....
....
....

(14 marks)

Translation

2. Translate the paragraph **into German**.

> At school I am hard-working and always try to get good marks. I do a lot of homework, because I think it is important to take responsibility for your own learning. Yesterday evening I spent three hours on German homework. That was hard, but I think that I understand it better now.

> If there's a word you don't know, try to use a sensible alternative rather than leave a gap.

> There are some complex structures here, so think carefully about word order / where to put the verbs.

....
....
....
....
....
....
....
....
....

(10 marks)

Had a go ☐ Nearly there ☐ Nailed it! ☐ 　　My school

Stress at school

How to deal with stress

1 Read this online advice for parents about helping young people with stress.

> Kinder und Jugendliche brauchen eine sichere Umgebung, die sie unterstützt. Sie müssen wissen, dass sie Ihre Unterstützung haben. Am wichtigsten ist es, mit dem / der Jugendlichen im Gespräch zu bleiben, damit es immer einen engen Kontakt gibt.
>
> Wenn Sie immer bereit sind, mit ihr / ihm zu sprechen, zeigt das, dass er / sie wichtig ist und dass Sie versuchen, seine / ihre Probleme zu verstehen.
>
> Stellen Sie sich die folgenden Fragen:
> - Schläft er / sie genug?
> - Gibt es eine klare Struktur mit festen Zeiten für Mahlzeiten und Hausaufgaben?
> - Gibt es einen Lernplan, damit er / sie Stück für Stück* die Arbeit schafft, erfolgreich wird und alle Probleme *überwinden* kann?

* *Stück für Stück* – bit by bit

(a) Complete the gap in each sentence using a word from the box below. There are more words than gaps.

study plans	surroundings	homework
support	conversation	contact
sleep	structure	meals

(i)   Children and young people need safe .... **(1 mark)**

(ii) They need to feel they have .... **(1 mark)**

(iii) The most important thing is .... **(1 mark)**

(iv) Parents should check that young people are getting enough .... **(1 mark)**

(v) A clear structure builds in set time for homework and .... **(1 mark)**

(b) Which of these is the best translation for the word *überwinden*?

Put a cross [×] in the correct box.

☐	**A** to fail
☐	**B** to overcome
☐	**C** to ignore

(1 mark)

Read aloud

2 Your friend Katharina has written to you about stress at school. Read out the text below.

> Ich bin jetzt gestresst.
> Es gibt bald wichtige Prüfungen.
> Ich habe Angst, dass ich dieses Jahr nicht genug gelernt habe.
> Ich werde heute Abend drei Stunden Hausaufgaben machen.
> Ich muss Deutsch, Englisch und Mathe lernen.

(8 marks)

Now play the recording of two questions related to what you have read.

You are expected to say a few words or a short phrase / sentence in response to each question. One-word answers will not be sufficient to gain full marks. **(4 marks)**

My school

Had a go ☐ Nearly there ☐ Nailed it! ☐

Preparing for exams

Listen to the recording

Role play

1 **Setting:** Interview on exam preparation

   Scenario:

   - You are doing an interview about exam preparation.
   - Scan the QR code for the teacher's voice. Pause the recording between each prompt to allow yourself time to answer.
   - The teacher will play the part of the interviewer and will speak first.
   - Your teacher will ask questions **in German** and you must answer **in German**.
   - You are expected to say a few words or a short phrase / sentence in response to each prompt. One-word answers will not be sufficient to gain full marks.   **(10 marks)**

> In the exam, you should plan your responses carefully during the preparation time.

Task:
1 Say how long you spend on schoolwork each evening.
2 Say where you do your work.
3 Say how often you have a break.
4 Say why you are working so hard.
5 Ask the interviewer a question about exams.

> Pay particular attention to formulating the question you need to ask for task 5. Keep the question simple. For example, you could ask *Wie findest du ... ?* or *Wie finden Sie ... ?*

Listen to the recording

Dictation

2 You are going to hear someone talking about preparing for exams.

   Sentences 1–2: write down the missing words in the gaps provided. In each gap, you will write one word **in German**.

   Example: Diese <u>Prüfungen</u> sind mir sehr <u>wichtig</u>.

   1 Man kann nicht .... in der .... Minute ....

   2 Ich habe .... vier Monaten .... in ....

   Sentences 3–6: write down the full sentences that you hear in the spaces provided, **in German**.

   Example: <u>Ich möchte gute Noten bekommen.</u>

   3 ....

   4 ....

   5 ....

   6 ....   **(10 marks)**

> Sounds to listen out for here:
> - final *-e* – always sounded as a separate syllable
> - *s* – note the difference between *s* and *z* at the start of a word: *s* sounds like a soft English 'z' (like 'zoo') and German *z* sounds like 'ts'
> - *g* – a hard sound, as in English 'get'
> - *ei* – sounds like the English word 'I'
> - *ä* – sounds like 'a' and 'e' combined
> - *ö* – sounds like 'o' and 'e' combined
> - *z* – sounds like 'ts'
> - *st* – sounds like 'sht'.

Had a go ☐ Nearly there ☐ Nailed it! ☐   My school

My ideal school

Picture task

See this photo in colour

You could write about the following:

1 The people in the photo – their clothes, age, appearance.
2 Where they are – outside, in front of a school.
3 What they are doing – leaving school, going home.
4 What the school building looks like.

1 Describe the photo. Write four short sentences **in German**.

.... (2 marks)
.... (2 marks)
.... (2 marks)
.... (2 marks)

Remember that *Es gibt …* or *Ich sehe …* are good starting points for your sentences.

Dictation

2 You are going to hear someone talking about an ideal school.

Sentences 1–2: write down the missing words in the gaps provided. In each gap, you will write one word **in German**.

Example: Meine Schule ist viel zu groß.

Sounds to listen out for here:
- sch – sounds like 'sh'
- äu – sounds like 'oy'
- ü – sounds like 'u' and 'e' combined, with pursed lips
- w – sounds like 'v'
- ä – sounds like 'a' and 'e' combined
- ch – a soft sound, as in *ich*
- -e – final -e is a syllable.

1 Alle .... finden das .... sehr ....

2 Die .... sind aber .... und .... sich um uns.

Sentences 3–6: write down the full sentences that you hear in the spaces provided, **in German**.

Example: Ich lerne gern Geschichte.

3 ....
4 ....
5 ....
6 .... (10 marks)

My future

Had a go ☐ Nearly there ☐ Nailed it! ☐

Plans for next year

What are your plans for next year?

1 Write a response to a survey about school and plans for next year.

You **must** include the following points:
- what you enjoy at school this year
- what you don't like about school this year
- what you want to do next year.

Write your answer **in German**. You should aim to write between 40 and 50 words.

> When you express an opinion (bullet points 1 and 2), try to explain why you think this.

> Bullet point 3 needs a future time frame. There are several ways to do this, so use the one you feel most confident about.

....
....
....
....
....
....
....

(14 marks)

Listen to the recording

Role play

2 **Setting:** At school

Scenario:
- You are talking to the headteacher at your school.
- Scan the QR code for the teacher's voice. Pause the recording between each prompt to allow yourself time to answer.
- The teacher will play the part of the headteacher and will speak first.
- Your teacher will ask questions **in German** and you must answer **in German**.
- You are expected to say a few words or a short phrase / sentence in response to each prompt. One-word answers will not be sufficient to gain full marks.

> **Task:**
> 1 Say what you would like to learn in the sixth form.
> 2 Say what your best subject is this year.
> 3 Ask a question about the exam grades you need.
> 4 Say whether you would like to go to university.
> 5 Ask a question about school trips.

> Keep your answers short – simply say enough to provide the information required by the task.

(10 marks)

Had a go ☐ Nearly there ☐ Nailed it! ☐

My future

Future studies

Picture task

1 Describe the photo. Write four short sentences **in German**.

   .... **(2 marks)**

   .... **(2 marks)**

   .... **(2 marks)**

   .... **(2 marks)**

> For the location, mention whether it is inside or outside. If outside, as here, comment on the weather.

How do you prepare for exams?

2 Describe this picture. Your description must cover:

   • people
   • location
   • activity.   **(8 marks)**

> To refer to the foreground figures, start with *Im Vordergrund ...*

> To say where you think the photo might have been taken, start with *Ich denke ... or Das ist vielleicht ...* (Perhaps it is ...).

When you have finished your description, scan the QR code to listen to two questions relating to your picture. Pause the recording between each question to allow yourself time to answer. You are expected to say a few words or a short phrase / sentence in response to each question. One-word answers will not be sufficient to gain full marks.   **(4 marks)**

65

My future

Had a go ☐ Nearly there ☐ Nailed it! ☐

Future career

My future career

1 Write a response to a survey about your future job.

You **must** include the following points:

- what sort of person you are
- what is important to you in a job
- which job you would like in the future.

> Make sure you answer each bullet point.
>
> Remember that bullet point 3 is in the future tense.

Write your answer **in German**. You should aim to write between 40 and 50 words.

....
....
....
....
....
....
....
....

(14 marks)

Read aloud

2 Mia, your friend, has sent you some information about her future career.

Read out the text below, then listen to the audio in the Answers section to check your pronunciation.

> Ich interessiere mich vor allem für die Umwelt.
>
> Heute ist Umweltverschmutzung ein enormes Problem, und es gibt viele Gefahren für unsere Welt.
>
> Aus diesem Grund möchte ich später im Bereich Umweltschutz arbeiten.
>
> Ich bin nicht sicher, welche beruflichen Möglichkeiten es gibt, aber ich denke, diese Arbeit ist wichtig.

(8 marks)

> Sounds to watch out for here:
> - *v* – sounds like a soft 'f'
> - short *e* – you need this sound in words like *allem* and *Umwelt*
> - long *e* – you need this sound in words like *Problem*
> - *ie* – sounds like the English 'ee', e.g. *diese*
> - *ei* – sounds like the English 'I', e.g. *Bereich, arbeiten*
> - *w* – sounds like 'v', e.g. *Welt, welche, wichtig*.
>
> Listen to the recording to practise these sounds.

Track 87

Listen to the recording

Now play the recording of two questions related to what you have read.

You are expected to say a few words or a short phrase / sentence in response to each question. One-word answers will not be sufficient to gain full marks.

(4 marks)

Had a go ☐ Nearly there ☐ Nailed it! ☐

My future

Pros and cons of some jobs

Discussing jobs

1 Write to an Austrian friend about possible future jobs.

You **must** include the following points:

- which job a relative or friend has
- your opinion of what makes a good job
- how you have earned money in the past
- which job you would like to have in the future.

Write your answer **in German**. You should aim to write between 80 and 90 words.

> For bullet point 1, say something about someone you know and their job – or invent someone!

> For bullet point 2, express a couple of opinions and explain them. For example – is good pay important? Why? Or nice colleagues? Or a pleasant working environment? Why?

> Remember that bullet point 3 needs a past time frame – if you haven't earned money in the past, say that and explain why. Or again, you can invent a way you have earned money. If you have less to say on this point, that's fine, as you can make up the word count on the other bullet points. (The sample response in the answer section demonstrates this.) But make sure you cover all four bullet points.

....
....
....
....
....
....
....

(14 marks)

Role play

2 **Setting:** At the careers office

Scenario:

- You are talking to a careers adviser.
- Scan the QR code for the teacher's voice. Pause the recording between each prompt to allow yourself time to answer.
- The teacher will play the part of the careers adviser and will speak first.
- Your teacher will ask questions **in German** and you must answer **in German**.
- You are expected to say a few words or a short phrase / sentence in response to each prompt. One-word answers will not be sufficient to gain full marks.

> **Task:**
> 1 Say which school subjects you like.
> 2 Say what interests you have.
> 3 Say what job you want in the future.
> 4 Say what is good about this job.
> 5 Ask a question about the adviser's job.

> Keep the questions simple. For example – What do you think of your job? Do you like your job?

(10 marks)

My future — Had a go ☐ Nearly there ☐ Nailed it! ☐

My dream job

Picture task

See this photo in colour

1 Describe the photo. Write four short sentences **in German**.

.... **(2 marks)**

.... **(2 marks)**

.... **(2 marks)**

.... **(2 marks)**

> For people, you can comment on their appearance and / or clothing and mention colours.

> You could begin your sentences with *Es gibt* … or *Ich sehe* … .

Read aloud

2 Elif, your friend, has sent you some comments about her ambitions.

Read out the text below.

> Ich träume davon, in der Zukunft mit Jugendlichen zu arbeiten.
>
> Ich würde gerne in einer Gesamtschule entweder Geschichte oder Englisch unterrichten.
>
> Wenn es möglich ist, möchte ich auch ein Jahr im Ausland arbeiten, vielleicht in Afrika.
>
> Dieses Jahr muss ich fleißig arbeiten, um in den Prüfungen gute Noten zu kriegen.

(8 marks)

Listen to the recording

Now play the recording of two questions related to what you have read.

You are expected to say a few words or a short phrase / sentence in response to each question. One-word answers will not be sufficient to gain full marks. **(4 marks)**

Had a go ☐   **Nearly there** ☐   **Nailed it!** ☐

My future

Gap year

Doing a gap year

1 Describe this picture. Your description must cover:
   - people
   - location
   - activity. **(8 marks)**

See this photo in colour

Practise using colour adjectives even if the picture is in black and white, or scan the QR code above to see it in colour.

Listen to the recording

When you have finished your description, scan the QR code to listen to two questions relating to your picture. Pause the recording between each question to allow yourself time to answer.
You are expected to say a few words or a short phrase / sentence in response to each question.
One-word answers will not be sufficient to gain full marks. **(4 marks)**

What are your plans for the future?

2 Broader conversation questions

   This is a conversation on the broader thematic context of **Studying and my future**.
   - Listen to the questions in the recording and give your answers in the pauses.
   - Pause the recording if you need more time.
   - There will be questions in the present, past and future tenses.
   - Your responses should be as full and detailed as possible. **(16 marks)**

Listen to the recording

This broader conversation follows the photo card part of the Speaking exam and can cover many questions in a conversation lasting around 5 minutes.

This is an opportunity to express and explain opinions, to use all three time frames and to use some elements of more complex language.

My future — Had a go ☐ Nearly there ☐ Nailed it! ☐

Equality and helping others

Read aloud

1. Your Swiss friend, Yasmin, has sent you some information about her town.

   Read out the text below, then listen to the audio in the Answers section to check your pronunciation.

   > Meine Stadt in Deutschland ist multikulturell.
   > Hier leben Menschen aus anderen Ländern der Welt.
   > Es gibt hier keine Diskriminierung.
   > Wir respektieren alle Religionen und Traditionen.
   > Ich habe viele Freundinnen – sie kommen aus Asien und aus Afrika.

   (8 marks)

   > Sounds to watch out for here:
   > - *st* – sounds like 'sht'
   > - final *-d* – sounds like 't'
   > - *ä* – sounds like 'a' and 'e' combined
   > - *ei* – sounds like the English word 'I'
   > - *w* – sounds like 'v'
   > - *g* – is a hard sound
   >
   > Listen to the recording to practise these sounds.

   Track 93

Now play the recording of two questions related to what you have read.

You are expected to say a few words or a short phrase / sentence in response to each question. One-word answers will not be sufficient to gain full marks. **(4 marks)**

Translation

2. Translate the following paragraph **into English**.

   > Ich wohne in Wien, der Hauptstadt von Österreich und einem berühmten Zentrum für Musik, Kunst und Kultur. Das Neujahrskonzert ist weltweit beliebt. Die Menschen in der Stadt stammen aus verschiedenen Ländern, deshalb ist die Kultur sehr interessant. Meine Mutter arbeitet mit Flüchtlingen, die wegen des Krieges ihre Heimat verlassen haben.

   ....
   ....
   ....
   ....
   ....
   ....
   .... **(10 marks)**

   > Don't be put off by nouns which appear long. They are usually compound nouns, composed of two or more shorter words. A good example here is *Neujahrskonzert*, which breaks down into *neu* (new) *Jahr* (year) and *Konzert* (concert).

Had a go ☐ Nearly there ☐ Nailed it! ☐

Tourism

Holiday activities

Holiday plans

1. Write a response to a survey about how you spend holidays.

   You **must** include the following points:
   - what you usually do in the holidays
   - your opinion of going abroad on holiday
   - your plans for the next summer holidays.

   Write your answer **in German**. You should aim to write between 40 and 50 words.

   > Bullet point 2 asks you to express opinions – also try to explain an opinion by saying why you think this.
   >
   > Bullet point 3 is in the future time frame – You could use a future tense (using *werden*) or a present tense with a future time marker, for example *Nächsten Sommer fahre ich ...*. You could also use *Ich will* or *ich möchte*.

   ....
   ....
   ....
   ....
   .... **(14 marks)**

Describing a beach holiday

2. Describe this picture. Your description must cover:
   - people
   - location
   - activity.

   (8 marks)

See this photo in colour

> You could also include details about the weather, the surroundings and where it might be.

Listen to the recording

When you have finished your description, scan the QR code to listen to two questions relating to your picture. Pause the recording between each question to allow yourself time to answer.
You are expected to say a few words or a short phrase / sentence in response to each question. One-word answers will not be sufficient to gain full marks. **(4 marks)**

71

Tourism

Had a go ☐ Nearly there ☐ Nailed it! ☐

Camping

Picture task

See this photo in colour

A good way to begin your sentences is *Es gibt ...* (There is / are ...) or *Ich sehe ...* (I can see ...).

1 Describe the photo. Write four short sentences **in German**.

    .... **(2 marks)**

    .... **(2 marks)**

    .... **(2 marks)**

    .... **(2 marks)**

Listen to the recording

Camping plans

2 Tim and Max are planning a camping weekend together.

   What do they discuss?

   Complete the gap in each sentence using a word from the box below.

   There are more words than gaps.

worried	excited	unhappy
boring	fun	interesting
café	forest	games room
cycling	hiking	boating
difficult	cold	romantic

As you listen for the first time, try to make quick notes of what each person says.

These notes will help you sort out who thinks what and will help you answer the questions.

   (a) Tim is .... about the camping trip. **(1 mark)**

   (b) Tim thinks it will be .... **(1 mark)**

   (c) Tim says the campsite has a lake and a .... **(1 mark)**

   (d) Tim says they will be able to go .... and swimming. **(1 mark)**

   (e) Max thinks it will be .... **(1 mark)**

Had a go ☐   Nearly there ☐   Nailed it! ☐

Tourism

Holiday accommodation

Dictation

1 You are going to hear someone talking about holidays.

Sentences 1–3: write down the missing words in the gaps provided. In each gap, you will write one word **in German**.

Example: Wir fahren nicht oft in den Urlaub.

1 Wir sind in einer .... am ....

2 Unsere Tante .... in einem .... Hotel.

3 Hinter dem .... gab es einen .... Garten.

Sentences 4–6: write down the full sentences that you hear in the spaces provided, **in German**.

Example: Ich verbringe zwei Wochen in Spanien.

4 ....

5 ....

6 ....   **(10 marks)**

Read aloud

2 Leon, your friend, has sent you some information about his holidays.

Read out the text below, then listen to the audio in the Answers section to check your pronunciation.

> Wir fahren nicht jedes Jahr in Urlaub, weil es heute so teuer ist.
> Manchmal bleiben wir hier in der Gegend und machen mit dem Auto Tagesausflüge.
> Letzten Sommer waren wir in einem Ferienhaus an der Küste, was sehr schön war.
> Während der Woche haben wir in der Nähe ein Schloss besucht.

(8 marks)

> Sounds to watch out for here:
> - w – sounds like 'v' (*wir, weil*)
> - eu – sounds like 'oy' (*heute, teuer*)
> - ei – sounds like English 'I' (*bleiben, einem*)
> - final -d – sounds like 't' (*Gegend, und, während*)
> - ä – sounds like 'a' and 'e' combined (*Nähe*).
> Listen to the recording to practise these sounds.

Track 98

Now play the recording of two questions related to what you have read.

You are expected to say a few words or a short phrase / sentence in response to each question. One-word answers will not be sufficient to gain full marks.   **(4 marks)**

73

Tourism

Had a go ☐ Nearly there ☐ Nailed it! ☐

Other holiday accommodation

Read aloud

1. Kim, your friend, has sent you some information about holidays.

   Read out the text below.

   > Ich fahre jedes Jahr nach Asien.
   > Dann kann ich meine Familie sehen.
   > Ich wohne bei meiner Tante und meinem Onkel.
   > Sie haben ein schönes Haus neben einem See.
   > Ich verbringe einen Monat mit meinen Cousinen.

   Sounds to watch out for here:
   - *-e* – at the end of the word is a separate syllable
   - *j* – sounds like 'y'
   - long *a* – sounds like 'aah' in *Asien*
   - *ö* – sounds like 'o' and 'e' combined
   - *ee* – not like the English 'ee' sound, but more like 'ay'.

   (8 marks)

Now play the recording of two questions related to what you have read.

You are expected to say a few words or a short phrase / sentence in response to each question. One-word answers will not be sufficient to gain full marks. **(4 marks)**

Read aloud

2. Maximilian, your friend, has sent you some information about holidays.

   Read out the text below.

   > In den Ferien fahren wir oft nach Europa, wo das Wetter besser ist.
   > Diesen Sommer bleiben wir aber in unserer Gegend und machen ein paar Ausflüge.
   > Für mich ist das Wichtigste, Zeit mit Familie und Freunden zu verbringen.
   > Wenn es Spaß macht, ist es mir egal, wo das geschieht.

   (8 marks)

   Sounds to watch out for here:
   - *eu* – sounds like 'oy'
   - *w* – sounds like 'v'
   - *s* – a soft 's' sound, not a 'z' sound
   - *ei* – sounds like the English 'I'
   - *ü* – sounds like 'u' and 'e' combined – purse your lips to make this sound!
   - *-e* – at the end of the word is a separate syllable
   - *z* – sounds like 'ts' and is a hard sound (not a soft sound, as in 'buzz')
   - *ie* – sounds like the English 'ee'.

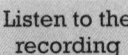

Now play the recording of two questions related to what you have read.

You are expected to say a few words or a short phrase / sentence in response to each question. One-word answers will not be sufficient to gain full marks. **(4 marks)**

Had a go ☐ Nearly there ☐ Nailed it! ☐

Tourism

Making a complaint

A restaurant review

1 Write a review of a restaurant for a website.

You **must** include the following points:
- where the restaurant is
- your opinion of the food
- whether you will eat at this restaurant in the future.

Write your answer **in German**. You should aim to write between 40 and 50 words. **(14 marks)**

> Note that the second bullet point asks you to express opinions, so you can use some or all of these:
> - *Ich denke …*
> - *Ich finde …*
> - *Meiner Meinung nach …*

> The third bullet point requires a future time frame, so you could use:
> - *Ich werde …* + infinitive
> - *In der Zukunft* + present tense
> - *Ich will …* + infinitive
> - *Ich möchte …* + infinitive

....
....
....
....
....

Listen to the recording

Role play

2 **Setting:** In a hotel

   Scenario:
   - You are at the hotel reception to complain about your room.
   - Scan the QR code for the teacher's voice. Pause the recording between each prompt to allow yourself time to answer.
   - The teacher will play the part of the receptionist and will speak first.
   - Your teacher will ask questions **in German** and you must answer **in German**.
   - You are expected to say a few words or a short phrase / sentence in response to each prompt. One-word answers will not be sufficient to gain full marks.

   > **Task:**
   > 1 Say what is wrong with your room.
   > 2 Say what your room number is.
   > 3 Ask a question about having a different room.
   > 4 Say when you are going out this morning.
   > 5 Ask a question about when the room will be ready.

   (10 marks)

   > If there's something you're not sure how to say, try to think of another way of asking the same question. For example, in task 5, if you don't know how to say 'ready', ask at what time you can have the room instead.

75

Tourism

Had a go ☐   Nearly there ☐   Nailed it! ☐

Pros and cons of travelling

Using public transport

1 Describe this picture. Your description must cover:

  • people
  • location
  • activity. **(8 marks)**

See this photo in colour

Listen to the recording

When you have finished your description, scan the QR code to listen to two questions relating to the picture. Pause the recording between each question to allow yourself time to answer. You are expected to say a few words or a short phrase / sentence in response to each question. One-word answers will not be sufficient to gain full marks. **(4 marks)**

> Always bear in mind that your answers to the follow-up questions need only be short.
>
> The key thing is to answer with relevant information the question you are asked, and to be clear and concise.

How do you travel?

2 Write a response to a survey about travelling.

You **must** include the following points:

  • how you travel to school
  • the positive aspects of public transport
  • where you would like to travel in the future.

Write your answer **in German**. You should aim to write between 40 and 50 words.

> Remember to answer each bullet point in a separate short paragraph. You could aim to write around 15 words for each task, or you can write a longer response to a task where you have more to say, as long as you include something about all the bullets. In the sample response, there are 18 words for point 2, but just 10 words for point 3.

> Make the most of the opportunities in points 1 and 2 to express ideas and opinions, and to explain them. Don't forget that bullet point 3 needs to be answered in a future time frame, so it's a good plan to start your response with an expression like *In Zukunft*.

....

....

....

....

(14 marks)

Had a go ☐ Nearly there ☐ Nailed it! ☐

Tourism

Plans for next summer

How I spend my summer holidays

1 Write a blog about summer holiday activities.

You **must** include the following points:
- what you usually do in the summer holidays
- the pros and cons of staying at home and travelling away
- a place you have visited in the past
- what you are going to do this summer.

Write your answer **in German**. You should aim to write between 130 and 150 words.

> Bullet point 2 gives you a great opportunity to express opinions and ideas and to explain them, so use it well.

....
....
....
....
....
....
....
....
....
....
....
....

(22 marks)

Plans for next summer

2 Charlotte is talking about her plans for the summer. What does she say? Listen to the recording and complete the sentences by putting a cross [×] in the correct box for each question.

(i) This summer, Charlotte is going to …

☐	A	go on a beach holiday.
☐	B	stay at home.
☐	C	get bored.

> Be careful to check **who** is going to do the activities – sometimes it may not be Charlotte!

(ii) At the beginning of the holidays, she is going to …

☐	A	go dancing.
☐	B	play handball.
☐	C	stay at her best friend's house.

(iii) In the evenings she will …

☐	A	go shopping.
☐	B	go to the cinema.
☐	C	watch films at home.

(3 marks)

Tourism

Had a go ☐ Nearly there ☐ Nailed it! ☐

Past holidays

Translation

1 Translate the following five sentences **into German**.

(a) The hotel was comfortable and modern.

....

(b) There was a beautiful beach.

....

(c) The people were very friendly.

....

(d) I bought some presents for my friends and family.

....

(e) The weather was good and it was warm every day.

....

> Because this topic is about a past holiday, all the tasks here are in the past tense to give you some practice. Usually, only one task will be in the past tense!

(10 marks)

Translation

2 Translate the paragraph **into German**.

> Last year we went to Austria on holiday. My grandparents live in the mountains there, so we do not need a hotel. We stayed for a week and the weather was good the whole time. I went swimming in the lake. On the last day we had a traditional lunch.

> Because this topic is about a past holiday, most of the tasks here are in the past tense to give you some practice.
>
> Usually, there will be only one past tense for you to tackle, so see this as a helpful challenge.

....
....
....
....
....
....
....
....
....

(10 marks)

Had a go ☐   Nearly there ☐   Nailed it! ☐

Tourism

Holiday problems

My holidays

1 Write a response to a survey about a past holiday.

You **must** include the following points:
- where you were on holiday
- what problems you had on holiday
- what you will do in the next holidays.

> Because this topic focuses on a **past** holiday, there are two tasks in the past tense, rather than in the present tense. This will not happen in the exam, but doing this question gives you extra practice in using past tense verbs.

Write your answer **in German**. You should aim to write between 40 and 50 words.

> Remember: you can use either the perfect tense (e.g. *ich bin … gefahren*) or the imperfect tense (*ich war, es gab*) to respond to tasks 1 and 2.

....
....
....
....
....
....
....
....

(14 marks)

Dictation

Listen to the recording

2 You are going to hear someone talking about a past holiday.

Sentences 1–2: write down the missing words in the gaps provided. In each gap, you will write one word **in German**.

Example: Ich habe die <u>Ferien</u> in einem <u>Kurort</u> <u>verbracht</u>.

1 .... Jahr war ich in einem .... in ....

2 Die .... in einer .... in den .... war schmutzig.

Sentences 3–6: write down the full sentences that you hear in the spaces provided, **in German**.

Example: <u>Von dem Hotel hatte man einen wunderschönen Blick.</u>

3 ....

4 ....

5 ....

6 ....

(10 marks)

> Sounds to listen out for here:
> - *j* – sounds like 'y'
> - *w* – sounds like 'v'
> - *ö* – sounds like a combination of 'o' and 'e'
> - *ü* – sounds like a combination of 'u' and 'e', with pursed lips
> - *z* – sounds like 'ts'
> - *-e* – at the end of the word is a separate syllable.

Tourism

Had a go ☐ Nearly there ☐ Nailed it! ☐

Lost property

Listen to the recording

Role play

1 **Setting:** At the station lost property office

   Scenario:

   - You are at the station lost property office.
   - Scan the QR code for the teacher's voice. Pause the recording between each prompt to allow yourself time to answer.
   - The teacher will play the part of the employee and will speak first.
   - Your teacher will ask questions **in German** and you must answer **in German**.
   - You are expected to say a few words or a short phrase / sentence in response to each prompt. One-word answers will not be sufficient to gain full marks.

> Because of the nature of this topic, there are two tasks here in the past tense. This will not usually be the case.

Task:
1 Say what you have lost.
2 Describe the lost item.
3 Say what time you arrived.
4 Say how long you are staying in Germany.
5 Ask whether they have your lost item.

> Use the exam preparation time to make some notes for each task, taking particular care to work out how to formulate the past tenses for tasks 1 and 3 and the question for task 5.

(10 marks)

Translation

2 Translate the paragraph **into German**.

> On Tuesday last week I travelled by train from Cologne to Munich. Unfortunately, because I was very tired, I left my mobile phone on the train. The next morning, I went back to the station. I was lucky because someone found my phone and took it to the office.

> Due to the topic, all of this text for translation is in the past tense, whereas in an exam, you will probably only have one past tense to deal with and most of the text will be in the present tense. This is a good opportunity for you to practise past tenses.

> Take particular care with verbs like *fahren* and *gehen* in the perfect tense. Because they denote movement from one place to another, they use *sein* rather than *haben* to form their perfect tenses.

....
....
....
....
....
....
....

(10 marks)

Had a go ☐ Nearly there ☐ Nailed it! ☐   **Tourism**

Places to visit

Read aloud

1 Your Swiss friend, Yasmin, has sent you some information about her city.

Read out the text below, then listen to the audio in the Answers section to check your pronunciation.

> Meine Stadt heißt Bern.
> Ich wohne in der Hauptstadt der Schweiz.
> Das alte Viertel ist sehr schön und historisch.
> Die Luft hier ist sauber und frisch.
> Im Juli gibt es ein großes und beliebtes Musikkonzert.

> To pronounce *Bern* correctly, mimic how you pronounce the common word *er* and just add the *b* and *n* consonant sounds at the beginning and end.

(8 marks)

> Other sounds to watch out for here:
> - *st* – sounds like 'sht'
> - *w* – sounds like 'v'
> - *schw* – sounds 'shv'
> - *v* – sounds like 'f'
> - *ö* – sounds like 'o' and 'e' combined
> - *j* – sounds like 'y'
> - *Musik* – has the stress on the second syllable in German.
> Listen to the recording to practise these sounds.

Track 107

Listen to the recording

Now play the recording of two questions related to what you have read.

You are expected to say a few words or a short phrase / sentence in response to each question. One-word answers will not be sufficient to gain full marks. **(4 marks)**

Translation

2 Translate the following paragraph **into English**.

> Ich wohne in München in Süddeutschland. Es ist eine große Stadt mit schönen Gebäuden. Es liegt in der Nähe der Berge, wo es eine schöne Landschaft gibt. Deshalb gibt es immer viele Touristen. Mein Freund arbeitet als Reiseführer und organisiert Touren durch die Altstadt. Als Kind habe ich oft den berühmten Botanischen Garten besucht.

> Look out for words like *wo*, which send the verb to the end of the clause.

> If there is a word you don't know, try to work it out from the surrounding text or by thinking of a related word you do know. So, with *Reiseführer*, you may recognise *Reise* (trip) and you may know the verb *führen* (to lead), so someone who leads trips is a guide.

....

....

....

....

....

(10 marks)

Tourism

Had a go ☐   Nearly there ☐   Nailed it! ☐

Holiday jobs

Plans for the summer

1 Three friends are talking about their plans for the summer.

What does each person say?

Listen to the recording and complete the sentences by putting a cross [×] in the correct box for each question.

(a) Samira plans to …

☐	**A** go away on holiday.
☐	**B** work in a shop.
☐	**C** help her parents.

(b) Layla will be …

☐	**A** moving house.
☐	**B** playing sport.
☐	**C** working one day a week.

(c) Malik is going to …

☐	**A** stay with friends.
☐	**B** work on his English.
☐	**C** go away with his parents.

(3 marks)

> Listen to the recording three times and try the following:
> First time: make quick notes.
> Second time: try to write in some answers.
> Third time: check your answers.

What I did last summer

2 Emily is talking about what she did last summer.

What does she say?

Complete the gap in each sentence using a word or phrase from the box below.

There are more words / phrases than gaps.

excited	nervous	confident
four	seven	fourteen
boring	noisy	helpful
the family	a restaurant	a cinema
cookery	childcare	vocabulary

(a) Before going to England, Emily felt .... **(1 mark)**

(b) She was in Cambridge for .... days. **(1 mark)**

(c) She found staying with a family .... **(1 mark)**

(d) Each day, she worked in .... **(1 mark)**

(e) She learned .... **(1 mark)**

> Remember that Listening exams often make use of synonyms, so you may not hear the exact word which appears in the box. For example – the word 'nervous' isn't spoken, but other words meaning the same thing are said!

Had a go ☐ Nearly there ☐ Nailed it! ☐   Tourism

Buying gifts and souvenirs

Listen to the recording

Role play

1 **Setting:** In a gift shop

   Scenario:

   - You are in a gift shop.
   - Scan the QR code for the teacher's voice. Pause the recording between each prompt to allow yourself time to answer.
   - The teacher will play the part of the shop owner and will speak first.
   - Your teacher will ask questions **in German** and you must answer **in German**.
   - You are expected to say a few words or a short phrase / sentence in response to each prompt. One-word answers will not be sufficient to gain full marks.

   > Remember that this is a formal transactional situation, so you will be addressed in the formal *Sie* form.

   Task:
   1 Say who you want to buy a present for.
   2 Say how much money you have.
   3 Say what you think of the item you are shown.
   4 Say you would like to buy it.
   5 Ask what the price is.

   > Plan how to formulate the question in the final task. Make a note of what you will say on your notes sheet.

   (10 marks)

2 Describe the picture. Your description must cover:
   - people
   - location
   - activity.

   (8 marks)

See this photo in colour

> You can make suppositions, by saying *ich denke* or by using *vielleicht*.

Listen to the recording

When you have finished your description, scan the QR code to listen to two questions relating to your picture. Pause the recording between each question to allow yourself time to answer.
You are expected to say a few words or a short phrase / sentence in response to each question. One-word answers will not be sufficient to gain full marks.

(4 marks)

> Note the instruction about answering these questions. A sentence is enough – you do not need to develop your responses in detail.

Tourism

Had a go ☐ Nearly there ☐ Nailed it! ☐

Weather

Picture task

See this photo in colour

1 Describe the photo. Write four short sentences **in German**.

.... **(2 marks)**

.... **(2 marks)**

.... **(2 marks)**

.... **(2 marks)**

| As they are outside, this is an opportunity to describe the weather. | Use colour adjectives to develop your answers where appropriate. The photo in the exam will be in colour. |

Road conditions

2 Read this weather report on driving conditions in Switzerland.

Straßenwetter

In der Nacht auf Donnerstag gibt es im Osten wenig Regen. Danach wird es neblig. Es bleibt sehr kalt mit Minusgraden, und in höheren Lagen sind die Straßen mit Schnee bedeckt.* Bei Fahrten in die Höhe brauchen Sie Winterausrüstung für Ihr Auto. Einige Straßen in den Alpen** sind geschlossen.

Das MeteoNews-Team wünscht Ihnen eine gute und sichere Fahrt.

* *bedeckt* – covered

** *Alpen* – Alps

Complete the gap in each sentence using a word from the box below.

There are more words than gaps.

sun	wind	rain
foggy	wet	windy
ice	snow	floods
dangerous	closed	icy

Remember that the questions follow the order of the information given in the text.

Use the words explained using asterisks to make the meaning clear.

(a) On Thursday night there will not be much .... **(1 mark)**

(b) It will be .... later. **(1 mark)**

(c) There will be .... on higher roads. **(1 mark)**

(d) Some roads in the Alps are .... **(1 mark)**

Had a go ☐   Nearly there ☐   Nailed it! ☐   **Tourism**

Tourism and the environment

Translation

1 Translate the following five sentences **into German**.

> Look at the verb forms first – there are a number of *er / sie / es* forms, so think about the ending you need for this form.

(a) I travel to Berlin by train.

....

(b) In the summer there are many tourists.

....

(c) Every year the weather is warmer.

....

(d) Planes are very bad for the environment.

....

(e) In August I had a good holiday in Austria.

....   **(10 marks)**

> There are a couple of irregular verbs, so remember that the *er / sie / es* form may have vowel changes.

> Note that sentence (e) is in the past tense, so you could use either the imperfect or the perfect tense. The other sentences are all in the present tense.

Translation

2 Translate the paragraph **into German**.

> I am afraid that we are destroying the world where we live. Today, many tourists want to fly abroad in the holidays, although they know how bad that is for the environment. Climate change is the biggest problem, but no one does anything to improve the situation. We are all responsible.

> This is quite a demanding topic, so here are some clues:
> - *Angst haben* – 'to be afraid'.
> - *Wo* is like *weil* and sends the verb to the end of the clause.
> - If you start a sentence with a time expression, invert the verb which follows.
> - Modal verbs like *wollen* need an infinitive at the end to complete their sense.
> - Remember the Time – Manner – Place word order rule.
> - *Obwohl* and *wie* work like *weil* and *wo*.
> - *Um … zu* + infinitive is needed in the penultimate sentence.
> - A few vocabulary items to guide you: *zerstören, niemand, verbessern, verantwortlich*.

....

....

....

....   **(10 marks)**

85

About the exams

Had a go ☐   Nearly there ☐   Nailed it! ☐

Practice for Paper 1: Speaking

Practise for the Speaking tasks with this selection of exam-style questions.

Read aloud

1 Elif, your friend, has sent you some information. Read out the text below.

> Meine Stadt ist sauber.
> Ich mag die frische Luft.
> Wir haben viele schöne Parks in der Gegend.
> Ich fahre jeden Tag mit dem Fahrrad zur Schule.
> Das ist besser für die Umwelt als ein Auto.

Track 113

Now play the recording of two questions related to what you have read. You are expected to say a few words or a short phrase / sentence in response to each question. One-word answers will not be sufficient to gain full marks. **(12 marks)**

Role play

2 **Setting:** At a swimming pool in Germany

Scenario: You are at a swimming pool in Germany.

- Scan the QR code for the teacher's voice. Pause the recording between each prompt to allow yourself time to answer.
- The teacher will play the part of the receptionist and will speak first.
- Your teacher will ask questions **in German** and you must answer **in German**.
- You are expected to say a few words or a short phrase / sentence in response to each prompt. One-word answers will not be sufficient to gain full marks.

Track 114

> **Task:**
> 1 Say how many tickets you want.   4 Say how you are paying.
> 2 Say what time you want to swim.   5 Ask a question about a café at the pool.
> 3 Say how long you want to stay at the pool.

(10 marks)

Picture task

3 Describe **ONE** of these pictures. Your description must cover:

- people
- location
- activity.

When you have finished your description, scan the corresponding QR code to listen to two questions relating to your chosen picture. You are expected to say a few words or a short phrase / sentence in response to each question. One-word answers will not be sufficient to gain full marks. **(12 marks)**

Track 115

Picture 1

See this photo in colour

You will then move on to a conversation on the broader thematic context of **Studying and my future**. Listen to the questions in the recording and give your answers in the pauses. There will be questions in the present, past and future tenses. Your responses should be as full and detailed as possible. **(16 marks)**

Track 116

Picture 2

See this photo in colour

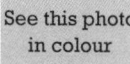

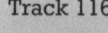

Had a go ☐   Nearly there ☐   Nailed it! ☐   **About the exams**

Practice for Paper 1: Speaking

Practise for the Speaking tasks with this selection of exam-style questions.

Target grade 5-9

Read aloud

Track 117

1 Max, your friend, has sent you some information about sport. Read out the text below.

> Ich versuche, jeden Tag Sport zu treiben, um gesund zu bleiben.
> Meine Lieblingssportart ist Tennis, denn man kann bei gutem Wetter draußen spielen.
> Ich bin Mitglied in einem Verein, der regelmäßig gegen andere Klubs in der Region spielt.
> Jeden August in den Sommerferien nehmen wir an einem nationalen Wettbewerb teil.

Now play the recording of two questions related to what you have read. You are expected to say a few words or a short phrase / sentence in response to each question. One-word answers will not be sufficient to gain full marks.   **(12 marks)**

Target grade 5-9

Role play

Track 118

2 **Setting:** In an Austrian tourist information office

Scenario: You are in a tourist information office in an Austrian town.

- Scan the QR code for the teacher's voice. Pause the recording between each prompt to allow yourself time to answer.
- The teacher will play the part of the tourist office employee and will speak first.
- Your teacher will ask questions **in German** and you must answer **in German**.
- You are expected to say a few words or a short phrase / sentence in response to each prompt. One-word answers will not be sufficient to gain full marks.

> **Task:**
> 1 Say you are looking for a chemist's shop.   4 Say what you will do today.
> 2 Ask how far it is.   5 Ask a question about buying food.
> 3 Say how long you are staying in Austria.

(10 marks)

Target grade 5-9

Picture task

Track 119

Track 120

3 Describe **ONE** of these pictures. Your description must cover:

   • people   • location   • activity.

When you have finished your description, scan the corresponding QR code to listen to two questions relating to your chosen picture. You are expected to say a few words or a short phrase / sentence in response to each question. One-word answers will not be sufficient to gain full marks.   **(12 marks)**

You will then move on to a conversation on the broader thematic context of **Media and technology**. Listen to the questions in the recording and give your answers in the pauses. There will be questions in the present, past and future tenses. Your responses should be as full and detailed as possible.   **(16 marks)**

Picture 1

See this photo in colour

Picture 2

See this photo in colour

About the exams

Had a go ☐   Nearly there ☐   Nailed it! ☐

Practice for Paper 2: Listening

Practise for the Listening tasks with this selection of exam-style questions.

Target grade 2-3

Track 121

Activities with friends

1 Jana and Malik are talking about activities with friends.

What do they say?

Listen to the recording and complete the sentences by putting a cross [×] in the correct box for each question.

(a) First of all, Jana and her friend will …

☐	**A** go to the café.
☐	**B** go to the book shop.
☐	**C** go to the library.

(b) After that they will …

☐	**A** go to the café.
☐	**B** go shopping.
☐	**C** go for a walk.

(c) Malik and his friend want to …

☐	**A** buy a computer.
☐	**B** buy a game.
☐	**C** buy a football.

(d) Jana prefers … to gaming.

☐	**A** dancing
☐	**B** fashion
☐	**C** music

(4 marks)

Target grade 1-5

Track 122

Dictation

2 You are going to hear someone talking to a sales assistant in a department store.

Sentences 1–3: write down the missing words in the gaps provided. In each gap, you will write one word **in German**.

Example: Dieses <u>Hemd</u> ist sehr <u>modisch</u>.

1 Ich .... ein .... für meine Schwester.

2 Was .... die rote ....?

3 Welche .... ist das .... Kleid?

Sentences 4–6: write down the full sentences that you hear in the spaces provided, **in German**.

Example: <u>Ich empfehle dieses Hemd.</u>

4 ....

5 ....

6 ....   **(10 marks)**

Had a go ☐   Nearly there ☐   Nailed it! ☐

About the exams

Practice for Paper 2: Listening

Practise for the Listening tasks with this selection of exam-style questions.

Target grade 5-6

Jobs

Track 123

1 Lara and Arda are talking about their jobs.

Which advantages and disadvantages do they mention?

Listen to the recording and complete the following tables **in English**.

You do not need to write in full sentences.

(a) Lara

Advantage	....
Disadvantage	....

(1 mark)

(1 mark)

(b) Arda

Advantage	....
Disadvantage	....

(1 mark)

(1 mark)

Target grade 5-9

Dictation

Track 124

2 You are going to hear someone talking about school.

Sentences 1–2: write down the missing words in the gaps provided. In each gap, you will write one word **in German**.

Example: Ich <u>lerne</u> <u>nicht</u> gern <u>Mathe</u>.

1 Dieses .... ist .... mein bestes ....

2 Mein .... ist .... ziemlich ....

Sentences 3–6: write down the full sentences that you hear in the spaces provided, **in German**.

Example: <u>Ich will nach der Schule ein Studium machen</u>.

3 ....

4 ....

5 ....

6 .... (10 marks)

89

Practice for Paper 3: Reading

Practise for the Reading tasks with this selection of exam-style questions.

Life in a town

1 Read Noah's blog about his town.

> Hallo!
> Meine Stadt war früher eine Industriestadt und hatte vor zwanzig Jahren viele Fabriken. Jetzt gibt es keine Industrie mehr, und die Stadt ist ruhiger und sauberer, als sie damals war.
> Die Stadt ist heute das kulturelle Zentrum der Region, und es gibt interessante Museen und Kunstgalerien, und auch ein sehr aktives Nachtleben, mit vielen Klubs und Bars, wo man einen lustigen Abend verbringen kann.
> Der Sonntagsmarkt neben dem Fluss ist auch sehr beliebt, und viele Touristen besuchen ihn, um Essen oder lokale Produkte zu kaufen. Es gibt zum Beispiel guten Käse und tolle Lederwaren wie Handtaschen und Hüte.
> Noah

Complete the gap in each sentence using a word or phrase from the box below.

There are more words / phrases than gaps.

shops	industry	traffic
outdoor activities	cuisine	night life
on Saturdays	on Sundays	every day
vegetables	handbags	magazines

(a) Noah's town used to have more .... **(1 mark)**

(b) The town is now known for .... **(1 mark)**

(c) There is a popular market .... **(1 mark)**

(d) At the market, tourists can buy local cheese and .... **(1 mark)**

Translation

2 Translate the following sentences **into English**.

(a) Ich bin gesund.

....

(b) Ich esse jeden Tag Obst und Gemüse.

....

(c) Einmal in der Woche gehe ich ins Fitnesszentrum.

....

(d) Gestern habe ich eine Tanzstunde gehabt.

....

(e) Ich bin glücklicher, wenn ich aktiv bleibe.

.... **(10 marks)**

90

Had a go ☐ Nearly there ☐ Nailed it! ☐

About the exams

Practice for Paper 3: Reading

Practise for the Reading tasks with this selection of exam-style questions.

Target grade 8-9

Environmental concerns

1 Read Sascha's blog about the environment.

> Unsere Welt leidet. Die Wälder werden zerstört und viele Tierarten verschwinden! Das ist klar, wenn man sich die Zeit nimmt, die Nachrichten zu hören oder eine Zeitung zu lesen. Viele Leute wollen diese schlimme Wahrheit aber nicht sehen, und machen so weiter, als ob alles OK wäre.
>
> Ich finde diese Einstellung nicht sehr intelligent. Deshalb bin ich Mitglied einer Umweltorganisation, die versucht, etwas Positives gegen Umweltverschmutzung zu tun. Wir haben keine Zeit zu *verschwenden*, und müssen hier und heute etwas machen. Die Lage ist jetzt echt ernst. Die einzige Lösung ist, dass wir unsere Lebensweise sofort verändern.

(a) Answer the following questions **in English**. You do not need to write in full sentences.

(i) What does Sascha say about the world?

.... **(1 mark)**

(ii) What **two** examples does he give of environmental damage?

.... **(2 marks)**

(iii) What attitude does Sascha find unintelligent?

.... **(1 mark)**

(iv) What does Sascha think is the only solution?

.... **(1 mark)**

(b) Which of these is the best translation of the word *verschwenden*?

Put a cross [×] in the correct box.

☐	**A** to die
☐	**B** to waste
☐	**C** to change things

(1 mark)

Target grade 5-9

Translation

2 Translate the following paragraph **into English**.

> Wenn die Schule vorbei ist, möchte ich auf die Uni gehen, um ein Studium zu machen. Mein Lieblingsfach ist Geschichte, denn ich interessiere mich sehr für die Ereignisse der Vergangenheit. Ich freue mich darauf, meine Heimatstadt zu verlassen, weil das Leben hier etwas langweilig sein kann. Ich hoffe, viele neue Leute kennenzulernen.

....

....

....

....

.... **(10 marks)**

Practice for Paper 4: Writing

Practise for the Writing tasks with this selection of exam-style questions.

My school

1. Write a review of your school.

   You **must** include the following points:
   - what your school is like
   - your opinion of studying there
   - what you will do next year.

   Write your answer **in German**. You should aim to write between 40 and 50 words.

   ....
   ....
   ....
   ....
   ....
   ....
   ....
   ....
   .... **(14 marks)**

A healthy lifestyle

2. Write to someone you know about healthy living.

   You **must** include the following points:
   - what you do to keep fit
   - your opinion of sport
   - what you did last week to be healthy
   - what you will do in the future to keep fit.

   Write your answer **in German**. You should aim to write between 80 and 90 words.

   ....
   ....
   ....
   ....
   ....
   ....
   ....
   ....
   ....
   .... **(18 marks)**

Had a go ☐ Nearly there ☐ Nailed it! ☐   **About the exams**

Practice for Paper 4: Writing

Practise for the Writing tasks with this selection of exam-style questions.

Target grade 4-6

A healthy living

1 Write to someone you know about healthy living.

   You **must** include the following points:
   - what you do to keep fit
   - your opinion of sport
   - what you did last week to be healthy
   - what you will do in the future to keep fit.

   Write your answer **in German**. You should aim to write between 80 and 90 words.

   ....
   ....
   ....
   ....
   ....
   ....
   ....
   ....
   ....
   ....

   (18 marks)

Target grade 5-9

Technology

2 Write a blog about technology in your life.

   You **must** include the following points:
   - what you think of mobile phones
   - the pros and cons of the internet
   - how you have used social media recently
   - how you think technology will improve your life in future.

   Write your answer **in German**. You should aim to write between 130 and 150 words.

   ....
   ....
   ....
   ....
   ....
   ....
   ....
   ....

   (22 marks)

Grammar

Had a go ☐ Nearly there ☐ Nailed it! ☐

Gender and plurals

German nouns are **masculine** (m), **feminine** (f) or **neuter** (nt).

With the **definite** article (the) they look like this:

der Mann / **der** Tisch   **die** Frau / **die** Tür   **das** Kind / **das** Buch

1 Circle the correct definite article.

(a) **der** / **die** / (**das**) Mädchen (*nt*)   (e) **der** / **die** / **das** Klassenzimmer (*nt*)

(b) **der** / **die** / **das** Lehrer (*m*)   (f) **der** / **die** / **das** Schule (*f*)

(c) **der** / **die** / **das** Karte (*f*)   (g) **der** / **die** / **das** Stuhl (*m*)

(d) **der** / **die** / **das** Flugzeug (*nt*)   (h) **der** / **die** / **das** Kino (*nt*)

2 Complete each sentence with *der*, *die* or *das*.

(a) ....Die.......... Lehrerin ist freundlich. (*f*)

(b) .... Zimmer ist bequem. (*nt*)

(c) .... Handy ist toll. (*nt*)

(d) .... Zug fährt schnell. (*m*)

(e) .... Bahnhof ist nicht weit von hier. (*m*)

(f) .... Umwelt ist wichtig. (*f*)

Plurals in German are formed in several different ways.

Some add *-e* or *-n* / *-en*, others add an umlaut or an umlaut plus another letter, and some don't change.

- (sg) Tisch –> (pl) Tisch**e**
- (sg) Karte –> (pl) Karte**n**
- (sg) Zahn –> (pl) Z**ä**hne
- (sg) Mann –> (pl) M**ä**nn**er**
- (sg) Freundin –> (pl) Freundin**nen**
- (sg) Mädchen –> (pl) Mädchen

3 Are these nouns singular (sg), plural (pl) or could they be either singular or plural (sg / pl)?

(a) Frauen   ....pl..........

(b) Welt   ....

(c) Kinder   ....

(d) Manager   ....

(e) Bücher   ....

(f) Geld   ....

(g) Arbeit   ....

(h) Hausaufgaben   ....

(i) Schwimmbad   ....

(j) Mädchen   ....

Had a go ☐ **Nearly there** ☐ **Nailed it!** ☐   Grammar

Indefinite articles and possessives

> German nouns are **masculine** (m), **feminine** (f) or **neuter** (nt).
>
> With the **indefinite** article (a / an) they look like this:
>
> **ein** Mann / **ein** Tisch   **eine** Frau / **eine** Schule   **ein** Kind / **ein** Buch

1 Circle the correct indefinite article.

(a) **(ein)** / **eine** Haus (*nt*)

(b) **ein** / **eine** Lehrerin (*f*)

(c) **ein** / **eine** Zug (*m*)

(d) **ein** / **eine** Hotel (*nt*)

(e) **ein** / **eine** Familie (*f*)

(f) **ein** / **eine** Zimmer (*nt*)

(g) **ein** / **eine** Stadt (*f*)

(h) **ein** / **eine** Stück (*nt*)

(i) **ein** / **eine** Kuchen (*m*)

(j) **ein** / **eine** Junge (*m*)

> *kein* / *keine* / *kein* (not a / no) follows the same pattern as *ein* / *eine* / *ein*.
>
> The plural of *kein* is *keine*.
>
> **kein** Mensch (*m*)   **keine** Idee (*f*)   **kein** Haus (*nt*)   **keine** Hausaufgaben (*pl*)

2 Write the correct form of *kein* / *keine* / *kein*.

(a) ....**kein**........ Buch (*nt*)

(b) .... Bruder (*m*)

(c) .... Schwestern (*pl*)

(d) .... Brot (*nt*)

(e) .... Lehrerin (*f*)

> The **possessives** follow the same pattern as *ein* and *kein*.
>
> **mein** Haus (*nt*)   **unser** Auto (*nt*)
>
> **dein** Bruder (*m*)   **eure** Freunde (*pl*)
>
> **seine** Schwester (*f*)   **Ihre** Arbeit (*f*)
>
> **ihre** Freundin (*f*)   **ihre** Interessen (*pl*)

3 Write these phrases **in German**.

(a) *my sister* ....**meine Schwester**........ (f) *my homework* ....

(b) *your family* (du form) .... (g) *his jacket* ....

(c) *his wife* .... (h) *her party* ....

(d) *her boyfriend* .... (i) *your clothes* ....

(e) *our town* .... (j) *my glass* ....

Grammar

Had a go ☐ Nearly there ☐ Nailed it! ☐

Nominative and accusative cases

The **nominative** case is used for the **subject** of the sentence.

With *der / die / das*:

Der Mann wartet auf den Bus. **Die** Frau ist jung. **Das** Kind ist klein. **Die** Bücher sind schwer.

With *ein*, *kein* or a possessive:

Mein Bruder ist groß. **Keine** Lehrerin ist da. **Unser** Haus ist klein. Wo sind **meine** Schuhe?

The **accusative** case is used for the **direct object** of the sentence. The word for 'the / a' changes in the **masculine accusative**. There is no change in the other genders or the plural.

With *der / die / das*:

	m	f	nt	pl
nominative	der	die	das	die
accusative	**den**	die	das	die

With *eine / kein* and possessives:

	m	f	nt	pl
nominative	ein	eine	ein	keine
accusative	**einen**	eine	ein	keine

Siehst du **den** Mann?   Hast du **einen** Bruder?

---

1 Complete the sentences with the correct missing form of *der / die / das*. Remember to check whether you need the nominative or accusative!

(a) ....*Der*........ Lehrer kommt spät.

(b) .... Mädchen sieht .... Film.

(c) .... Junge hat .... Buch.

(d) .... Frau kauft .... Zeitung.

(e) .... Kinder haben .... Ball verloren.

(f) .... Touristen besuchen .... Museum.

(g) .... Mann hat .... Karten gekauft.

(h) .... Straße ist schmutzig.

2 Complete the sentences with the correct missing form of *ein / eine / ein*. Remember to check whether you need the nominative or accusative!

(a) Hat sie ....*einen*........ Bruder oder .... Schwester?

(b) Wir haben .... großes Frühstück gegessen.

(c) Hast du .... Garten zu Hause?

(d) .... Junge wartet auf dich.

(e) Ich habe .... Koffer verloren.

(f) Haben Sie .... Straßenplan?

3 Circle the correct possessives needed to complete each sentence.

(a) **Mein** / **Meine** / **Mein** Schwester hat **meinen** / **meine** / **mein** Hut.

(b) Ist **dein** / **deine** / **dein** Freund hier?

(c) **Mein** / **Meine** / **Mein** Onkel liest **seinen** / **seine** / **sein** Zeitung.

(d) **Ihr** / **Ihre** / **Ihr** Mann arbeitet im Ausland.

(e) Das ist **unser** / **unsere** / **unser** Problem.

(f) **Mein** / **Meine** / **Mein** Noten sind nicht so gut.

Had a go ☐ Nearly there ☐ Nailed it! ☐

Grammar

Other cases and prepositions

In addition to the nominative (used for the subject of the sentence) and the accusative (used for the direct object and after some prepositions), you also need to know how to use the **genitive** and **dative** cases. You only need to know about the genitive case at Higher tier. Here is a reminder of what happens to articles in these cases.

Definite articles (*der / die / das*) and *dieser / jener / jeder / welcher*:

	m	f	nt	pl
dative	dem	der	dem	den
genitive	des	der	des	der

Indefinite articles (*eine / kein*) and possessives:

	m	f	nt	pl
dative	einem	einer	einem	keinen
genitive	eines	einer	eines	keiner

Note that the endings are the same with both the definite and indefinite articles, so you only need to learn them once.

1 Underline the dative article and noun in each sentence.

(a) Ich gebe <u>der Lehrerin</u> meine Hausaufgaben.

(b) Wir laufen aus dem Haus.

(c) Er kauft seiner Mutter eine Pflanze.

(d) Ich habe meinem Vater im Garten geholfen.

(e) Sie geht mit ihren Freunden aus.

(f) Ich erzähle meinen Eltern alles.

> Note that when you use a noun in the dative plural, you add an *-n* to the end of the noun if it does not already end in *-n*.

2 Some set phrases use the dative case. What do these ones mean?

(a) im Ausland ....

(b) an der Küste ....

(c) auf dem Land ....

(d) bei uns ....

(e) vor allem ....

(f) im Gegenteil ....

3 Complete each sentence with the correct form of *der / die / das* in the genitive case. You may sometimes need to add an *-s* to the noun!

(a) Der Bruder .... *des* .... Mädchen .... *s* .... ist ziemlich sportlich.

(b) In der Mitte .... Stadt ist ein Markt.

(c) Trotz .... Wetter .... gehen wir zelten.

(d) Während .... Sommerferien spiele ich Basketball.

(e) Die Arbeit .... Ärzte ist sehr hart.

4 Translate the sentences from exercise 3 **into English**.

(a) ....

(b) ....

(c) ....

(d) ....

(e) ....

Grammar Had a go ☐ Nearly there ☐ Nailed it! ☐

Prepositions with the accusative or dative

> The **dual case** prepositions are:
>
> an *on (vertically), at*
> auf *on (horizontally)*
> hinter *behind*
> in *in*
> neben *next to*
> über *over / above*
> unter *under / below*
> vor *in front of / before*
> zwischen *between*
>
> - Use the **accusative** case to express *movement towards* something.
> - Use the **dative** when there is a fixed position and *no movement*.

1. Circle the correct article to complete each sentence.

    (a) Wir wohnen neben **(dem)**/ **der** Fluss.

    (b) Gehst du heute in **die** / **der** Stadt?

    (c) Der Hund schläft in **den** / **dem** Garten.

    (d) Wir schwimmen in **das** / **dem** Meer.

    (e) Die Bücher sind auf **den** / **dem** Tisch.

    (f) Die Geschenke sind unter **den** / **dem** Baum.

    (g) Die Bilder sind an **die** / **der** Wand.

    (h) Die Katze läuft unter **das** / **dem** Bett.

    (i) Es gibt einen Parkplatz hinter **den** / **dem** Fitnesszentrum.

    (j) Ich setze mich vor **den** / **dem** Computer.

    (k) Das Café ist zwischen **den** / **dem** Kino und **die** / **der** Bibliothek.

    (l) Sie gehen schnell in **das** / **dem** Haus.

Some verbs are used with a preposition followed by the **accusative** case.

2. Complete the sentences with an accusative definite article (the).

    (a) Wir freuen uns auf .... *die* .... Ferien.

    (b) Meine Schwester und ich sprechen über .... Problem.

    (c) Ich warte auf .... nächsten Zug.

    (d) Die Schüler denken an .... Zukunft.

3. Now translate the sentences from exercise 2 **into English**.

    (a) ....

    (b) ....

    (c) ....

    (d) ....

Had a go ☐ **Nearly there** ☐ **Nailed it!** ☐   Grammar

Dieser, jener and jeder

Dieser, *jener* and *jeder* (also *welcher*) all follow the *der* / *die* / *das* pattern.

	masculine	feminine	neuter	plural
nominative	dieser	diese	dieses	diese
accusative	diesen	diese	dieses	diese
dative	diesem	dieser	diesem	diesen
genitive	dieses	dieser	dieses	dieser

1 Add the correct ending to each word. Check whether you need to use the nominative, accusative or dative case.

(a) Dies................ Stadt ist klein. (*f*)

(b) In jed................ Stadt gibt es ein Kino. (*f*)

(c) Ich mag dies................ Film. (*m*)

(d) Ich besuche dies................ Schule. (*f*)

(e) Jed................ Kinder sind sehr laut. (*pl*)

(f) Dies................ Junge wohnt in der Nähe. (*m*)

(g) Ich habe dies................ Buch schon gelesen. (*nt*)

(h) Jen................ Fluss ist der längste in der Schweiz. (*m*)

(i) Mit dies................ Bus kann man zum Stadion fahren. (*m*)

(j) Er geht mit jen................ Mädchen aus. (*nt*)

> Remember that *jener* is only needed at Higher tier.

2 Complete the sentences with the correct word endings.

(a) Welch................ Mann hast du gesehen?

(b) Mit welch................ Zug fahren Sie?

(c) Ich übernachte in dies................ Hotel.

(d) Dies................ Woche bin ich in München.

(e) Am Ende dies................ Jahres werde ich ein Auto kaufen.

(f) Warum hast du dies................ Buch mit?

(g) Jed................ Schülerin muss eine Uniform tragen.

(h) Jed................ Mensch braucht eine Pause.

(i) Jed................ Schulstunde dauert 40 Minuten.

(j) In jed................ Klassenzimmer gibt es Laptops.

(k) Jed................ Flugzeug kommt heute spät an.

(l) Es gibt ein Geschenk für jed................ Kind.

> *Dieser* and *jeder* are often used in **time expressions**.
> In this context, they are used in the **accusative** case.
> jed**en** Monat – *every month*   dies**en** Freitag – *this Friday*

3 Complete each word to give a time expression in the accusative case.

(a) jed................ Jahr

(b) dies................ Woche

(c) dies................ Monat

(d) jed................ Wochenende

(e) jed................ Sonntag

Grammar

Had a go ☐ Nearly there ☐ Nailed it! ☐

Adjective endings

Adjectives after definite articles

	masculine	feminine	neuter	plural
nominative	der alte Mann	die alte Frau	das alte Haus	die alten Häuser
accusative	den alten Mann	die alte Frau	das alte Haus	die alten Häuser
dative	dem alten Mann	der alten Frau	dem alten Haus	den alten Häusern
genitive	des alten Mannes	der alten Frau	des alten Hauses	der alten Häuser

1 Complete the sentences with the correct adjective endings. Check the gender, case and number (whether the noun is singular or plural).

  (a) Die schwarz ......e...... Hose gefällt mir am besten. (*f*)

  (b) Hast du den neu .... Lehrer gesehen? (*m*)

  (c) Ich habe die weiß .... Blumen gekauft. (*pl*)

  (d) Ich liebe den braun .... Hund. (*m*)

  (e) Wo ist das bekannt .... Museum? (*nt*)

Adjectives after indefinite articles

	masculine	feminine	neuter	plural
nominative	ein alter Mann	eine alte Frau	ein altes Haus	keine alten Häuser
accusative	einen alten Mann	eine alte Frau	ein altes Haus	keine alten Häuser
dative	einem alten Mann	einer alten Frau	einem alten Haus	keinen alten Häusern
genitive	eines alten Mannes	einer alten Frau	eines alten Hauses	keiner alten Häuser

2 Complete the sentences with the correct adjective endings. Check the gender, case and number.

  (a) Mein klein .... Bruder ist sehr sportlich. (*m*)

  (b) Hast du eine älter .... Schwester? (*f*)

  (c) Ich habe gestern ein interessant .... Buch gekauft. (*nt*)

  (d) Wir versuchen, ein gesund .... Leben zu haben. (*nt*)

  (e) Die Familie sucht eine klein .... Wohnung in der Nähe. (*f*)

  (f) Seine best .... Freunde feiern seinen Geburtstag. (*pl*)

Adjectives without an article

	masculine	feminine	neuter	plural
nominative	schwarzer Kaffee	kalte Milch	gutes Wetter	nette Leute
accusative	schwarzen Kaffee	kalte Milch	gutes Wetter	nette Leute
dative	schwarzem Kaffee	kalter Milch	gutem Wetter	netten Leuten
genitive	schwarzen Kaffees	kalter Milch	guten Wetters	netter Leute

3 Complete the sentences with the correct adjective endings. Check the gender, case and number.

  (a) Trinkst du gern schwarz .... Tee? (*m*)

  (b) Frisch .... Wasser schmeckt gut. (*nt*)

  (c) Wir haben freundlich .... Lehrer. (*pl*)

  (d) Habt ihr schön .... Wetter gehabt? (*nt*)

Had a go ☐ **Nearly there** ☐ **Nailed it!** ☐   Grammar

Comparative and superlative adjectives

Comparing adjectives and adverbs
Describing nouns:

adjective	comparative form + -er	superlative form + -(e)st
schnell	schneller	schnellst-
lustig	lustiger	lustigst-
interessant	interessanter	interessantest-

Describing verbs:

adverb	comparative form + -er	superlative form am ... + -(e)sten
schnell	schneller	am schnellsten
lustig	lustiger	am lustigsten
interessant	interessanter	am interessantesten

1. Complete the sentences with the correct comparative form of the adjective in brackets.
   (a) Ich finde Deutsch ....interessanter.... als Mathe. (interessant)
   (b) Mein Bruder ist .... als ich. (intelligent)
   (c) Es ist ...., mit dem Rad zu fahren, als zu Fuß zu gehen. (schnell)
   (d) Ist deine Schwester .... als du? (klein)

2. Complete the sentences with the correct superlative form of the adjective in brackets.
   (a) Dies ist das ....modernste.... Haus auf der Straße. (modern)
   (b) Ich finde Physik das .... Fach. (schwer)
   (c) Cricket ist das .... Spiel. (langsam)
   (d) Diese Hose ist die .... im Geschäft. (teuer)

3. Complete the sentences with the correct comparative and superlative forms of the adverb in **bold**.
   (a) Lea singt **schön**, aber Matteo singt ....schöner.... und Anna singt ....
   (b) Ich arbeite **fleißig**, aber Kim arbeitet .... und Yusuf arbeitet ....
   (c) Max läuft **schnell**. Yuki läuft .... als Max, aber ich laufe ....

   Some comparative / superlative forms are **irregular**. Many common single syllable adjectives add an umlaut too: w**ä**rmer / k**ä**lter / l**ä**nger. And some are even more irregular! gut / besser / best-, gern / lieber / liebst- and hoch / höher / höchst-

4. Translate these sentences **into English**.
   (a) Mein Vater ist größer als ich. ....
   (b) Wie heißt der höchste Berg in der Schweiz? ....
   (c) Was für Filme siehst du am liebsten? ....

Personal pronouns

Here's a reminder of how the personal pronouns work in the three main cases.

nominative	accusative	dative
ich	mich	mir
du	dich	dir
er / sie / es	ihn / sie / es	ihm / ihr / ihm
wir	uns	uns
ihr	euch	euch
Sie	Sie	Ihnen
sie	sie	ihnen

Plural dative forms are only needed at Higher tier.

1 Complete the sentences with the correct pronoun in the appropriate case.

(a) Was machst .... *du* .... heute Abend? (*you, familiar sg*)

(b) Kommt ihr mit ....? (*us*)

(c) Meine Mutter ist lieb. Ich verstehe mich gut mit .... (*her*)

(d) Kannst du .... helfen? (*me*)

(e) Ich zeige .... den Weg. (*you, formal*)

(f) Ich rufe .... später an. (*you, familiar sg*)

(g) Er hat .... nicht gekannt. (*her*)

(h) Ich schicke .... eine Geburtstagskarte. (*him*)

(i) Hast du .... heute gesehen? (*them*)

(j) Warte! Ich komme mit .... (*you, familiar sg*)

> Some set phrases are always used with a **dative** pronoun.
> Es geht mir gut. *I'm fine.*
> Wie geht es dir? *How are you?*
> Das schmeckt mir. *It tastes good / I like the taste.*
> Mir ist kalt / warm! *I'm cold / hot.*
> Es gelingt uns, ... zu + infinitive. *We manage to ...*
> Es tut mir leid. *I'm sorry.*
> Es ist mir egal. *I'm not bothered.*
> ... gefällt mir. *I like ...*

2 Complete the sentences with the correct pronoun in the dative case.

(a) Wie geht es .... *euch* ....? (*you, familiar pl*)

(b) Es tut .... leid. (*we / us*)

(c) Das ist .... egal. (*I / me*)

(d) Der Film gefällt .... (*he / him*)

(e) Wie schmeckt es ....? (*you, familiar, sg*)

(f) Es ist .... gelungen, den Berg zu steigen. (*she / her*)

Had a go ☐ **Nearly there** ☐ **Nailed it!** ☐ Grammar

Word order 1

> The first rule of German word order is that **the verb is the second 'idea'** (chunk of language) in a sentence. If something else is added at the front, the verb inverts (the subject and verb swap places). Ich **fahre** nach Köln. –> Morgen **fahre** ich nach Köln.

1 Rewrite these sentences after adding the phrase in brackets at the front.

   Example: Ich gehe zu Fuß zur Schule. (Jeden Tag) –> Jeden Tag **gehe** ich zu Fuß zur Schule.

   (a) Wir fahren in die Schweiz. (Nächstes Jahr)

   ....

   (b) Mein Bruder geht im Park laufen. (Jeden Morgen)

   ....

   (c) Ich lerne am liebsten Englisch. (In der Schule)

   ....

   (d) Meine Freunde spielen Fußball. (In den Ferien)

   ....

> **Word order in the perfect tense**
>
> The key rule is that the past participle stands at the end of the clause / sentence. The part of *haben* or *sein* is the main verb and is the second idea. Inversion rules still apply.

2 Rewrite these jumbled sentences in the correct order. Start with the word / phrase in **bold**.

   (a) gehabt / mein Freund / hat / **Letzte Woche** / eine Party

   ....

   (b) aus dem Fenster / ist / gesprungen / die Katze / **Plötzlich**

   ....

   (c) sind / wegen des Wetters / angekommen / spät / **Wir** / in Berlin

   ....

> **Word order in the future tense and with modal verbs**
>
> With these structures, the infinitive stands at the end of the clause or sentence, while the part of *werden* (for the future tense) or the modal verb (e.g. *ich will, wir konnten, ich musste, man darf,* etc.) is the main verb and is the second idea. Inversion rules still apply.

3 Rewrite these present tense sentences in the future tense.

   (a) Er spielt morgen Golf. ....

   (b) Wann gehst du einkaufen? ....

   (c) Nächstes Jahr verlasse ich die Schule. ....

4 Rewrite these sentences to include the modal verb in brackets.

   (a) Ich mache zuerst meine Hausaufgaben. (müssen) ....

   (b) Meine Schwester fährt nach London. (wollen) ....

   (c) Bald haben wir endlich mehr Freizeit. (können) ....

103

Grammar — Had a go ☐ Nearly there ☐ Nailed it! ☐

Conjunctions

A really useful and important **subordinating conjunction** is *weil* (because). By using this word, you can not only explain ideas and opinions, but you can also use some complex language, as *weil* moves the verb to the end of the clause or sentence.

Ich mag Mathe, **weil** ich einen tollen Lehrer **habe**.

1 Link these pairs of sentences together using *weil*.

   Example: Ich bin heute müde. Ich habe zu viele Hausaufgaben. –>
            Ich bin heute müde, **weil** ich zu viele Hausaufgabe **habe**.

   > Remember to use a comma before *weil* and move the verb to the end.

   (a) Wir bleiben diesen Sommer zu Hause. Reisen ist sehr teuer.

   ....

   (b) Ich will nach der Schule studieren. Ich will Arzt werden.

   ....

   (c) Er geht auf dem Land wandern. Das Wetter ist schön.

   ....

   (d) Mein Bruder geht zu jedem Fußballspiel. Er ist ein großer Fan.

   ....

   (e) Wir sollen die Umwelt besser schützen. Es gibt nur eine Welt.

   ....

Other conjunctions which work exactly like *weil* are: *als, bevor, bis, da, damit, dass, nachdem, ob, obwohl, während, was, wie* and *wenn*.

2 Rewrite these sentences, adding the conjunction shown in brackets.

   > Check your punctuation and word order!

   (a) Es war sehr spät. Ich bin nach Hause gekommen. (als)

   ....

   (b) Ich bin nach Hause gekommen. Es war sehr spät. (als)

   ....

   (c) Er geht zur Arbeit. Er isst das Frühstück. (bevor)

   ....

   (d) Die Lehrerin hilft uns. Wir verstehen besser. (damit)

   ....

   (e) Wir wollten ausgehen. Ich hatte Geburtstag. (da)

   ....

3 Translate the sentences in exercise 2 **into English**.

   (a) ....
   (b) ....
   (c) ....
   (d) ....
   (e) ....

Had a go ☐ Nearly there ☐ Nailed it! ☐

Grammar

Word order 2

> An *um ... zu* + infinitive (in order to ...) clause is a great way to develop an initial idea and use complex language. All you need to remember is to put a comma before *um* and put *zu* and the infinitive at the end.
>
> Ich gehe ins Einkaufszentrum, **um** ein Geschenk für meinen Freund **zu kaufen**.

1 Link these pairs of sentences and rephrase them using *um ... zu*.

   Example: Ich gehe jeden Tag schwimmen. Ich bleibe fit. –>
   　　　　 Ich gehe jeden Tag schwimmen, **um** fit **zu** bleiben.

   (a) Wir fahren dieses Jahr in den Urlaub. Wir genießen die Sonne.

   ....

   (b) Ich werde nach London fahren. Ich suche eine Arbeitsstelle.

   ....

   (c) Er fährt auf dem Land Rad. Er ist an der frischen Luft.

   ....

   > Similarly, you can use *zu* + infinitive clauses after certain verbs. This is another great way of expressing yourself in more extended sentences.
   >
   > Try these: *hoffen ... zu, versuchen ... zu, beginnen ... zu*.

2 Rewrite these sentences to include the verb shown in brackets.

   Example: Ich verdiene genug Geld. (versuchen) –>
   　　　　 Ich **versuche**, genug Geld **zu verdienen**.

   (a) Ich mache nächstes Jahr ein Auslandsjahr.* (hoffen)

   ....

   (b) Wir leben gesünder. (versuchen)

   ....

   (c) Mein Freund treibt mehr Sport. (beginnen)

   ....

   * *ein Auslandsjahr* – a year abroad

   > **Relative clauses** can also be used to develop and extend an initial idea. These clauses are introduced by the correct form of *der / die / das*, etc. (meaning 'who / whom / which / that'), depending on the thing they refer to and its case. The relative clause is divided from the main clause by commas and the verb goes at the end of the clause.
   >
   > Die Prüfungen, **die** wir dieses Jahr machen, beginnen im Mai.

3 Complete each sentence by selecting the correct relative pronoun from the three options provided. Consider both the gender and number of the noun it refers to and the case required within the relative clause.

   (a) Der Mann, **(der)** / **den** / **das** da steht, ist der neue Mathelehrer.
   (b) Das Mädchen, **das** / **die** / **der** rote Haare hat, heißt Hanna.
   (c) Kennst du die Frau, **der** / **das** / **die** neben dir wohnt?
   (d) Der Film, **den** / **der** / **dem** wir gestern Abend gesehen haben, war eine Komödie.
   (e) Die Bücher, **das** / **die** / **den** wir lesen, sind nicht so spannend.

105

Grammar

Had a go ☐ Nearly there ☐ Nailed it! ☐

The present tense

Regular verbs in the present tense
Remove the *-en* ending to find the stem, then add these endings according to the person doing the action of the verb.

ich	spiel**e**	*I play / am playing*
du	spiel**st**	*you play / are playing*
er / sie / es	spiel**t**	*he / she / it plays / is playing*
wir	spiel**en**	*we play / are playing*
ihr	spiel**t**	*you play / are playing*
Sie	spiel**en**	*you play / are playing*
sie	spiel**en**	*they play / are playing*

1 Complete each sentence with the correct form of the verb in brackets. All these verbs are regular in the present tense.

   (a) Ich ....*wohne*........ in Köln. (wohnen)

   (b) Wir .... Handball. (spielen)

   (c) Wie oft .... du schwimmen? (gehen)

   (d) Er .... oft Computerspiele. (kaufen)

   (e) Wo .... Sie? (übernachten)

   (f) Was .... ihr heute Abend? (machen)

   (g) Mein Bruder .... das Abendessen. (kochen)

   (h) .... du ihn? (lieben)

   (i) Die Freunde .... sich E-Mails. (schicken)

   (j) .... du heute das Schloss? (besuchen)

   (k) Die Klasse .... hart. (arbeiten)

   (l) Wann .... die Sendung? (beginnen)

Some common verbs have a vowel change in the *du* and the *er / sie / es* forms.
For example, *fahren -> er fährt   geben -> er gibt   sehen -> er sieht*
You can check for vowel changes in column 2 of the irregular verb tables on pages 108–109 of the Revision Guide. The endings are regular.

2 Complete each sentence with the correct form of the verb in brackets.

   (a) Wann ....*fährst*........ du nach Österreich? (fahren)

   (b) Ich .... am Montagabend. (fahren)

   (c) Wir .... einen Roman. (lesen)

   (d) Was .... du? (lesen)

   (e) Lena .... sehr gut Englisch. (sprechen)

   (f) Was .... er dir zum Geburtstag? (geben)

   (g) Mein Bruder .... immer noch. (schlafen)

   (h) Er .... uns später. (treffen)

   (i) Meine Freundin .... modische Kleidung. (tragen)

   (j) Das Kind .... seiner Mutter. (helfen)

Had a go ☐   Nearly there ☐   Nailed it! ☐   **Grammar**

Reflexive and separable verbs

1. Match these reflexive verbs to their English meanings.

(a)	sich anziehen	(i)	*to meet*
(b)	sich konzentrieren	(ii)	*to concentrate*
(c)	sich treffen	(iii)	*to get dressed*
(d)	sich äußern	(iv)	*to feel*
(e)	sich fühlen	(v)	*to apologise / excuse yourself*
(f)	sich entschuldigen	(vi)	*to express yourself*

2. Complete each sentence with the correct reflexive pronoun.

   (a) Wir freuen .... auf das Wochenende.

   (b) Ich fühle .... nicht sehr gut.

   (c) Er soll .... entschuldigen.

   (d) Sie zieht .... schnell an.

   (e) Wir treffen .... in dem Park.

   (f) Konzentrierst du .... in Mathe?

3. Complete each sentence in the **present** tense with the two correct parts of the separable verb in brackets.

   Example: Wir ...*stehen*... zu spät ......*auf*...... . (aufstehen)

   (a) Er .... immer früh .... (ankommen)

   (b) Ich .... meine Mutter .... (anrufen)

   (c) Meine Eltern .... bald .... (zurückkommen)

   (d) Heute Abend .... ich einen Film .... (herunterladen)

   (e) Mein Freund und ich .... samstags .... (ausgehen)

4. Complete these sentences in the **perfect** tense with the correct past participle of the verb in brackets.

   Example: Er ist am Nachmittag ......*ausgegangen*...... . (ausgehen)

   (a) Ich bin heute Morgen .... (zurückkommen)

   (b) Der Lehrer hat meine Eltern .... (anrufen)

   (c) Ich habe lustige Fotos .... (hochladen)

   (d) Meine Tante ist gestern bei uns .... (ankommen)

   (e) Wir haben zusammen .... (fernsehen)

5. Rewrite these sentences in the correct order. All use separable verbs in the **future** tense. Start with the words in **bold**.

   (a) ankommen / in der Schweiz / morgen / **Ich** / werde

   (b) **Später** / Musikvideos / wird / im Internet / er / ansehen

   (c) Lichter / ausmachen / **Meine Eltern** / werden / die

Grammar — Had a go ☐ Nearly there ☐ Nailed it! ☐

Irregular verb tables 1

Refer to the irregular verb tables on page 108 of the Revision Guide to check the verb forms.

> **Irregular verbs in the present tense**
>
> Look at column 2 of the verb table to show you which, if any, changes happen to the *er / sie / es* form of the verb. Any change will apply to the *du* form too.

1 Circle the correct form of the verb to complete each sentence.

(a) Was **esse** / **(isst)** / **esst** du zu Mittag?

(b) Er **fährst** / **fährt** / **fahrt** mit dem Zug.

(c) Es **gibt** / **gebe** / **gebt** zu viele Leute.

(d) Was **habe** / **habt** / **hast** du in der Tasche?

(e) Die Lehrerin **helft** / **hilft** / **helfe** uns mit der Aufgabe.

(f) Wie oft **lauft** / **läufst** / **läuft** du?

> **Irregular verbs in the imperfect tense**
>
> Use column 3 of the verb tables to find the imperfect tense *er / sie / es* form. This is also the *ich* form and it acts as the stem to which appropriate endings are added for the other parts of the verb, e.g. *-st* for the *du* form and *-en* for the *wir / Sie / sie* forms.

2 Complete each sentence with the correct imperfect form of the verb in brackets.

Both tiers:

(a) Ich .... *mochte* .... nicht in die Schule gehen. (mögen)

(b) Er .... zu Hause helfen. (müssen)

(c) Wir .... einen schönen Urlaub. (haben)

(d) Mein Bruder .... nicht schwimmen. (können)

(e) Wir .... eine Party zu Hause. (haben)

Higher tier only:

(a) Das Konzert .... *begann* .... um 20:30 Uhr. (beginnen)

(b) Ich .... zu Hause. (bleiben)

(c) Wir .... spät zu Abend. (essen)

(d) Ich .... in die Schweiz. (fahren)

(e) Der Lehrer .... uns viele Hausaufgaben. (geben)

> **Irregular verbs in the perfect tense**
>
> Use column 4 of the verb tables to check the past participles of irregular verbs. Most end in *-en*. The asterisk (*) tells you that the verb forms its perfect tense with *sein*.

3 Complete each sentence in the perfect tense with the correct part of *haben* or *sein* and the past participle.

(a) Ich .... *bin* .... gestern nicht in die Schule .... *gegangen* .... (gehen*)

(b) Was .... du .... ? (essen)

(c) Die Kinder .... zum Schloss .... (fahren*)

Had a go ☐ Nearly there ☐ Nailed it! ☐   **Grammar**

Irregular verb tables 2

Refer to the irregular verb tables on page 109 of the Revision Guide to check the verb forms.

Irregular verbs in the present tense

Look at column 2 of the verb tables to show you which, if any, changes happen to the *er / sie / es* form of the verb. Any change will apply to the *du* form too.

---

1 Circle the correct form of the verb to complete each sentence.

   (a) Ich **(nehme)** / **nimmst** / **nimm** diese Hose.

   (b) Sie **siehst** / **seht** / **sieht** eine Sendung an.

   (c) Er **spreche** / **sprecht** / **spricht** mit meinen Eltern.

   (d) Was **trägst** / **tragt** / **trage** du in der Schule?

   (e) Die Lehrerin **trefft** / **trifft** / **treffe** uns nach der Schule.

   (f) Du **vergesse** / **vergisst** / **vergesst** immer meinen Geburtstag.

Irregular verbs in the imperfect tense

Use column 3 of the verb tables to find the imperfect tense *er / sie / es* form. This is also the *ich* form and it acts as the stem to which appropriate endings are added for the other parts of the verb, e.g. *-st* for the *du* form and *-en* for the *wir / Sie / sie* forms.

---

2 Complete each sentence with the correct imperfect form of the verb in brackets.

   Both tiers:

   (a) Ich ....*wollte*........ ausgehen. (wollen)

   (b) Die Lehrerin .... sehr nett. (sein)

   (c) Man .... mehr für die Umwelt machen. (sollen)

   (d) Wir .... in der Schweiz im Urlaub. (sein)

   (e) Meine Freunde .... nicht mitkommen. (wollen)

   Higher tier only:

   (a) Wir ....*nahmen*........ unseren Hund mit. (nehmen)

   (b) Ich .... meinen Freund an. (rufen)

   (c) Wir .... die E-Mails. (schreiben)

   (d) Ich .... in dem See. (schwimmen)

   (e) Wir .... in dem Park. (sitzen)

Irregular verbs in the perfect tense

Use column 4 of the verb tables to check the past participle of irregular verbs. Most end in *-en*. The asterisk (*) tells you that the verb forms its perfect tense with *sein*.

---

3 Complete each sentence in the perfect tense with the correct part of *haben* or *sein* and the past participle.

   (a) Ich ......*bin*...... im Meer ......*geschwommen*...... (schwimmen*)

   (b) Was .... du ....? (nehmen)

   (c) Wir .... über das Problem .... (sprechen)

   (d) Er .... nichts .... (wissen)

109

Grammar — Had a go ☐ Nearly there ☐ Nailed it! ☐

Using irregular verbs in different tenses

Refer to the irregular verb tables on pages 108 and 109 of the Revision Guide to check the verb forms you need to use here.

The present tense

1 Complete each sentence with the correct present tense form of the verb in brackets.

   (a) Die Mädchen .... *singen* .... sehr schön. (singen)

   (b) Du .... immer deine Bücher. (vergessen)

   (c) Welchen Film .... wir? (sehen)

   (d) Mein Bruder .... Horrorfilme. (mögen)

   (e) Wann .... der Bus ab? (fahren)

   (f) Ich .... keine Schwestern. (haben)

2 Circle the correct form of the verb to complete each present tense sentence.

   (a) Wann **beginnst / beginnt / beginnen** der Film?

   (b) Meine Mutter **schreibe / schreiben / schreibt** viele E-Mails.

   (c) Der Lehrer **spricht / sprecht / sprechen** gut Deutsch.

   (d) Was **tragt / trägst / tragen** du heute Abend?

   (e) Die Kinder **trinkt / trinken / trinkst** oft Milch.

The perfect tense

3 Rewrite these present tense sentences in the **perfect** tense.

   Examples: Ich **fahre*** nach Österreich. –> Ich **bin** nach Österreich **gefahren**.

   (a) Das Konzert **beginnt** spät.   (f) Wir **helfen** unseren Freunden.

   (b) Was **isst** er in der Pause?   (g) Ich **laufe*** jeden Morgen am Strand.

   (c) Ich **gehe*** zu Fuß zur Schule.   (h) Meine Eltern **kommen*** spät nach Hause.

   (d) Wir **bringen** dir ein Geschenk.   (i) Er **trinkt** viel Kaffee.

   (e) Ich **lese** einen neuen Krimi.

The imperfect tense

4 Complete each sentence with the correct imperfect form of the verb in brackets.

   Both tiers:

   (a) Ich .... zu viel Arbeit. (haben)

   (b) Wir .... nichts sehen. (können)

   (c) Er .... eine Stunde auf den Zug warten. (müssen)

   Higher tier only:

   (a) Ich .... meine Freundin an. (rufen)

   (b) Wir .... mit dem Arzt. (sprechen)

   (c) Er .... die Stunde langweilig. (finden)

Had a go ☐ **Nearly there** ☐ **Nailed it!** ☐

Grammar

Sein and *haben*

Sein and *haben* are perhaps the most useful verbs of all, because they occur so frequently, and also because we use them to form the perfect tense of every other verb. Refer to page 1 and the irregular verb tables on pages 108 and 109 of the Revision Guide for the verb forms you need to use here.

Here are their key forms:			
	present tense *er / sie / es* **form**	**imperfect tense** *er / sie / es* **form**	**past participle**
haben	hat	hatte	gehabt
sein	ist	war	gewesen*

* This means that the verb takes *sein* in the perfect tense. You won't meet *gewesen* in the exam, but it is good to know.

1 Complete the sentences with the correct present tense form of *haben* (a)–(e) or *sein* (f)–(j).

(a) ......*Hast*...... du Geschwister?

(b) Man .... nie genug Zeit.

(c) Ich .... nächste Woche Geburtstag.

(d) Die Mädchen .... lange blonde Haare.

(e) .... ihr Geld mit?

(f) Mein Onkel .... heute fünfzig Jahre alt.

(g) Diese Städte .... sehr historisch.

(h) .... du krank?

(i) Ich .... in der Handballmannschaft.

(j) .... Sie Touristen?

2 Complete the sentences with the correct imperfect tense form of *haben* (a)–(e) or *sein* (f)–(j).

(a) Wir ......*hatten*...... schönes Wetter.

(b) Ich .... Angst.

(c) Die Kinder .... Hunger.

(d) Er .... Durst.

(e) Die Touristen .... einen schönen Tag.

(f) Ich .... letzte Woche im Krankenhaus.

(g) Wo .... deine Freunde?

(h) Es .... echt spannend!

(i) .... Sie in Berlin?

(j) Du .... nicht auf der Party?

Grammar

Had a go ☐ Nearly there ☐ Nailed it! ☐

Modal verbs in the present tense

> Modal verbs need the **infinitive** of another verb to complete their sense.
>
> This infinitive appears at the end of the clause or sentence.
>
> Modal verbs in the **present** tense follow a regular pattern in the plural, but they have some irregular singular forms.
>
> - dürfen – ich / er / sie / es darf
> - können – ich / er / sie / es kann
> - mögen – ich / er / sie / es mag
> - müssen – ich / er / sie / es muss
> - sollen – ich / er / sie / es soll
> - wollen – ich / er / sie / es will

1 Circle the correct form of the modal verb to complete each sentence.

(a) Mein Bruder **will** / **wollen** / **wollt** auf die Uni gehen.

(b) Wir **soll** / **sollt** / **sollen** die Umwelt schützen.

(c) Welches Hemd **mag** / **magst** / **mögt** du?

(d) Hier **dürfen** / **darf** / **darfst** man nicht rauchen.

(e) Ich **muss** / **musst** / **müsst** bis morgen diese Wörter lernen.

(f) Wann **kann** / **können** / **könnt** wir dich besuchen?

2 Translate the sentences in exercise 1 **into English**.

(a) ....

(b) ....

(c) ....

(d) ....

(e) ....

(f) ....

> Modals can also be useful in the **imperfect** tense to say what you had to / wanted to / were able to do. Here are the *ich* forms (which are also the *er* / *sie* / *es* forms). Just add the usual endings for the other persons of the verb.
>
> ich durfte   ich konnte   ich mochte   ich musste   ich sollte   ich wollte

3 Complete each sentence with the imperfect tense form of the verb in brackets.

(a) Wir ......*konnten*...... nicht mit dem Zug fahren. (können)

(b) Wohin .... du in Urlaub fahren? (wollen)

(c) Ich .... den Jungen nicht. (mögen)

(d) Leider .... meine Freundin nicht mitkommen. (dürfen)

(e) Man .... mehr tun, um anderen zu helfen. (sollen)

(f) Er .... lange auf einen Bus warten. (müssen)

(g) Die Kinder .... ein Eis kaufen. (dürfen)

(h) Jugendliche .... aktiver sein. (sollen)

(i) Ich .... kein Wort verstehen. (können)

(j) Ich .... Schriftsteller werden. (wollen)

(k) Das Hotel .... wir nicht sehr. (mögen)

Had a go ☐   Nearly there ☐   Nailed it! ☐   **Grammar**

The perfect tense with *haben*

> Most verbs form their **perfect** tense with the auxiliary verb *haben*.
>
> The past participle stands at the end of the clause / sentence.
>
> Regular past participles form like this:
>
> - **mach**en –> **mach** –> **gemacht**
>   Ich **habe** einen Sprachkurs **gemacht**.
> - Note that if the stem ends in *-d* or *-t*, you should add an extra *e* before the final letter.
>   Hast du gearbei**tet**?
> - If the verb has an inseparable prefix like **be**nutzen, no *ge-* is added to the front.
>   Ich habe meinen Laptop **be**nutzt.
> - If the infinitive ends in *-ieren*, no *ge-* is added to the front, but the past participle ends, as normal, in *-t*.
>   Ich habe in Berlin **studiert**.

1 Complete the sentences with the correct part of *haben* and the regular past participle of the verb in brackets.

(a) Ich .... habe .... Golf .... gespielt .... (spielen)

(b) .... er Souvenirs .... ? (kaufen)

(c) Wir .... Nachrichten .... (schicken)

(d) Meine Freunde .... lange .... (warten)

(e) Ich .... in diesem Café .... (arbeiten)

(f) Die Klasse .... Mathe .... (lernen)

> Some verbs have irregular past participles, which often end in *-en* rather than the regular *-t*.
>
> Here's a reminder of some common ones you need to know.
>
> essen –> geg**essen**   finden –> gefund**en**   geben –> gegeb**en**
> helfen –> gehol**fen**   lesen –> geles**en**   nehmen –> genomm**en**
> schreiben –> geschrieb**en** sprechen –> gesproch**en**   trinken –> getrunk**en**
>
> Use the irregular verb tables on pages 108 and 109 of the Revision Guide to check other irregular past participles. You'll find them in column 4.

2 Complete the sentences with an appropriate past participle from the box below.

| gegessen | geholfen | gegeben | geschrieben |
| getroffen | getrunken | ~~gelesen~~ | gesprochen |

(a) Habt ihr diesen spannenden Roman .... gelesen .... ?

(b) Wir haben Schnitzel und Würste ....

(c) Meine Schwester hat keinen Kaffee ....

(d) Er hat mit der Lehrerin über meine Noten ....

(e) Hast du dem armen Kind .... ?

(f) Ich habe die E-Mail noch nicht ....

(g) Wir haben uns im Park ....

(h) Der Mathelehrer hat uns nochmal viele Hausaufgaben ....

The perfect tense with *sein*

Which verbs form their perfect tense with *sein*?

Verbs which denote:

- movement from A to B
  - ankommen *to arrive*
  - fahren* *to travel* (note than when *fahren* means 'to drive' and has a direct object (car, etc.), it takes *haben* in the perfect tense: Er **hat** sein neues Auto **gefahren**.)
  - fliegen *to fly*
  - gehen *to go / walk*
  - kommen *to come*
  - laufen *to run*
- a state
  - bleiben *to stay / remain*
  - sein *to be*
- a change of state
  - werden *to become*
- to happen
  - passieren *to happen*
  - geschehen *to happen*

> Verbs ending in *-ieren* are all regular and never add *ge-* to the past participle: *Was ist passiert?* What happened?

1 Complete each sentence with the correct part of *sein*.

(a) Ich .... bin .... ins Kino gegangen.

(b) Wann .... du in die Schule gekommen?

(c) Wir .... dahin geflogen.

(d) Die Touristen .... nach Wien gefahren.

(e) Wo .... der Unfall passiert?

(f) Mila .... immer meine beste Freundin gewesen.

(g) Viele Flüchtlinge .... angekommen.

(h) Ich .... dieses Jahr fleißiger geworden.

(i) Was .... hier geschehen?

2 Translate these perfect tense sentences **into German**.

(a) Have you been to Berlin? (use *fahren* in the *du* form)

....

(b) We arrived late yesterday evening.

....

(c) How did the accident happen?

....

(d) They have been ill.

....

(e) She has become more sporty.

....

Had a go ☐ **Nearly there** ☐ **Nailed it!** ☐   Grammar

The imperfect tense

> You can use the **imperfect** tense to write about events in the past. Many common verbs are used in the imperfect in spoken language too. Examples include: *war, hatte, musste, konnte* and *wollte*.
> - For **regular** verbs: add *-t* to the stem and then the endings *-e / -ste / -e* in the singular and *-en* for all the plural forms except *ihr*, which ends in *-et*.
>   Ich mach**te** Gartenarbeit.
> - For **irregular** verbs: try to get to know the *er / sie / es* form, which is also the *ich* form. The plural endings are as for regular verbs.
>   Er **trug** eine Jacke.

1 Circle the correct imperfect form of these regular verbs to complete each sentence.

(a) Ich **spielten** / (**spielte**) / **spieltet** gestern Fußball.

(b) Die Schüler **lerntest** / **lernten** / **lernte** viel über das Klima.

(c) Wir **kämpfte** / **kämpften** / **kämpftest** gegen Diskriminierung.

(d) Er **kochtest** / **kochte** / **kochten** etwas zu essen.

(e) Meine Tante **malte** / **maltest** / **malten** ein schönes Bild.

(f) Ich **kaufte** / **kauftest** / **kauftet** eine blaue Jacke.

> At Foundation tier you only need to know the imperfect for *haben* and *sein* (all persons) and modal verbs for *ich*, *du* and *er/sie/es*.

2 Complete the sentences with the correct imperfect form of the irregular verb in brackets.

(a) Meine Familie ………… war ………… im Urlaub in der Türkei. (sein)

(b) Das Kind ………………… nach Hause. (laufen)

(c) Wann ………………… der Zug an? (kommen)

(d) Ich ………………… im Bett. (bleiben)

(e) Wir ………………… nicht ausgehen. (können)

(f) Meine Freunde ………………… Fastfood. (essen)

(g) Wir ………………… jeden Morgen. (schwimmen)

(h) Ich ………………… spät nach Hause. (gehen)

(i) Die Schülerin ………………… mir ein Geschenk. (geben)

(j) Er ………………… mit dem Auto in die Berge. (fahren)

(k) ………………… Sie eine gute Reise? (haben)

(l) Wir ………………… nicht, wo das Hotel war. (wissen)

> Use the irregular verb tables on pages 108 and 109 of the Revision Guide to check any forms you are not sure of. Look at column 3 for the imperfect tense.

Grammar

Had a go ☐ Nearly there ☐ Nailed it! ☐

The future tense

Correct form of *werden* + *infinitive*			
ich	werde	in die Stadt	gehen
du	wirst	nicht genug Zeit	haben
er / sie / es	wird	Flüchtlingen	helfen
wir	werden	nicht mit dem Flugzeug	fliegen
ihr	werdet	heute Handball	spielen
Sie	werden	in diesem Restaurant	essen
sie	werden	in den Sommerferien	zelten

1 Complete each sentence with the correct part of *werden*.

   (a) Was ....*wirst*........ du nach den Prüfungen machen?

   (b) Ich .... in der Oberstufe Fremdsprachen lernen.

   (c) Meine Schwester .... einen Job in London suchen.

   (d) Wir .... nächstes Jahr nicht in den Urlaub fahren.

   (e) Meine Freundinnen .... am Samstag tanzen gehen.

2 Rewrite these jumbled sentences in the correct order, starting with the words in bold.

   (a) gehen / **Mein Freund** / auf die Uni / im Oktober / wird

   (b) werde / sein / **Ich denke** / ich / Tierärztin

   (c) haben / nächstes Jahr / eine Party / werden / **Wir**

   (d) Wasser / nicht / in der Zukunft / genug / **Es wird** / geben

   (e) unsere Welt / **Flugzeuge** / weiter / zerstören / werden

> Remember that you can use a **future time marker** (e.g. nächste Woche, in der Zukunft) and a **present** tense verb to indicate a future time frame.
> Nächsten Samstag arbeite ich in einem Restaurant.
> Another alternative is to use *ich will* (I want to), *ich möchte* (I would like to) or *ich hoffe ... zu*. All these expressions need an infinitive at the end.

3 Translate these sentences **into English**, each time referring to the future!

   (a) Nächsten September gehe ich in die Oberstufe.

   ....

   (b) Heute Abend wollen wir mit meinen Großeltern essen.

   ....

   (c) In der Zukunft heirate ich bestimmt nicht.

   ....

4 Translate these sentences **into German**.

   (a) In the future I would like to work with animals. ....

   (b) I hope to be an actor. ....

   (c) Next week I want to buy some new clothes. ....

Had a go ☐ **Nearly there** ☐ **Nailed it!** ☐   Grammar

The conditional

> The structure is the same as for the future tense, except that you use *würde* instead of *werde*.
>
> Ich würde gerne ins Ausland fahren.
> Ich würde lieber Geld verdienen.
> Ich würde am liebsten ein Studium machen.
>
> You can use *gern / lieber / am liebsten* (I would like / I would prefer / best of all I would like ...) to intensify your idea.

1 Rewrite these future tense sentences in the conditional.

   (a) Ich werde Geschichte studieren. ....

   (b) Mein Bruder wird eine Lehre machen. ....

   (c) Unsere Lehrerin wird nicht zufrieden sein. ....

   (d) Was werden sie machen? ....

   (e) Vielleicht werde ich die Schule verlassen. ....

> A full conditional sentence often uses a *wenn* clause to say what you would do **if** ...
>
> The verb in the *wenn* clause can either be a **conditional** or a **past subjunctive** form, which has the same meaning but often sounds more natural.
>
> | conditional | past subjunctive alternative | meaning |
> | --- | --- | --- |
> | Ich würde ... haben | Ich hätte | *I would have* |
> | Wir würden ... können | Wir könnten | *We would be able to* |
> | Es würde ... sein | Es wäre | *It would be* |
> | Wir würden ... mögen | Wir möchten | *We would like* |

2 Translate these conditional sentences **into English**.

   (a) Was würde er machen, wenn er reich wäre?

   ....

   (b) Ich würde einen teuren Urlaub auf einer Insel buchen.

   ....

   (c) Wenn er könnte, würde mein Bruder mit seiner Freundin zusammenleben.

   ....

   (d) Wenn ich Schuldirektor wäre, hätten wir keine Hausaufgaben mehr.

   ....

Paper 1: Speaking (Foundation)

Pearson Edexcel publishes official Sample Assessment Material on its website. This test has been written to help you practise what you have learned across the four skills and may not be representative of a real exam paper.

Read aloud

My neighbourhood

1 Mia, your friend, has sent you some information about where she lives. Read out the text below.

> Ich wohne in Europa.
> Meine Stadt ist die Hauptstadt von Österreich und heißt Wien.
> Ich mag die historischen kleinen Straßen im Zentrum.
> Es gibt oft viele Touristen, die im Urlaub sind.
> Ich will in der Zukunft hier bleiben.

Now play the recording of two questions related to what you have read. You are expected to say a few words or a short phrase / sentence in response to each question. One-word answers will not be sufficient to gain full marks. **(12 marks)**

Role play

2 **Setting:** In a café

Scenario: You are in a café in Germany.

Listen to the recording of the teacher's part. The teacher will play the part of the waiter / waitress and will speak first. They will ask questions **in German** and you must answer **in German**.
You are expected to say a few words or a short phrase / sentence in response to each prompt. One-word answers will not be sufficient to gain full marks.

> **Task:**
> 1 Say for how many people you want a table.
> 2 Say what you would like to drink.
> 3 Say what you want to eat.
> 4 Give your opinion of the town.
> 5 Ask a question about the price.

(10 marks)

Photo card

 Picture 1

 Picture 2

See this photo in colour

See this photo in colour

3 Describe **ONE** of these pictures. Your description must cover:

- people
- location
- activity.

Now listen to the recording. You will hear two questions related to each picture. Answer the two questions related to your chosen picture. You are expected to say a few words or a short phrase / sentence in response to each question. One-word answers will not be sufficient to gain full marks. **(12 marks)**

You will then move on to a conversation on the broader thematic context of **My personal world**. Play the recording of an example of a teacher's question. In the real exam, your teacher will ask you more than one question. Practise saying your answer – it should be as full and detailed as possible and could use a variety of tenses. Then listen to the recording of different levels of student answers in the Answer section. **(16 marks)**

TOTAL FOR PAPER = 50 MARKS

Had a go ☐ Nearly there ☐ Nailed it! ☐   **Practice papers**

Paper 2: Listening (Foundation)

Favourite things

1 Alina, Joel and Mika are talking about their favourite things. What do they say?

   Listen to the recording and complete the sentences by putting a cross [×] in the correct box for each question.

   (a) Alina's favourite thing is …

☐	**A** her home.
☐	**B** her dog.
☐	**C** her clothes.

   (b) Joel's favourite thing is …

☐	**A** his phone.
☐	**B** his friend.
☐	**C** his computer.

   (c) Mika's favourite thing is …

☐	**A** his new football.
☐	**B** his football team.
☐	**C** his football shirt.

   (3 marks)

Holidays

2 Tim is talking about his summer holidays. Which activities does he mention? Listen to the recording and put a cross [×] in each one of the **three** correct boxes.

☐ **A** walking	☐ **C** swimming	☐ **E** camping
☐ **B** cycling	☐ **D** horse riding	☐ **F** climbing

   (3 marks)

Being green

3 Mia is talking about the environment. What does she say? Complete the gap in each sentence using a word or phrase from the box. There are more words than gaps.

   > bus   car   train
   > on foot   by bike   by underground
   > heating   computer   lights

   (a) Mia does not use the ……………………………………………………… .

   (b) When it is possible she goes ……………………………………………………… .

   (c) She tries to save electricity by switching off the ……………………………… .   **(3 marks)**

School subjects

4 Malik is talking about school. Which subjects does he mention?

   Listen to the recording and put a cross [×] in each one of the **three** correct boxes.

☐ **A** Maths	☐ **C** Languages	☐ **E** Art
☐ **B** Games	☐ **D** Geography	☐ **F** History

   (3 marks)

Family relationships

5 Sofie is talking about her family. What does she say? Listen to the recording and complete the sentences by putting a cross [×] in the correct box for each question.

   (a) Sofie gets on best with her …

☐	**A** mother.
☐	**B** father.
☐	**C** stepfather.

   (b) Sofie has a lot in common with her …

☐	**A** brother.
☐	**B** mother.
☐	**C** sister.

119

Practice papers — Had a go ☐ Nearly there ☐ Nailed it! ☐

(c) Sofie's sister is …

☐	**A** pretty.
☐	**B** noisy.
☐	**C** funny.

(d) Helmut is Sofie's …

☐	**A** uncle.
☐	**B** grandfather.
☐	**C** stepbrother.

(4 marks)

Helping others

6 Sascha is talking about what he has done to help others. What does he say? Listen to the recording and complete the following tables **in English**. You do not need to write in full sentences.

(a) The group of people the band wanted to help	
(b) Why these families have come to Germany	
(c) What the band did on Saturday	

(3 marks)

An active holiday

7 Listen to an advert for an active holiday. What do you learn? Listen to the recording and complete the sentences by putting a cross [×] in the correct box for each question.

(a) The advert is for a holiday in …

☐	**A** Austria.
☐	**B** Switzerland.
☐	**C** Germany.

(b) In the mountains you can hike and …

☐	**A** camp.
☐	**B** ski.
☐	**C** cycle.

(c) Every day there are …

☐	**A** cultural visits.
☐	**B** boat trips.
☐	**C** fishing trips.

(3 marks)

Technology

8 Jonas is talking about technology. What does he say? Complete the gap in each sentence using a word or phrase from the box below.

There are more words / phrases than gaps.

> do research   do homework   keep in touch
> affordable   possible   safe
> day   week   month
> stupid   dangerous   fun
> faster   easier   cheaper

(a) Jonas uses technology to ……………………………………………………………………………………

(b) Without the internet it would not be ……………………………………………………………………

(c) He talks to his family every ……………………………………………………………………………

(d) Jonas thinks social networks are ………………………………………………………………………

(e) Jonas likes shopping online as it's convenient and ………………………… than local shops.

(5 marks)

Getting around

9 Frida is talking about getting around. What does she mention? Listen to the recording and put a cross [×] in each one of the **three** correct boxes.

☐	**A** car	☐	**D** bike
☐	**B** train	☐	**E** bus
☐	**C** tram	☐	**F** taxi

(3 marks)

Had a go ☐ Nearly there ☐ Nailed it! ☐ **Practice papers**

Future plans

10 Jana, Yusuf and Robin are talking about the future. What do they say?

Listen to the recording and complete the sentences by putting a cross [×] in the correct box for each question.

(a) Jana used to want to be …

☐	**A** a vet.
☐	**B** a teacher.
☐	**C** a doctor.

(b) Jana has now decided to …

☐	**A** go to university.
☐	**B** travel.
☐	**C** get married.

(c) Yusuf wants to …

☐	**A** go to university.
☐	**B** go travelling.
☐	**C** earn money.

(d) Robin wants to become …

☐	**A** a musician
☐	**B** an actor.
☐	**C** a writer.

(4 marks)

Places of interest

11 (a) Yannie is talking about a recent visit. What does he say?

Listen to the recording and answer the following questions **in English**. You do not need to write in full sentences.

(i) What did Yannie visit in London? .... **(1 mark)**

(ii) Why was he not looking forward to the visit? .... **(1 mark)**

(iii) What did he enjoy about the visit? .... **(1 mark)**

(b) Samira is describing a school trip. What did she like and dislike?

Listen to the recording and complete the following tables **in English**. You do not need to write in full sentences.

| (i) | Samira did not like … | .... | **(1 mark)** |
| (ii) | She liked … | .... and .... | **(2 marks)** |

(Total for Question 11 = 6 marks)

Dictation

12 You are going to hear someone talking about a healthy lifestyle.

Sentences 1–3: write down the missing words in the gaps provided. In each gap, you will write one word **in German**.

Example: Ich <u>esse</u> immer <u>gesund</u>.

1 Ich .... Obst und ....

2 Ich bin .... in der ....

3 .... sind gut für die ....

Sentences 4–6: write down the full sentences that you hear in the spaces provided, **in German**.

Example: <u>Wir kaufen nie Fastfood.</u>

4 ....

5 ....

6 ....

(10 marks)

TOTAL FOR PAPER = 50 MARKS

Practice papers   Had a go ☐ Nearly there ☐ Nailed it! ☐

Paper 3: Reading (Foundation)

My town

1 Read these comments from an online forum.

> **Anna:** Ich liebe meine Stadt, denn es gibt ein tolles Kino und gute Geschäfte. Ich gehe gern samstags einkaufen.
>
> **Jonas:** Meine Kleinstadt ist auf dem Land und hat nicht viel für Jugendliche. Das Leben hier ist langweilig.
>
> **Yusuf:** Ich wohne gern an der Küste. Schwimmen im Meer ist meine Lieblingsaktivität.

Who says what? Choose the correct answers. Put a cross [×] in the correct column for each question.

	Who …	Anna	Jonas	Yusuf
(a)	… lives near the sea?			
(b)	… is not happy in their town?			
(c)	… likes shopping?			
(d)	… lives in the countryside?			
(e)	… enjoys a sporting activity?			
(f)	… thinks the facilities are great?			

(6 marks)

School uniform

2 Read Mika's blog about school uniform.

> Ich finde die Uniform schlecht, denn ich mag grün nicht und ich denke, es ist nicht nötig, eine Krawatte zu tragen. Die schwarze Hose ist nicht schlecht, aber die Jacke ist nie bequem, weil sie im Sommer zu warm und im Winter nicht warm genug ist! Vergessen wir nicht, dass eine Uniform auch teuer ist.

Put a cross [×] in each one of the **three** correct boxes.

Mika mentions the …

☐ **A** colour.	☐ **C** comfort.	☐ **E** discipline.
☐ **B** style.	☐ **D** individuality.	☐ **F** cost.

(3 marks)

A restaurant flyer

3 Read this flyer for a local restaurant.

> Unser Angebot für Januar!
>
> Mittwochabends im Januar zwischen 17:00 Uhr und 19:00 Uhr darf ein Kind / eine junge Person unter 18 Jahren bei uns kostenlos essen, wenn Mutter oder Vater zu Abend isst.
>
> Probieren Sie unser **Schaschlik** mit leckerem Fleisch und frischem Gemüse. Reservieren Sie auf unserer Webseite oder rufen Sie uns an.

Had a go ☐ **Nearly there** ☐ **Nailed it!** ☐   **Practice papers**

(a) Complete the sentences below.

Put a cross [×] in the correct box for each question.

(i) The offer lasts …

☐ **A** a month.
☐ **B** 2 weeks.
☐ **C** 2 months.

(ii) The offer is available on …

☐ **A** Mondays.
☐ **B** Tuesdays.
☐ **C** Wednesdays.

(iii) You can eat …

☐ **A** at lunchtime.
☐ **B** in the evening.
☐ **C** at any time.

(iv) You can book …

☐ **A** online only.
☐ **B** by phone only.
☐ **C** online or by phone.

(b) What is *Schaschlik*?

☐ **A** cake
☐ **B** food
☐ **C** wine

(5 marks)

Family

4 Read Alina's description of her family.

Complete the following tables **in English**. You do not need to write in full sentences.

> Ich habe eine große Familie. In unserem Haus leben drei Generationen, weil meine Großmutter jetzt bei uns wohnt. Ich denke, ich bin glücklich, dass wir alle zusammen sind, denn viele Familien in anderen Ländern der Welt haben diese Chance nicht.

(a) Why Alina feels fortunate	…………………………………………………
(b) One reason she feels this way	…………………………………………………

(2 marks)

Holiday survey

5 Read the results of a survey.

> Viele Deutsche wollen den Urlaub in einem warmen Land verbringen, aber nicht viele nehmen jetzt einen Flug ins Ausland, weil sie die Umwelt schützen wollen. Mehr Deutsche bleiben heute in Europa und fahren mit dem Auto in den Süden, vielleicht nach Italien*, in die Türkei oder auch nach Süddeutschland, wo das Wetter meistens besser ist. Nicht so viele Touristen wie früher fahren mit der Bahn.

Italien – Italy

Put a cross [×] in each one of the **three** correct boxes. The survey says …

☐	**A** many Germans want hot weather on holiday.	☐	**D** environmental concerns play a part in holiday choices.
☐	**B** flying to a holiday destination is increasingly popular.	☐	**E** many people go on holiday by train.
☐	**C** more Germans now spend their holiday outside Europe.	☐	**F** many people drive to their holiday destination.

(3 marks)

Practice papers   Had a go ☐   Nearly there ☐   Nailed it! ☐

Plans for the future

6 Read Robin's email about her future plans.

> ✉
> Ich bin nicht sicher, aber ich denke, ich möchte in der Zukunft etwas Praktisches machen. Deshalb ist ein Studium an der Uni für mich nicht nötig, obwohl mein Vater darauf hofft. Ich interessiere mich für die Natur, für Pflanzen und Bäume, und ich arbeite gern draußen. Mein Plan ist, einen Beruf als Gärtnerin zu haben. Ich möchte zuerst im Stadtpark arbeiten und später meine eigene Firma haben.

Complete the gap in each sentence using a word from the box below.

There are more words than gaps.

> interesting   interesting   well-paid
> necessary   necessary   useful
> in a team   outside   alone

(a) Robin wants a job which is ....

(b) Studying at university is not ....

(c) She enjoys working ....   **(3 marks)**

A local cinema

7 Read this information about a local cinema.

> Unser Kino ist klein und freundlich. Wir haben drei Räume mit bequemen Sitzplätzen. In jedem Raum sind besondere Plätze für Rollstühle, und wenn man im Rollstuhl kommt, gibt es einen kostenlosen Platz für die Person, die mitkommt.
>
> Wir zeigen neue Filme und haben ein Café, wo man vor dem Film etwas essen oder nach dem Film einen Kaffee trinken und über den Film diskutieren kann.
>
> Donnerstagabends gibt es Filmkurse für Jugendliche. Hier sprechen wir über einen modernen Film und lernen etwas über die **Schauspieler**, die die Rollen der Filmcharaktere spielen und oft weltweit berühmt sind.

(a) Complete the sentences below.

Put a cross [×] in the correct box for each question.

(i) The cinema has …

☐ A one screen.
☐ B two screens.
☐ C three screens.

(ii) There is designated space for …

☐ A groups.
☐ B wheelchair users.
☐ C children.

(iii) There are free places for …

☐ A carers.
☐ B children.
☐ C pensioners.

(iv) Young people can take part in a film course on …

☐ A Wednesdays.
☐ B Thursdays.
☐ C Fridays.

(b) Which of these is the best translation for the word **Schauspieler**?

Put a cross [×] in the correct box.

☐ A actors
☐ B authors
☐ C filmmakers

(5 marks)

Had a go ☐   **Nearly there** ☐   **Nailed it!** ☐   **Practice papers**

Technology

8 Read what Katharina says about technology.

> Ich bin ein großer Fan der Technologie*. Ich liebe mein Handy, kann ohne meinen Laptop nichts machen und finde das Internet eine tolle Sache. Ich benutze täglich die sozialen Netzwerke, um zu wissen, was alle meine Freundinnen und Freunde machen, und um ihre Fotos zu sehen. Im Internet bekomme ich alle Infos, die ich brauche, entweder für meine Hausaugaben oder um zu verstehen, was in der Welt passiert.

Technologie – technology

(a) Complete the gap in each sentence using a word from the box. There are more words than gaps.

> today   rarely   every day
> pictures   comments   achievements
> fashion tips   news   weather reports

  (i)   Katharina uses technology ....

  (ii) She likes to see her friends' ....

  (iii) She relies on the internet for ....

Katharina's comments continue.

> In der Zukunft möchte ich viel mehr über Computer lernen und ich will an der Uni **Informatik** studieren, damit ich später bei einer großen Computerfirma arbeiten kann. Meiner Meinung nach ist Technologie unsere Zukunft. Sie wird viele Arbeiten von Menschen übernehmen und wird mit der Zeit eine immer größere Rolle in unserem Alltagsleben spielen, damit wir mehr Freizeit haben.

(b) Complete the sentence.
    Put a cross [×] in the correct box.

    Katharina wants to work …

    | ☐ | A in industry. |
    | ☐ | B independently. |
    | ☐ | C in education. |

(c) Which of these is the best translation for the word *Informatik*?

    Put a cross [×] in the correct box.

    | ☐ | A management studies |
    | ☐ | B computer science |
    | ☐ | C media studies |

(d) Answer the following questions **in English**. You do not need to write in full sentences.

  (i) What impact will technology have on the jobs market? ....

  (ii) What difference will technology make to our lives? ....

(7 marks)

Lifestyle choices

9 Read these posts on a social media site.

> **Elias:** Als ich jünger war, habe ich nichts für meine Gesundheit gemacht, aber heute weiß ich, dass es wichtig ist, aktiv zu sein. Deshalb bin ich in der Handballmannschaft und habe zweimal pro Woche Trainingsstunden.
>
> **Layla:** Ich habe früher geraucht, als ich gestresst war. Ich rauche nicht mehr und mache jeden Morgen einen Online-Tanzkurs. Wenn ich Musik höre, bin ich immer glücklicher.
>
> **Kim:** Ich bin jetzt Veganer und fühle mich viel gesünder, wenn ich meistens Obst und Gemüse esse. Früher habe ich ungesund gegessen und war oft krank. Jetzt habe ich viel mehr Energie und Lebenslust.

Practice papers

Had a go ☐ Nearly there ☐ Nailed it! ☐

Complete the tables **in English**. You do not need to write in full sentences. Give **one** detail for each answer.

(a) Elias

His lifestyle in the past.	....
His lifestyle now.	....

(b) Layla

Her lifestyle in the past.	....
Her lifestyle now.	....

(c) Kim

His lifestyle in the past.	....
His lifestyle now.	....

(6 marks)

Translation

10 Translate the following sentences **into English**.

(a) Mein bester Freund ist sportlich und lustig.

....

(b) Ich verstehe mich gut mit ihm.

....

(c) Wir haben zusammen Spaß, weil wir viel gemeinsam haben.

....

(d) Letzten Samstag haben wir in der Stadt gegessen.

....

(e) Danach sind wir zum Fußballspiel gegangen.

....

(10 marks)

TOTAL FOR PAPER = 50 MARKS

Had a go ☐ Nearly there ☐ Nailed it! ☐   **Practice papers**

Paper 4: Writing (Foundation)

In the real exam, you will write your answers on the question paper. Here some lines are provided but you may need to write the rest of your answer on your own paper.

Picture task

See this photo in colour

1 Describe the photo. Write four short sentences **in German**.

....

....

....

.... **(8 marks)**

A review

2 Choose either Question 2(a) or Question 2(b).

| (a) Write a review of a local cinema.

You **must** include the following points:

• where the cinema is located
• your opinion of the cinema
• the next film you will see there.

Write your answer **in German**. You should aim to write between 40 and 50 words.

(14 marks) | (b) Write a review of a new shopping centre.

You **must** include the following points:

• where you usually go shopping
• your opinion of the new shopping centre
• what you will buy on your next shopping trip.

Write your answer **in German**. You should aim to write between 40 and 50 words.

(14 marks) |

....

....

....

....

....

Practice papers — Had a go ☐ Nearly there ☐ Nailed it! ☐

A letter

3 Choose either Question 3(a) or Question 3(b).

(a) Write to someone you know about your school life. You **must** include the following points: • what your school is like • your opinion of school subjects with reasons • a good lesson you have had recently • what you will do next year. Write your answer **in German**. You should aim to write between 80 and 90 words. **(18 marks)**	(b) Write to someone you know about friends. You **must** include the following points: • what you like to do with friends • how important your friends are and why • what you have done with friends recently • what you will do this weekend with your friends. Write your answer **in German**. You should aim to write between 80 and 90 words. **(18 marks)**

....
....
....
....
....
....
....
....
....
....

Translation

4 Translate the following five sentences **into German**.

(a) I like the warm weather.

....

(b) In the summer there are lots of visitors here.

....

(c) We do not go abroad in the holidays.

....

(d) Today I want to play tennis with friends.

....

(e) Last week I did a boat trip.

....

(10 marks)

TOTAL FOR PAPER = 50 MARKS

Had a go ☐ **Nearly there** ☐ **Nailed it!** ☐ **Practice papers**

Paper 1: Speaking (Higher)

Pearson Edexcel publishes official Sample Assessment Material on its website. This test has been written to help you practise what you have learned across the four skills and may not be representative of a real exam paper.

Read aloud

Lifestyle and wellbeing

1 Malik, your friend, has sent you information about healthy living. Read out the text below.

> Meiner Meinung nach ist es wichtig, dass man seine Gesundheit ernst nimmt.
> Ich möchte ein langes Leben haben, deshalb versuche ich, mich täglich zu bewegen.
> Ich treibe regelmäßig Sport und finde das besonders nützlich, wenn ich gestresst bin.
> Zu Hause essen wir gesund, weil wir alle Vegetarier sind, und ich esse kein Fastfood.

Now play the recording of two questions related to what you have read. You are expected to say a few words or a short phrase / sentence in response to each question. One-word answers will not be sufficient to gain full marks. **(12 marks)**

Role play

2 **Setting: A shop**

Scenario: You are being interviewed for a weekend job in a shop.

Listen to the recording of the teacher's part. The teacher will play the part of the manager and will speak first. They will ask questions **in German** and you must answer **in German**. You are expected to say a few words or a short phrase / sentence in response to each prompt. One-word answers will not be sufficient to gain full marks.

> **Task:**
> 1 Say why you want the job.
> 2 Say what sort of person you are.
> 3 Say when you would like to start work.
> 4 Ask a question about the hours of work.
> 5 Ask a question about the pay.

(10 marks)

Photo card

Picture 1

See this photo in colour

Picture 2

See this photo in colour

3 Describe **ONE** of these pictures. Your description must cover:

- people
- location
- activity.

Now listen to the recording. You will hear two questions related to each picture. Answer the two questions related to your chosen picture. You are expected to say a few words or a short phrase / sentence in response to each question. One-word answers will not be sufficient to gain full marks. **(12 marks)**

You will then move on to a conversation on the broader thematic context of **Travel and tourism**. Play the recording and give your answers in the pauses. There will be present, past and future tense questions. Make your responses full and detailed. **(16 marks)**

TOTAL FOR PAPER = 50 MARKS

Paper 2: Listening (Higher)

An active holiday

1 Listen to an advert for an active holiday. What do you learn? Listen to the recording and complete the sentences by putting a cross [×] in the correct box for each question.

(a) The advert is for a holiday in …
- ☐ **A** Austria.
- ☐ **B** Switzerland.
- ☐ **C** Germany.

(c) Every day there are …
- ☐ **A** city visits.
- ☐ **B** boat trips.
- ☐ **C** fishing trips.

(b) In the mountains you can hike and …
- ☐ **A** camp.
- ☐ **B** ski.
- ☐ **C** cycle.

(3 marks)

Technology

2 Jonas is talking about technology. What does he say? Complete the gap in each sentence using a word or phrase from the box below. There are more words / phrases than gaps.

do research	do homework	keep in touch
affordable	possible	safe
day	week	month
stupid	dangerous	fun
faster	easier	cheaper

(a) Jonas uses technology to ………………… .
(b) Without the internet it would not be ………… .
(c) He talks to his family every ………………… .
(d) Jonas thinks social networks are …………… .
(e) Jonas likes shopping online because it's convenient and ……………… than local shops.

(5 marks)

Getting around

3 Frida is talking about getting around. What does she mention? Listen to the recording and put a cross [×] in each one of the **three** correct boxes.

| ☐ **A** car | ☐ **C** tram | ☐ **E** bus |
| ☐ **B** train | ☐ **D** bike | ☐ **F** taxi |

(3 marks)

Future plans

4 Jana, Yusuf and Robin are talking about the future. What do they say? Listen to the recording and complete the sentences by putting a cross [×] in the correct box for each question.

(a) Jana used to want to be …
- ☐ **A** a vet.
- ☐ **B** a teacher.
- ☐ **C** a doctor.

(b) Jana has now decided to …
- ☐ **A** go to university.
- ☐ **B** find a job.
- ☐ **C** get married.

(c) Yusuf wants to …
- ☐ **A** go to university.
- ☐ **B** go travelling.
- ☐ **C** earn money.

(d) Robin wants to become …
- ☐ **A** a musician.
- ☐ **B** an actor.
- ☐ **C** a writer.

(4 marks)

Had a go ☐ Nearly there ☐ Nailed it! ☐

Practice papers

Wellbeing

5 Leonie and Yasmin are talking about wellbeing. What do they say? Listen to the recording and complete the following tables **in English**. You do not need to write in full sentences.

(a) One thing Leonie admires about Yasmin	....
(b) How Yasmin tries to organise her life	....
(c) One thing, apart from studying, which is important to Yasmin	....

(3 marks)

Planning a holiday

6 Noah and his boyfriend, Tim, are planning a holiday together. What do they say? Complete the gap in each sentence using a word or phrase from the box below. There are more words / phrases than gaps.

> restaurants   gardens   entertainment
> beach   village   shops
> cheaper   quieter   more practical

(a) Noah likes the look of the hotel as it has a pool and ....

(b) Tim thinks the hotel is too far from the ....

(c) Tim prefers a holiday house because it's ....

(3 marks)

Future study

7 Matteo, Paula and Milan are talking about future studies. Which advantages and disadvantages do they mention? Listen to the recording and complete the following tables **in English**. You do not need to write in full sentences.

	Advantage	Disadvantage
(a) Matteo		
(b) Paula		
(c) Milan		

(6 marks)

Environmental issues

8 You hear a podcast about the environment. What does the speaker say? Listen to the recording and complete the sentences by putting a cross [×] in the correct box for each question.

(a) The environment is now …
- ☐ **A** an important issue.
- ☐ **B** a popular issue.
- ☐ **C** a necessary issue.

(b) At stake is the …
- ☐ **A** survival of the world.
- ☐ **B** habitat of animals.
- ☐ **C** supply of fresh water.

(c) Protecting the environment is the job of …
- ☐ **A** government.
- ☐ **B** industry.
- ☐ **C** everyone.

(d) People should …
- ☐ **A** join action groups.
- ☐ **B** use less electricity.
- ☐ **C** not drive cars.

(e) Instead of heating the house, you should …
- ☐ **A** heat one room.
- ☐ **B** wear more clothes.
- ☐ **C** do more exercise.

(f) Too many people are …
- ☐ **A** lazy.
- ☐ **B** thoughtless.
- ☐ **C** selfish.

(6 marks)

Practice papers — Had a go ☐ Nearly there ☐ Nailed it! ☐

Interests

9 (a) Lukas is talking about his main interests. What does he say? Listen to the recording and put a cross [×] in each one of the **three** correct boxes.

Lukas ...

☐	A recently discovered a love of films.	☐	D recommends films for his peers.
☐	B sees a film every week.	☐	E helps to run a film club at school.
☐	C never reads what film critics say.	☐	F wants to study drama.

(3 marks)

(b) Lukas now talks about the last film he saw. Listen to the recording and answer the following questions **in English**.

You do not need to write in full sentences.

(i) Why is it difficult to say what genre this film belongs to? ....

(ii) What is special about the actors? ....

(iii) What does Lukas say about the plot of the film? ....

(iv) What can only be decided by seeing the film for yourself? ....

(4 marks)

(Total for Question 9 = 7 marks)

Dictation

10 You are going to hear someone talking about relationships with family and friends. Sentences 1–2: write down the missing words in the gaps provided. In each gap, you will write one word **in German**.

Example: Ich habe viele Freunde.

1 Ich .... mich gut mit meiner ...., weil sie .... ist.

2 Mein .... zu meinem Bruder ist schlecht, denn er ist .... und ....

Sentences 3–6: write down the full sentences that you hear in the spaces provided, **in German**.

Example: Ich finde meinen Onkel sehr lustig.

3 ....

4 ....

5 ....

6 ....

(10 marks)

TOTAL FOR PAPER = 50 MARKS

Had a go ☐ Nearly there ☐ Nailed it! ☐   **Practice papers**

Paper 3: Reading (Higher)

Plans for the future

1 Read Robin's email about her future plans.

> Ich bin nicht sicher, aber ich denke, ich möchte in der Zukunft etwas Praktisches machen. Deshalb ist ein Studium an der Uni für mich nicht nötig, obwohl mein Vater darauf hofft. Ich interessiere mich für die Natur, für Pflanzen und Bäume, und ich arbeite gern draußen. Mein Plan ist, einen Beruf als Gärtnerin zu haben. Ich möchte zuerst im Stadtpark arbeiten und später meine eigene Firma haben.

Complete the gap in each sentence using a word from the box below.

There are more words than gaps.

interesting	well-paid	practical
necessary	important	useful
in a team	outside	alone

(a) Robin wants a job which is ....

(b) Studying at university is not ....

(c) She enjoys working ....

(3 marks)

A local cinema

2 Read this information about a local cinema.

> Unser Kino ist klein und freundlich. Wir haben drei Räume mit bequemen Sitzplätzen. In jedem Raum sind besondere Plätze für Rollstühle, und wenn man im Rollstuhl kommt, gibt es einen kostenlosen Platz für die Person, die mitkommt.
>
> Wir zeigen neue Filme und haben ein Café, wo man vor dem Film etwas essen oder nach dem Film einen Kaffee trinken und über den Film diskutieren kann.
>
> Donnerstagabends gibt es Filmkurse für Jugendliche. Hier sprechen wir über einen modernen Film und lernen etwas über die **Schauspieler**, die die Rollen der Filmcharaktere spielen und oft weltweit berühmt sind.

(a) Complete the sentences below.

Put a cross [×] in the correct box for each question.

(i) The cinema has …

☐ **A** one screen.
☐ **B** two screens.
☐ **C** three screens.

(ii) There is designated space for …

☐ **A** groups.
☐ **B** wheelchair users.
☐ **C** children.

(iii) There are free places for …

☐ **A** carers.
☐ **B** children.
☐ **C** pensioners.

(iv) Young people can take part in a film course on …

☐ **A** Wednesdays.
☐ **B** Thursdays.
☐ **C** Fridays.

133

Practice papers — Had a go ☐ Nearly there ☐ Nailed it! ☐

(b) Which of these is the best translation for the word *Schauspieler*?

Put a cross [×] in the correct box.

☐ **A** actors   ☐ **B** authors   ☐ **C** filmmakers

(5 marks)

Technology

3 Read what Katharina says about technology.

> Ich bin ein großer Fan der Technologie*. Ich liebe mein Handy, kann ohne meinen Laptop nichts machen und finde das Internet eine tolle Sache. Ich benutze täglich die sozialen Netzwerke, um zu wissen, was alle meine Freundinnen und Freunde machen, und um ihre Fotos zu sehen. Im Internet bekomme ich alle Infos, die ich brauche, entweder für meine Hausaugaben oder um zu verstehen, was in der Welt passiert.

Technologie – technology

(a) Complete the gap in each sentence using a word from the box below.

There are more words than gaps.

> today   rarely   every day
> pictures   comments   achievements
> fashion tips   news   weather reports

(i) Katharina uses technology ....

(ii) She likes to see her friends' ....

(iii) She relies on the internet for ....

Katharina's comments continue.

> In der Zukunft möchte ich viel mehr über Computer lernen und ich will an der Uni **Informatik** studieren, damit ich später bei einer großen Computerfirma arbeiten kann. Meiner Meinung nach ist Technologie unsere Zukunft. Sie wird viele Arbeiten von Menschen übernehmen und wird mit der Zeit eine immer größere Rolle in unserem Alltagsleben spielen, damit wir mehr Freizeit haben.

(b) Complete the sentence.

Put a cross [×] in the correct box.

(i) Katharina wants to work …

☐ **A** in industry.
☐ **B** independently.
☐ **C** in education.

(ii) Which of these is the best translation for the word *Informatik*?

Put a cross [×] in the correct box.

☐ **A** management studies
☐ **B** computer science
☐ **C** media studies

(c) Answer the following questions **in English**. You do not need to write in full sentences.

(i) What impact will technology have on the jobs market? ....

(ii) What does she say about the future role of technology in our lives? ....

(7 marks)

Supporting refugees

4 Read Max's post about helping refugees.

> Deutschland ist das neue Heimatland für viele Flüchtlinge, die aus verschiedenen Gründen ihr Land verlassen müssen, weil die Situation dort wegen Religionsunterschieden oder **Krieg** zu gefährlich ist, mit viel Gewalt und sogar Straßenkämpfen.
> Hier sind sie sicher, aber sie haben alles verloren und müssen wieder bei null anfangen.
> Eine Gruppe von Schülern*innen in meiner Klasse will etwas Positives für diese armen Menschen tun. Wir gehen zweimal pro Woche und helfen ihnen mit der deutschen Sprache. Sie bekommen schon Sprachkurse, aber wir sprechen über nichts Besonderes und spielen mit den Kindern, was für sie eine gute Übung ist.

Had a go ☐ **Nearly there** ☐ **Nailed it!** ☐

Practice papers

(a) Answer the following questions **in English**.

You do not need to write in full sentences.

(i) Why do refugees come to Germany? ....

(ii) Why does Max say these people have to start from scratch? ....

(b) Which of these is the best translation for the word *Krieg*?

Put a cross [×] in the correct box.

☐	**A** famine
☐	**B** war
☐	**C** drought

(3 marks)

Holidays

5 Read Lea's and Arda's blog posts.

> Meine Eltern haben ein Restaurant an der Küste, wo wir wohnen, und wir können im Sommer nicht wegfahren, weil das die beste Zeit für ihr Geschäft ist. Touristen wollen essen! Deshalb sind meine Schwester und ich in den Sommerferien immer zu Hause. Ich helfe ab und zu als Kellnerin und verdiene dabei Geld für mein Studium, und meine Schwester macht einen Theaterkurs, weil sie Schauspielerin werden will.

(a) What does Lea say?

Put a cross [×] next to each one of the **three** correct statements.

☐	**A** Her parents run a shop.	☐	**D** She works full time in the holidays.
☐	**B** The family doesn't have a summer holiday.	☐	**E** She is saving for her future education.
☐	**C** They live in the city centre.	☐	**F** Her sister wants to be an actor.

> Meine Eltern kommen aus der Türkei und sind vor zwanzig Jahren nach Deutschland gekommen. Wir haben noch viele Verwandte im Heimatland und fahren fast jeden Sommer dahin, um Zeit mit meinem Opa, meinen beiden Onkeln und ihren Familien zu verbringen.
>
> Das Land ist ein wunderschönes Urlaubsziel und hat das perfekte Klima, wenn man draußen an der frischen Luft sein will. Letztes Jahr habe ich mit meinen Cousinen viel Wassersport getrieben. Ich habe zum Beispiel sogar **Tauchen** probiert. Das war spannend! Unter dem Wasser ist es eine andere Welt, mit bunten Fischen und Seepflanzen.

(b) What do we learn about Arda?

Complete the tables **in English**. You do not need to write in full sentences.

(i) Reason for going to Turkey	....
(ii) What Turkey is like as a holiday destination	....
(iii) What he and his cousins did last year	....

(c) Which of these is the best translation for the word *Tauchen*?

Put a cross [×] in the correct box.

☐	**A** windsurfing
☐	**B** diving
☐	**C** water skiing

(7 marks)

Practice papers   **Had a go** ☐   **Nearly there** ☐   **Nailed it!** ☐

A new gym

6 Read this flyer about a new gym opening soon.

> Das neue Fitnesszentrum wird in vierzehn Tagen öffnen!
> Am Samstag haben wir einen Tag der offenen Tür.
> Kommen Sie herein und sehen Sie, was Sie erwartet!
> - Swimmingpool mit einer Länge von zwanzig Metern
> - Zwei Fitnessräume mit modernen Trainingsgeräten
> - Kinderpool
> - Fantastisches Programm – Fitnesskurse für alle
> - Sparen Sie 15%, wenn Sie am Samstag Mitglied werden
> - Café mit Terrasse
> - Persönliche Trainer innen

(a) What do you find out?

Put a cross [×] next to each one of the **two** correct statements.

☐	A	The gym opens next week.
☐	B	Saturday is an open day.
☐	C	The gym has a 25-metre pool.
☐	D	There are special membership deals on Saturday.

The flyer continues.

> Wenn Sie Mitglied werden, haben Sie das Recht, an so vielen kostenlosen Kursen teilzunehmen, wie Sie wollen. Sie können alles online buchen, aber erst acht Tage vor dem Kurs, an dem Sie teilnehmen wollen. Unser Angebot bietet ein komplettes und diverses Programm von Aktivitäten – von Aerobic bis Zumba – täglich zwischen 6:00 und 21:00 Uhr. Sie werden auch die Gelegenheit haben, Spiele im Freien zu genießen, weil wir Tennisplätze haben. Handball und Basketball gibt es auch.
>
> Es ist noch günstiger, wenn Sie das ganze Jahr im Voraus* bezahlen. Weitere Infos bekommen Sie von unseren Mitarbeitern.

im Voraus – in advance / up front

(b) What else does the flyer say?

Complete the tables **in English**. You do not need to write in full sentences.

(i) Number of classes members can book	....
(ii) When you can book a class	....
(iii) The cheapest way to pay for membership	....

(5 marks)

An online influencer

7 Read this description of Anna Paula Paulsen, a social media influencer.

> Anna Paula Paulsen, auch APP oder Paulschi genannt, ist ein bekannter Star der deutschsprachigen sozialen Netzwerke und hat weltweit über 2,2 Millionen Fans. Paulschi kommt aus Österreich, aber sie wohnt zurzeit teilweise in Berlin, teilweise in London. Man weiß nicht genau, wie alt sie ist, aber man denkt vielleicht sechsundzwanzig. Paulschi hat auf der Hochschule Architektur studiert, hat zwei Jahre bei einer Fluggesellschaft gearbeitet und hat dann diesen Beruf aufgegeben. Jetzt ist sie Mode-Fanatikerin.
>
> Was an ihr ungewöhnlich* ist, ist dass sie nie Designerkleidung anhat. Sie ist originell, da sie verschiedene Stile trägt und billige Kleidungsstücke auf einem Markt oder in einem Charity-Shop findet. Sie hat aber die fantastische Fähigkeit, diverse Kleidung cool zu kombinieren, ohne viel Geld auszugeben.

ungewöhnlich – unusual

Had a go ☐ **Nearly there** ☐ **Nailed it!** ☐   **Practice papers**

What do you learn about Anna Paula Paulsen?

(a) Complete the sentences below. Put a cross [×] in the correct box for each question.

(i) Anna Paula is …
- ☐ **A** German.
- ☐ **B** Austrian.
- ☐ **C** Swiss.

(ii) Anna Paula trained as …
- ☐ **A** an architect.
- ☐ **B** a doctor.
- ☐ **C** a pilot.

(iii) She then worked for …
- ☐ **A** an airline.
- ☐ **B** a designer.
- ☐ **C** a model agency.

(3 marks)

(b) Answer the following questions **in English**.

You do not need to write in full sentences.

(i) What makes Anna Paula unusual? (**1** detail) ………………………………… **(1 mark)**

(ii) What is her particular skill? (**2** details) ………………………………… **(2 marks)**

(Total for Question 7 = 6 marks)

A local environment plan

8 Read the poster about a local environment group's action plan.

> In unserer Stadt haben wir einen Plan gemacht, damit wir alle mehr tun, um unsere Umwelt zu schützen. Dadurch wollen wir ein Beispiel für andere Städte sein und wir hoffen, dass alle Einwohner mitmachen werden.
>
> - **Verkehrsmittel** – Es ist klar, dass die Zahl der Autos auf unseren Straßen steigt, und dass die Luftverschmutzung deshalb immer schlimmer wird. Unsere Bitte*: Lassen Sie das Auto drei Tage pro Woche zu Hause und fahren Sie mit dem Bus oder gehen Sie zu Fuß.
> - **Müll zu Hause** – Trennen Sie den Müll, damit mehr recycelt werden kann. Versuchen Sie, sehr wenig wegzuwerfen! Gemüse- und Obstreste sollte man kompostieren.
> - **Müll auf der Straße** – Wir treffen uns jeden Samstagmorgen um 10:00 Uhr auf dem Marktplatz, um Müll zu sammeln. Machen Sie mit, damit unsere Stadt sauberer wird und besser aussieht!

*_Bitte_ – request

Answer the following questions **in English**. You do not need to write in full sentences.

(a) What does the plan aim to achieve? (**1** detail) ……………………………… **(1 mark)**

(b) What is the challenge regarding car use? (**1** detail) ……………………………… **(1 mark)**

(c) What are the aims of the litter pickers? (**2** details) ……………………………… **(2 marks)**

(Total for Question 8 = 4 marks)

Translation

9 Translate the following paragraph **into English**.

> Zu Hause essen wir meistens gesund, obwohl wir manchmal Pommes machen. Das ist die Lieblingsmahlzeit meines Bruders. Ich versuche, mich regelmäßig zu bewegen. Entweder treibe ich mit Freunden Sport oder ich gehe schwimmen. Gestern bin ich im Meer geschwommen, weil ich mit meiner Schularbeit gestresst war. Wegen der Prüfungen gibt es eine Menge Druck.

………………………………………………………………………………………………

………………………………………………………………………………………………

………………………………………………………………………………………………

………………………………………………………………………………………………

(10 marks)

TOTAL FOR PAPER = 50 MARKS

Practice papers   Had a go ☐   Nearly there ☐   Nailed it! ☐

Paper 4: Writing (Higher)

In the real exam, you will write your answers on the question paper. Here lines are provided for the translation but you will need to write the other answers on your own paper.

An email

1   Choose either Question 1(a) or Question 1(b).

(a) Write to someone you know about your school life. You **must** include the following points: • what your school is like • your opinion of school subjects with reasons • a good lesson you have had recently • what you will do next year. Write your answer **in German**. You should aim to write between 80 and 90 words. **(18 marks)**	(b) Write to someone you know about friends. You **must** include the following points: • what you like to do with friends • how important your friends are and why • what you have done with friends recently • what you will do this weekend with your friends. Write your answer **in German**. You should aim to write between 80 and 90 words. **(18 marks)**

A blog

2   Choose either Question 2(a) or Question 2(b).

(a) Write a blog about your local environment. You **must** include the following points: • how clean your environment is • the pros and cons of living where you do • what you have done recently to protect the environment • what you will do in future to be greener. Write your answer **in German**. You should aim to write between 130 and 150 words. **(22 marks)**	(b) Write a blog about technology. You **must** include the following points: • how you use technology • the pros and cons of using the internet • what you have recently done online • a website you will use in the future. Write your answer **in German**. You should aim to write between 130 and 150 words. **(22 marks)**

Translation

3   Translate the paragraph **into German**.

> I do not often go on holiday, but I love travelling. At the moment, I have a job and I am saving in order to buy travel tickets. In two years, I will have enough money. It is my dream in the future to fly to America and to experience life there.

....

....

....

....

....   **(10 marks)**

TOTAL FOR PAPER = 50 MARKS

Answers

The answers to the Speaking and Writing activities below are sample answers – there are many ways you could answer these questions.

1. Physical descriptions
1. (a) B (b) C (c) A (d) C (e) B
2. (a) Ich bin sechzehn Jahre alt und ziemlich groß.
   (b) Ich habe kurze blonde Haare.
   (c) Mein Freund / Meine Freundin hat ein rundes Gesicht und blaue Augen.
   (d) Meine Brüder sind kleiner als ich.
   (e) Sie ist schön und sieht sportlich aus.

2. Character and personality
1. **Sample answer:**
   Ich glaube, dass ich normalerweise lustig und positiv bin. Ich denke, ich bin auch offen und freundlich. Ein guter Freund von mir heißt Finn. Er ist auch sechzehn Jahre alt und ein sehr guter Freund, denn er ist lieb und hat immer Zeit für mich. Meine Lehrer finden mich ruhig und fleißig.
2. **Read aloud and sample answers to follow-on questions:**
   (a) Ich bin nett, freundlich und meistens zufrieden. Ich habe viele Freunde und ich bin glücklich.
   (b) Meine beste Freundin heißt Mia. Sie ist immer nett und lieb und ist sehr lustig.

3. My family
1. (a) A (b) B (c) B (d) C
2. **Sample answers:**
Picture 1
Es gibt eine große Familie. Ich sehe neun Personen: sechs Erwachsene und drei Kinder. Ich denke, die Großeltern sind auch da. Der Opa sieht ziemlich alt aus und hat graue Haare. Es ist vielleicht eine Party zu Hause. Ein Mädchen hat lange braune Haare.

Picture 2
Eine Mutter und ihre Tochter sind im Park. Vielleicht spielt das Mädchen gern hier. Das Wetter sieht gut aus. Die Mutter hat lange schwarze Haare und braune Augen und trägt eine schwarze Jacke. Die Tochter ist sehr glücklich und hat auch lange dunkle Haare.

Sample answers to follow-on questions:
Picture 1
(a) Meine Familie ist nicht sehr groß. Es gibt meine Mutter, meinen Stiefvater, meine Schwester und mich. Wir verstehen uns gut. Meine Mutter ist sehr lieb, mein Stiefvater ist lustig, und meine Schwester und ich sind beide sportlich.
(b) Gestern habe ich mit Freunden einen Spaziergang gemacht. Wir sind in den Park gegangen und haben dort Eis gegessen.

Picture 2
(a) Ich verstehe mich meistens gut mit meiner Mutter, weil sie so nett ist. Mein Vater ist manchmal ein bisschen streng, und das finde ich nicht so gut.
(b) Am Samstag bin ich mit Mutti in der Stadt einkaufen gegangen. Das war toll, denn wir haben Kleidung und Schuhe gekauft. Danach haben wir Pizza gegessen.

4. Friends
1. **Sample answer:**
Ich habe viele Freundinnen und Freunde, aber ein sehr guter Freund von mir heißt Can. Er ist sechzehn Jahre alt. Ich finde, er ist ein guter Freund, weil er immer nett und nie böse ist. Meine Freunde sind wichtig für mich, weil wir immer etwas zusammen machen.
Am Samstag werden wir im Park Fußball spielen.

2. **Sample answers:**
Teacher: Guten Tag. Sag mir etwas über deine Freunde und Freundinnen.
Student: Ich habe viele Freunde und Freundinnen. Sie sind alle nett und lustig.
Teacher: Sehr schön.
Teacher: Kannst du deinen besten Freund oder deine beste Freundin beschreiben?
Student: Mein bester Freund heißt Tim. Ich mag ihn sehr, weil er sehr sportlich ist.
Teacher: Interessant.
Student: Haben Sie viele Freunde?
Teacher: Ja, ich habe viele nette Freunde.
Teacher: Warum sind deine Freunde und Freundinnen wichtig für dich?
Student: Freunde sind für mich wichtig, weil sie das Leben schöner machen.
Teacher: Das stimmt.
Student: Was machen Sie gern mit Freunden?
Teacher: Ich gehe gern mit Freunden ins Restaurant.

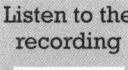

5. Relationships
1. (a) Not getting on / Difficult to talk to them.
   (b) They don't want to listen.
   (c) He's their son / He's gay.
   (d) He has a boyfriend / He loves him.
   (e) A better relationship with his parents.
2. (a) I have a lot of nice friends.
   (b) One of my good friends is very intelligent and hard-working.
   (c) I like him because he always has time for me.
   (d) We do our homework together every day.
   (e) Yesterday we played computer games.

6. Dealing with problems
1. **Sample answer:**
   Es gibt zwei Mädchen.
   Sie trinken Kaffee.
   Sie sprechen.
   Sie sind nicht glücklich.
2. **Sample answers:**
Picture 1
Es gibt ein Paar, eine junge Frau und einen Mann. Vielleicht ist er ihr Mann. Sie sehen nicht glücklich aus, und ich denke, sie diskutieren und es gibt einen Streit. Die Frau hat schwarze Haare und trägt einen Pullover. Der Mann trägt ein Hemd.

Picture 2
Es gibt zwei Personen, vielleicht eine Mutter und ihren Sohn. Die Mutter hat hellbraune Haare und sieht nicht glücklich aus. Der Junge trägt ein weißes T-Shirt und ein blaues Hemd. Ich denke, sie verstehen sich nicht gut, und dass es ein Problem gibt. Der Sohn hört nicht zu.

Sample answers to follow-on questions:
Picture 1
(a) Ich komme meistens gut mit meinen Freunden aus. Wir machen viel zusammen.
(b) Ich habe mit meiner Freundin Streit gehabt, weil sie immer ausgehen will und ich kein Geld habe. Ich finde das traurig, weil ich sie wirklich liebe.

Picture 2
(a) Ich verstehe mich gut mit meiner Schwester. Sie ist sehr lieb. Sie ist älter als ich und hilft mir mit meinen Hausaufgaben.

139

(b) Letztes Wochenende bin ich mit meinen Freunden in die Stadt gefahren. Ich habe Sportschuhe gekauft. Das war toll, denn meine alten Schuhe sind kaputt.

7. Daily routine
1 Sample answer:
Montag bis Freitag stehe ich immer früh auf, weil ich natürlich in die Schule gehen muss. Normalerweise stehe ich um sieben Uhr auf, damit ich genug Zeit habe, etwas zu essen.
Zum Frühstück esse ich meistens Brot mit Käse und ich trinke eine heiße Schokolade. Das schmeckt immer gut und gibt mir Energie für den Tag. Dann sammle ich meine Schulbücher ein und verlasse um halb acht das Haus.
Gestern bin ich zu Fuß zur Schule gegangen. Das mache ich fast jeden Tag, aber nicht, wenn es regnet.
Am Samstagmorgen werde ich lange schlafen!

2 Read aloud and sample answers to follow-on questions:
(a) Ich stehe um sieben Uhr auf und ziehe mich an. Ich höre Musik und spreche mit meiner Mutter. Um acht Uhr verlasse ich das Haus und ich fahre mit dem Zug zur Schule.
(b) Ich esse gern Brot mit Fleisch oder Käse und ich trinke normalerweise Tee. Am Wochenende esse ich manchmal Eier. Sie schmecken mir sehr gut.

8. Clothing and fashion
1 Sample answer:
Es gibt zwei Personen: eine junge Frau und einen Mann.
Das Wetter ist schön und warm.
Sie gehen spazieren.
Die Frau trägt ein weißes Kleid und einen Hut.

2
1 Sind **deine** neuen **Sandalen bequem**?
2 Es ist mir **absolut wichtig**, auf Modetrends zu **achten**.
3 Ich mag diese Hose am liebsten.
4 Mein Vater trägt nicht gern eine Krawatte.
5 In der Schule müssen wir eine Uniform tragen.
6 Wir werden bunte Kleidung anziehen.

9. Identity
1 Sample answers:
Picture 1
Auf dem Foto gibt es vier Jugendliche: zwei Jungen und zwei Mädchen.
Ein Junge sitzt in einem Rollstuhl und spricht mit seinen Freunden. Ich denke, sie sind in der Schule, vielleicht in der Schulbibliothek. Alle haben Bücher mit und sprechen wahrscheinlich über ihre Hausaufgaben. Sie helfen einander und sehen glücklich aus. Ein Mädchen trägt eine rosarote Hose, und ein Junge hat kurze schwarze Haare und trägt einen dunklen Pullover.

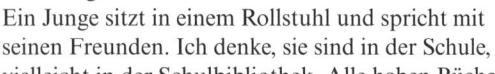

Picture 2
Auf dem Foto sehe ich zwei Jungen. Sie sind vielleicht sechzehn oder siebzehn Jahre alt. Ich denke, sie sind ein Paar und dass sie sich lieben. Sie sehen glücklich aus. Die Jugendlichen sind in der Küche zu Hause. Ein Junge trägt ein weißes Hemd, und der andere trägt ein graues T-Shirt. Beide Jungen haben schwarze Haare und dunkle Augen.

Sample answers to follow-on questions:
Picture 1
(a) Ich arbeite manchmal mit einem Freund zusammen, wenn ich Mathehausaufgaben habe. Ich finde Mathe sehr schwierig, aber mein Freund Alex findet Mathe einfach und versteht alles. Er hilft mir sehr!
(b) Letzten Samstag war ich mit einer Gruppe Freunden im Kino. Wir haben eine tolle Komödie gesehen, und das hat Spaß gemacht.

Picture 2
(a) Ein guter Freund von mir heißt Yusuf. Er kommt aus der Türkei und wohnt jetzt in Deutschland. Wir sind sehr gute Freunde und machen viel zusammen. Yusuf ist nett, freundlich und nie böse. Er ist größer als ich, und wir spielen beide gern Basketball.
(b) Letztes Wochenende waren zwei Freunde bei mir zu Hause. Ich habe Pizza gemacht, und wir haben zusammen gegessen und dann Musik gehört.

2 Sample answer:
Ich bin sehr zufrieden mit meinem Leben, und ich weiß, dass ich Glück habe, keine großen Probleme zu haben. Meine Familie und meine Freunde sind mir wichtig – ohne sie würde ich traurig sein / wäre ich traurig.
Ich treibe gern Sport mit Freunden und manchmal hören wir gern Musik zusammen.
Vor zwei Wochen habe ich meiner Freundin Samira mit dem Einkaufen geholfen. Samiras Mutter ist krank, und die Familie hat kein Auto. Wir sind mit dem Bus zum Supermarkt gefahren und haben alles nach Hause gebracht.
Dieses Wochenende werde ich wahrscheinlich Hausaufgaben machen!

10. Celebrations
1 Sample answer:
Es gibt sechs junge Leute: zwei Männer und vier Frauen.
Eine Frau hat Geburtstag.
Es gibt einen großen Kuchen.
Sie trinken und lächeln.

2 Sample answer:
In meiner Familie feiern wir jeden Geburtstag. Wir machen das, um Zeit zusammen zu verbringen und Spaß zu haben. Mein älterer Bruder hat im April Geburtstag. Letztes Jahr sind wir für das Wochenende auf einen Campingplatz gefahren / gegangen. Nächstes Jahr möchte ich eine große Party zu Hause haben.

11. When I was younger
1 Read aloud and sample answers to follow-on questions:
(a) Meine letzte Schule war ziemlich klein. Ich hatte gute Freunde und Freundinnen.
(b) Ich spiele nicht gern Fußball, aber ich mag Tennis und Basketball.

2 Sample answers:
Picture 1
Auf dem Foto sehe ich sechs Kinder, die ziemlich jung sind. Sie gehen in die Schule. Sie tragen alle eine Schultasche.

Picture 2
Es gibt fünf Kinder, die Fußball spielen. Sie sind ziemlich jung. Sie sind im Park. Das Wetter ist gut, und sie sehen glücklich aus.

Sample answers to follow-on questions:
Picture 1
(a) Meine letzte Schule war ziemlich klein. Es hat Spaß gemacht.
(b) Als ich jünger war, spielte ich oft Fußball.

Picture 2
(a) Ich spielte oft Fußball, als ich jünger war.
(b) Meine Schule war ziemlich klein, aber ich hatte viele Freunde.

12. My life in the future
1
1 Meine **Pläne** sind **klar**.
2 Ich **kann** es in England nicht **aushalten**.
3 Das Wetter **hier** ist so **wechselhaft**.
4 Es regnet jeden Tag.
5 Ich möchte in Deutschland wohnen.
6 Ich werde in einem Hotel arbeiten.

2 Sample answer:
In der Woche muss ich natürlich jeden Tag zur Schule gehen. Ich stehe früh auf und esse schnell das Frühstück und verlasse gegen halb acht das Haus. Ich bin den ganzen Tag in der Schule und wenn ich nach Hause komme, muss ich immer Hausaufgaben machen.
Ich bin meistens glücklich, aber ich finde den Tag in der Schule zu lang, weil ich immer müde bin. Ich habe aber viele Freundinnen, die sehr lieb sind, und das ist ein positiver Aspekt in meinem Leben.
Am Wochenende habe ich meine Großeltern gesehen und habe mit ihnen zu Mittag gegessen. Das hat wirklich Spaß gemacht, weil sie sehr lustig sind.
In Zukunft möchte ich mehr Freizeit und weniger Stress in meinem Leben haben. Ich hätte gerne mehr Zeit für Sport und Lesen. Später will ich heiraten, wenn ich den richtigen Mann finde, aber ich will keine Kinder haben.

13. Food and drink

1 (a) meat (b) vegetables (c) cake (d) chocolate / coffee
2 (a) C (b) A (c) C

14. Meals at home

1 (a) I don't like / enjoy (eating) vegetables.
(b) In the morning(s) I drink hot chocolate, which is delicious.
(c) My father cooks dinner / the evening meal every day.
(d) Yesterday we ate sausage and / with chips.
(e) When / If I'm hungry, I like eating chips.

2 Read aloud and sample answers to follow-on questions:

SPEAKING TRACK 163 – Listen to the recording

(a) Ich esse jeden Morgen Brot mit Käse und dann ein Stück Obst. Ich trinke Kaffee.
(b) Ich mag Fastfood, obwohl ich weiß, dass es nicht so gesund ist.

15. Shopping for food

1 Sample answers:

SPEAKING TRACK 164 – Listen to the recording

Teacher: Guten Tag. Kann ich Ihnen helfen?
Student: Guten Tag. Ich möchte Milch, bitte.
Teacher: Bitte schön. Sonst noch etwas?
Student: Ich brauche auch Brot.
Teacher: Gerne.
Teacher: Ist das alles?
Student: Ich möchte auch Eier, bitte.
Teacher: Wie viele Eier möchten Sie?
Student: Ich möchte bitte sechs Eier.
Teacher: Kein Problem.
Teacher: Haben Sie eine Frage?
Student: Ab wann ist das Geschäft geöffnet?
Teacher: Das Geschäft macht um acht Uhr morgens auf.

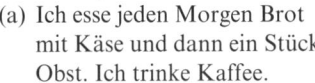

2 Sample answers:

SPEAKING TRACK 165 – Listen to the recording

Teacher: Guten Tag. Kann ich Ihnen helfen?
Student: Guten Tag. Ich hätte gern Tee, bitte.
Teacher: Bitte schön. Sonst noch etwas?
Student: Ich brauche auch Kaffee.
Teacher: Gerne.
Student: Gibt es eine Bäckerei in der Nähe?
Teacher: Eine Bäckerei gibt es hier um die Ecke.
Student: Danke. Das ist alles.
Teacher: Danke. Das macht 12 Euro.
Student: Wo kann ich Obst kaufen?
Teacher: Auf dem Markt am Ende der Straße.

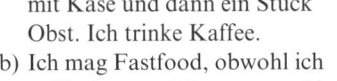

16. Eating out

1 Sample answers:

SPEAKING TRACK 166 – Listen to the recording

Teacher: Guten Tag. Kann ich Ihnen helfen?
Student: Ich möchte bitte einen Tisch für zwei Personen.
Teacher: Kein Problem.
Teacher: So … Bitte schön.
Student: Ich möchte die Karte sehen.
Teacher: Natürlich.
Teacher: So … meine Damen und Herren … was möchten Sie essen?
Student: Ich möchte den Fisch mit Gemüse, bitte.
Teacher: Alles klar.
Teacher: Und zu trinken?
Student: Ich trinke Wasser. Danke schön.
Teacher: Kommt sofort.
Teacher: Haben Sie noch eine Frage?
Student: Haben Sie WLAN hier?
Teacher: Ja, natürlich.

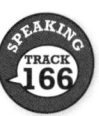

2 Sample answers:

SPEAKING TRACK 167 – Listen to the recording

Teacher: Guten Tag. Kann ich Ihnen helfen?
Student: Ich möchte bitte einen Tisch für drei Personen.
Teacher: Kein Problem.
Teacher: Wo möchten Sie sitzen?
Student: Ich möchte einen Tisch in der Ecke.
Teacher: Natürlich.
Teacher: Bitte schön.
Student: Darf ich die Karte sehen?
Teacher: Alles klar.
Teacher: Was darf es sein?
Student: Ich werde das Schnitzel essen und Wasser trinken. Danke.
Teacher: Kommt sofort.
Teacher: Haben Sie noch eine Frage?
Student: Ich habe kein Messer. Darf ich ein Messer haben?
Teacher: Das hole ich sofort.

17. A healthy diet

1 (a) Stops you feeling hungry.
(b) Give you energy.
(c) Occasionally / Every now and then / From time to time.
(d) Cheese and other dairy products.
(e) Drink enough water.
(f) Eating slowly / calmly.
(g) Green foods / vegetables.
(h) Start the day with a good breakfast.

2 Sample answer:
I usually eat healthily, although I sometimes enjoy chips. They are delicious when you're hungry. For me, breakfast is the most important meal of the day, because it gives me the energy I need for the whole morning. Yesterday I ate eggs with bread and tomorrow I'm going to prepare lots of fruit.

18. Sport

1 Sample answer:
Auf dem Foto gibt es zwei Mädchen.
Sie spielen Fußball.
Ein Mädchen trägt ein rotes T-Shirt.
Das andere Mädchen trägt ein gelbes T-Shirt und gelbe Schuhe.

2 Sample answers:

SPEAKING TRACK 168 – Listen to the recording

Picture 1
Es gibt vier junge Leute: zwei Männer und zwei Frauen. Sie sehen glücklich aus, vielleicht weil das Wetter gut ist.
Sie wandern auf dem Land. Sie sind vielleicht im Urlaub. Die Landschaft ist schön, und es gibt viele Bäume. Eine junge Frau trägt ein gelbes T-Shirt, und die andere trägt ein rosarotes T-Shirt.

Picture 2
Auf dem Foto sehe ich ein Mädchen, das ziemlich jung ist. Sie trägt ein rotes T-Shirt und spielt Tennis. Es gibt auch einen Mann. Er ist vielleicht der Vater des Mädchens oder ihr Trainer. Das ist eine Tennisstunde. Sie sind auf einem Tennisplatz, und das Wetter ist schön. Ich denke, es ist Sommer. Im Hintergrund gibt es große Bäume.

Sample answers to follow-on questions:
Picture 1
(a) Ich mag Wandern, aber ich gehe nicht sehr oft wandern, weil ich in der Stadt wohne. Ich spiele meistens Fußball oder Handball. Ich bin in der Fußballmannschaft in meiner Schule.
(b) Gestern habe ich Handball gespielt, und das hat Spaß gemacht, weil ich mit Freunden gespielt habe. Am Wochenende bin ich ins Schwimmbad gegangen.

Picture 2
(a) Ich gehe manchmal schwimmen, aber ich spiele meistens Fußball, weil das mein Lieblingssport ist. Ich spiele gerne mit meiner Mannschaft.
(b) Ich habe am Samstag Tennis gespielt, weil das Wetter schön war. Ich bin auch mit meiner Familie spazieren gegangen, und die Landschaft war wunderschön.

19. Advantages of sport
1 (a) I often (do / take) exercise.
   (b) I go running every morning.
   (c) Sport is healthy and also a lot of fun.
   (d) Yesterday my brother and I played handball.
   (e) When I go swimming, I am no longer so stressed.
2 **Read aloud and sample answers to follow-on questions:**
   (a) Ich denke, der größte Vorteil für mich ist, dass ich besser schlafe und mich positiver fühle.
   (b) Ich gehe jeden Tag laufen und spiele oft Handball mit meiner Mannschaft. Das macht immer Spaß.

20. Physical wellbeing
1 (a) I always sleep well.
   (b) My friend and I like playing football.
   (c) When / If I have time, I go running in the morning(s).
   (d) Last weekend I went swimming with my stepbrother.
   (e) In the future I would like to play tennis.
2 **Sample answers:**
Teacher: Guten Tag. Kann ich Ihnen helfen?
Student: Ich möchte bitte Tennis spielen.
Teacher: Kein Problem.
Teacher: Für wann möchten Sie das reservieren?
Student: Ich möchte bitte für 18:00 Uhr reservieren.
Teacher: Kein Problem.
Teacher: Das ist für wie viele Personen?
Student: Das ist für vier Personen, bitte.
Teacher: Alles klar.
Teacher: Sonst noch etwas?
Student: Um wie viel Uhr schließt das Sportzentrum heute?
Teacher: Wir schließen um 20:00 Uhr.
Student: Was kostet das?
Teacher: Das macht 21 Euro.

21. Mental wellbeing
1 1 Ich **bin** oft **gestresst**.
   2 Für **Jugendliche** sind gute Freunde **unersetzlich**.
   3 Bewegung und **Entspannung** sind mir **wichtig**.
   4 Ich höre gern Musik.
   5 Das Leben ist manchmal schwierig.
   6 Man muss gut schlafen.

2 **Sample answer:**
Ich fühle mich manchmal gestresst, weil es in der Schule viel Druck gibt. Wenn ich Sorgen habe, spreche ich mit meiner Lehrerin / meinem Lehrer. Das hilft immer. Meiner Meinung nach ist es wichtig, mich zu bewegen, Zeit mit Freunden / Freundinnen zu verbringen und über Probleme zu reden / sprechen. Es ist eine schlechte Idee, allein zu leiden.

22. Feeling unwell
1 **Sample answer:**
Ich sehe einen Arzt und ein Mädchen.
Das Mädchen trägt ein Hemd und Jeans.
Der Arzt trägt ein weißes Hemd und hat graue Haare.
Das Mädchen ist krank und hat Kopfschmerzen.
2 **Sample answer:**
Teacher: Guten Tag. Was ist los?
Student: Ich habe Kopfschmerzen.
Teacher: So …
Teacher: Seit wann?
Student: Ich bin seit Montag krank.
Teacher: Ich verstehe.
Student: Was soll ich machen?
Teacher: Ich denke, Sie sollten zu Hause bleiben.
Teacher: Was werden Sie heute Nachmittag machen?
Student: Ich werde nach Hause gehen und schlafen.
Teacher: Gute Idee.
Teacher: Haben Sie noch eine Frage?
Student: Wie lange wird das dauern?
Teacher: Vielleicht zwei oder drei Tage.

23. Avoiding health risks
1 **Sample answer:**
Es gibt fünf junge Menschen.
Sie tanzen und bewegen sich.
Sie sind in einem Klub.
Ein Mädchen hat blonde Haare.

2 **Sample answer:**
Ich treibe Sport, um gesund zu sein. Ich mag Fußball und ich bin in der Schulmannschaft für Tennis. Ich bin sehr aktiv.
Sport ist für mich wichtig, und ich finde Rauchen sehr schlecht und total ungesund. Es macht krank und es ist sehr teuer. Ich weiß nicht, warum junge Leute rauchen wollen.
Letzte Woche bin ich zweimal laufen gegangen und danach habe ich sehr gut geschlafen. Genug Schlaf ist auch wichtig.
Nach den Prüfungen werde ich mit meinen Freunden eine Party haben. Wir wollen zusammen feiern.

24. Sports stars
1 (a) B (b) A (c) A (d) B
2 **Sample answers:**
Picture 1
Auf dem Foto sehe ich eine Frau im Rollstuhl. Sie spielt Tennis. Sie trägt weiße Kleidung und sie hat dunkle Haare. Sie ist auf einem Tennisplatz. Der Tennisplatz ist in einem Sportzentrum und ist blau. Die Frau ist stark. Der Ball ist gelb.

Picture 2
Auf dem Foto gibt es zwei Frauen, die Fußball spielen. Sie sind draußen auf einem Fußballplatz, und das Wetter ist nicht schlecht. Es gibt Bäume im Hintergrund. Eine Frau trägt ein blaues T-Shirt, und die andere trägt ein weißes T-Shirt. Beide Frauen haben lange dunkle Haare. Der Ball ist weiß.

Sample answers to follow-on questions:
Picture 1
(a) Ich mag Tennis und ich spiele oft im Sommer. Ich mag lieber draußen spielen.
(b) Letztes Wochenende bin ich mit meinen Freunden schwimmen gegangen. Das war schön.

Picture 2
(a) Fußball interessiert mich nicht sehr. Ich laufe gern und mache am liebsten Leichtathletik.
(b) Gestern habe ich Handball gespielt – das macht immer Spaß, weil ich mit meinen Freunden spiele.

25. Hobbies and interests
1 Sample answers:
Picture 1
Ich sehe sechs Personen, vier Männer und zwei junge Frauen. Sie sind in einem Kunstmuseum und sehen die Bilder an. Ein Mann spricht über ein Bild.

Picture 2
Es gibt einen See und drei Boote. Ein Jugendlicher sitzt im Boot. Es ist Sommer, und das Wetter ist schön und sonnig. Ich sehe Bäume im Hintergrund.

Sample answers to follow-on questions:
Picture 1
(a) Ich mag Kunst in der Schule, denn es ist einfach.
(b) Ich gehe gern ins Kino und ich spiele Fußball.

Picture 2
(a) Ich liebe Schwimmen und Surfen. Das macht Spaß.
(b) Ich gehe gern einkaufen und tanzen.

2 (a) (i) working in the garden / gardening (ii) 26%
(iii) going to the gym
(b) B

26. Music and dance
1 Sample answers:
Picture 1
Es gibt eine Band. Es gibt zwei Männer und zwei junge Frauen. Drei Personen spielen Instrumente. Die Sängerin sieht cool aus. Sie hat dunkle Haare und trägt eine schwarze Hose. Sie sind vielleicht in einem Klub.

Picture 2
Auf dem Foto gibt es drei Freundinnen. Sie sind in einem Klub. Sie tanzen und sehen glücklich aus. Zwei Mädchen haben braune Haare, und die andere hat blonde Haare. Sie tragen schöne Kleidung.

Sample answers to follow-on questions:
Picture 1
(a) Ich mag Live-Musik. Ich gehe manchmal zu einem Konzert.
(b) Ich höre gern Metal und Rapmusik, aber ich mag nicht Pop.

Picture 2
(a) Ich tanze gern auf Partys oder in einem Club. Das macht Spaß und ist lustig.
(b) Ich höre sehr gern Popmusik. Ich finde Miley Cyrus sehr gut.
2 (a) A (b) C (c) A (d) B

27. Arranging to go out
1 (a) B (b) A (c) C (d) A (e) B
2 1 Ich **habe** einen **neuen italienischen** Freund.
2 Wir haben **uns** zu **Ostern** auf der **Kegelbahn** kennengelernt.
3 Wir gehen oft zusammen aus.
4 Am liebsten tanzen wir.
5 Letzte Woche hat er mich in ein Restaurant eingeladen.
6 Wir haben einen wunderbaren Abend gehabt.

28. Reading
1 Sample answer:
Ich lese nicht sehr oft, denn ich habe nicht viel Freizeit. Ich mag Liebesgeschichten für Jugendliche, und mein Lieblingsroman ist Heartstopper von Alice Oseman. Ich mag Krimis und Actionromane nicht. Ich denke, sie sind langweilig. Ich will nächste Woche den neuen Roman von Alice Oseman lesen.

2 Sample answer:
Ich lese gerne und habe immer ein Buch mit. Als ich jünger war, habe ich die ganzen / alle Harry-Potter-Bücher gelesen. Jetzt lese ich lieber Krimis. Zurzeit / Im Moment lese ich einen neuen Roman, der Die Regeln heißt. Die Hauptperson ist ein Junge, der Computer liebt.

29. Television
1 Read aloud and sample answers to follow-on questions:
(a) Ich sehe gern Serien und ich mag auch Krimis.
(b) Ich sehe gern Tennis und Leichtathletik im Fernsehen, aber Fußball finde ich laut und langweilig.

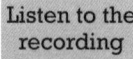

2 Sample answers:
Teacher: Guten Tag. Wie oft sehen Sie fern?
Student: Ich sehe einmal oder zweimal pro Woche fern.
Teacher: Interessant.
Teacher: Und was für Sendungen sehen Sie gern?
Student: Ich mag Krimis und Dokumentarsendungen.
Teacher: Alles klar.
Teacher: Glauben Sie, es gibt zu viel Gewalt im Fernsehen?
Student: Können Sie die Frage bitte wiederholen?
Teacher: Ja …
Teacher: Glauben Sie, es gibt zu viel Gewalt im Fernsehen?
Student: Ich sehe selten Gewalt im Fernsehen.
Teacher: Gut. Danke.
Teacher: Haben Sie eine Frage?
Student: Sehen Sie oft fern?
Teacher: Ja, jeden Abend.

30. Film and cinema
1 Sample answers:
Teacher: Guten Tag. Kann ich Ihnen helfen?
Student: Ich möchte einen Horrorfilm sehen.
Teacher: Kein Problem.
Teacher: Für wann möchten Sie Karten kaufen?
Student: Ich möchte für 20:00 Uhr Karten kaufen.
Teacher: Alles klar.
Teacher: Wie viele Karten möchten Sie?
Student: Ich möchte zwei Karten, bitte.
Teacher: Bitte schön.
Teacher: Wie finden Sie unser Kino?
Student: Ich finde das Kino sehr schön und modern.
Teacher: Gut.
Teacher: Haben Sie eine Frage?
Student: Was kostet das?
Teacher: Das macht 21 Euro. Danke.

2 Sample answer:
I rarely go to the cinema because the tickets are so expensive nowadays, but I always think it's a good experience when I see a film with friends. In my opinion, the best films are action films, because everything happens very fast and it's always exciting. Last month I saw a German detective film / thriller.

31. Mobile technology
1 (a) Knows what's happening (in the world).
(b) Can find his way (around town).
(c) Can get messages (from friends).
(d) Can see funny photos.

2 1 Ich **finde** die **Technologie** toll und **nützlich**.
2 Ich kann **Bilder** von meinen **Tätowierungen hochladen**.
3 Es macht Spaß, soziale Netzwerke zu benutzen.
4 Für meine Hausaufgaben ist das Internet wichtig.

5 Es ist notwendig, mit Freunden in Kontakt zu bleiben.
6 Ich habe eine App, mit der ich täglich Musik höre.

32. Social media
1 Sample answer:
Ich finde die sozialen Medien lustig. Ich sehe gerne die Fotos, die meine Freundinnen teilen, denn das macht Spaß.
Es ist gut, Instagram-Posts zu sehen, aber es gibt Risiken. Ich bin immer vorsichtig, denn ich teile meine Fotos nur mit Freunden. Heute Abend werde ich auf YouTube Musik hören.

2 Sample answer:
Ich benutze nicht sehr oft die sozialen Medien, aber manchmal gehe ich auf Instagram, wo es viele lustige Fotos gibt. Ich finde WhatsApp nützlich, um mit meinen Freunden und Freudinnen in Kontakt zu bleiben, besonders wenn sie nicht mehr in der Nähe wohnen und ich sie nur selten sehen kann.
Das schlimmste Risiko ist, dass man Cybermobbing erleben kann. Das ist meiner Meinung nach ein schlimmer Aspekt der digitalen Welt, weil es Angst verursachen kann. Man soll immer vorsichtig sein, und nur mit Freunden chatten. Das ist sicherer.
Letzte Woche habe ich Fotos von unserem letzten Handballspiel heruntergeladen. Es war unser bestes Spiel dieses Jahr. Wir haben gewonnen, und es war toll, die Fotos zu sehen.
In Zukunft werde ich mein Passwort regelmäßiger ändern, um meine privaten Daten zu schützen. Ich werde auch vorsichtig sein, welche Online-Freunde ich akzeptiere, und nur ja sagen, wenn ich diese Personen schon kenne.

33. Internet
1 Sample answers:
Picture 1
Auf dem Foto gibt es ein Mädchen, das in der Bibliothek arbeitet. Sie macht vielleicht Hausaufgaben.
Sie schreibt und hat ein Tablet in einer Hand und Bücher und ein Heft auf dem Tisch. Hinter ihr sind auch viele Bücher. Das Mädchen hat lange dunkelblonde Haare und trägt ein weißes Hemd. Sie sieht ernst aus.

Picture 2
Hier gibt es drei Jugendliche: einen Jungen und zwei Mädchen. Sie sitzen im Wohnzimmer zu Hause. Ich sehe eine Pflanze. Ich denke, sie sehen einen Film im Internet an. Vielleicht ist das ein Horrorfilm, denn sie sehen überrascht aus. Der Junge hat kurze braune Haare und trägt ein T-Shirt. Beide Mädchen haben lange Haare.

Sample answers to follow-on questions:
Picture 1
(a) Ich benutze jeden Tag das Internet, in der Schule und auch zu Hause. Ich finde es sehr nützlich.
(b) Ich habe gestern eine Webseite für Fremdsprachen besucht. Die Webseite heißt Duolingo, und ich mag sie sehr.

Picture 2
(a) Ich sehe gern Filme online, denn man kann immer einen guten Film finden. Am liebsten sehe ich Krimis.
(b) Ich habe Musikvideos gesehen und habe eine neue Hose bei Boohoo gekauft. Das ist eine sehr modische Webseite.

2 Sample answer:
(a) I find the internet necessary. / I think that the internet is necessary.
(b) We have a new computer at home.
(c) My parents think (that) I spend too much time online.
(d) Yesterday I downloaded a film.
(e) When / If I have time, I like playing video / computer games.

34. Computer games
1 Sample answer:
Ich mag Gaming und spiele jeden Tag Videospiele, entweder allein oder mit Freunden. Im Internet kann man viele spannende Spiele finden, die man mit anderen Jugendlichen online spielen kann.
Es gibt natürlich Nachteile, und ich habe Freunde, die zu viel Zeit beim Gaming verbringen. Das heißt, dass sie in ihrem Zimmer bleiben und nicht mehr ausgehen, um Freunde zu treffen. Das kann nicht gesund sein.
Gestern habe ich mit meinem Bruder Minecraft gespielt. Das hat Spaß gemacht.
Ich möchte die neue Version von SuperMario spielen. Die sieht toll aus!

2 Sample answers:
Teacher: Kann ich Ihnen helfen?
Student: Ich möchte ein Abenteuerspiel.
Teacher: Kein Problem.
Teacher: Was für Spiele spielen Sie normalerweise?
Student: Ich spiele meistens Actionspiele.
Teacher: Interessant.
Teacher: Haben Sie eine Frage?
Student: Haben Sie die neue Version von SuperMario?
Teacher: Ja, die haben wir.
Teacher: Welches Spiel nehmen Sie?
Student: Danke … ich hätte gerne Wonder.
Teacher: Gut.
Teacher: Haben Sie noch eine Frage?
Student: Was kostet das Spiel?
Teacher: Das macht 25 Euro. Danke.

35. Pros and cons of technology
1 Sample answer:
Auf dem Foto gibt es fünf Jugendliche: zwei Jungen und drei Mädchen.
Sie sitzen in einem Garten.
Sie haben alle ein Laptop oder ein Tablet.
Das Wetter ist schön und sie sind glücklich.

2 Sample answer:
Ich benutze jeden Tag Technologie, entweder mein Handy, einen Computer in der Schule oder mein Laptop zu Hause. Das Leben ohne digitale Geräte würde nicht mehr möglich sein. Ich schicke zum Beispiel viele SMS-Nachrichten, ich lade Filme herunter und ich mag Gaming.
Diese sind einige Vorteile, aber es gibt auch andere. Meine Eltern können oft von zu Hause arbeiten, und wir sehen uns mehr, und manchmal finde ich es praktischer, etwas online zu kaufen. Auf der anderen Seite gibt es Risiken wie Cyberkriminalität, und man muss immer vorsichtig sein, weil Daten oft nicht sicher sind.
Neulich habe ich neue Sportschuhe online gekauft. Das hat mir gefallen, weil sie billiger waren als in einem Geschäft. Ich habe auch über Skype mit meinem Onkel in Amerika gesprochen – das war kostenlos!
In ein paar Jahren hoffe ich, auch von zu Hause arbeiten zu können und nicht jeden Tag in ein Büro fahren zu müssen.

36. Films on the internet
1 (a) B (b) A (c) C (d) B
2 Sample answer:
In the twenty-first / 21st century we no longer need traditional television because it's very old-fashioned. Today, we have the internet and the possibility to watch all types of programmes. With Netflix, you can watch what you like and also choose the time. Yesterday, I watched an interesting documentary about higher education.

37. My home
1 Sample answer:
(a) Mein Haus ist ziemlich modern.
(b) Es gibt eine große Küche.
(c) Ich mag mein Schlafzimmer, denn es ist bequem.
(d) Am Abend sehen wir oft einen Film.
(e) Letztes Wochenende haben wir in dem / im Garten gearbeitet.
2 1 Ich **wohne** in einem kleinen **Doppelhaus** in der **Stadt**.
2 **Unser** Haus hat einen **Dachboden** und einen **Keller**.
3 Ich mag es, weil es ruhig ist.
4 Mein Schlafzimmer ist bequem.

5 Im Garten haben wir schöne Bäume.
6 In der Gegend gibt es wenig Verschmutzung.

38. My town

1 Sample answer:
Ich sehe fünf Mädchen.
Sie sind in der Stadt.
Es regnet und es ist kalt.
Ein Mädchen trägt eine schwarze Jacke.

2 A, C, E

39. Facilities in town

1 Sample answers:
Picture 1 (Foundation tier)
Es gibt viele Leute in der Stadt. Es ist vielleicht Samstag, und sie gehen einkaufen. Ich sehe kleine Geschäfte auf der Straße. Es ist Sommer, und die Leute tragen T-Shirts. Ein Mann links hat braune Haare und trägt eine kurze Hose.

Picture 2 (Foundation tier)
Es gibt vier junge Leute: zwei Mädchen und zwei Jungen. Sie sind in der Stadt und gehen einkaufen. Die Mädchen tragen modische Kleidung und haben lange Haare. Sie haben Taschen in der Hand. Es ist Sommer, und das Wetter ist schön.

Picture 1 (Higher tier)
Auf dem Foto sehe ich viele Leute in einer historischen Stadtmitte. Ich denke, die Stadt ist klein, weil die Straße sehr eng ist. Es gibt hier keine Autos, und alle gehen zu Fuß einkaufen. Sie tragen Sommerkleidung, also denke ich, das Wetter ist warm und sonnig. Einige Leute haben etwas gekauft und tragen Taschen.

Picture 2 (Higher tier)
Ich sehe vier Teenager, die in der Stadt sind. Ich denke, sie gehen zusammen einkaufen. Die beiden Mädchen tragen Taschen und haben schon etwas gekauft. Die Mädchen sehen modisch und glücklich aus. Ein Mädchen trägt einen Hut und ein weißes T-Shirt. Das andere Mädchen trägt rote Schuhe. Ich denke, das Wetter ist gut, weil sie keine Jacken oder Pullover tragen.

Sample answers to follow-on questions:
Picture 1 (Foundation tier)
(a) Ich finde meine Stadt nicht schlecht.
(b) Es gibt ein Kino in der Stadt.

Picture 2 (Foundation tier)
(a) Ich finde meine Stadt schön und freundlich.
(b) Ich gehe nicht oft einkaufen. Ich kaufe nicht gerne ein.

Picture 1 (Higher tier)
(a) Ich mag meine Stadt, obwohl sie ein bisschen klein ist.
(b) Letzten Samstag bin ich mit meiner Freundin einkaufen gegangen. Ich habe ein T-Shirt gekauft.

Picture 2 (Higher tier)
(a) Ich mag meine Stadt, obwohl sie ein bisschen klein ist. Die Geschäfte sind gut.
(b) Letzten Samstag bin ich mit meinen Freunden zum Fußballspiel gegangen. Das hat Spaß gemacht.

2
1 Ich **wohne** gern **hier**.
2 Für junge **Leute** gibt es viele **Attraktionen**.
3 Wir **haben** eine tolle **Eisbahn**.
4 Man kann Sport spielen.
5 Die Geschäfte sind meistens gut.
6 Meine Stadt gefällt mir sehr.

40. Finding the way

1 Sample answers:
Teacher: Guten Tag. Kann ich Ihnen helfen?
Student: Ich suche ein Restaurant.
Teacher: Kein Problem.
Teacher: Ja, es gibt ein gutes Restaurant.
Student: Wie komme ich zum Restaurant?
Teacher: Immer geradeaus und dann die erste Straße links.
Teacher: Wie lange sind Sie in der Stadt?
Student: Ich bin für eine Woche hier.
Teacher: Alles klar.
Teacher: Wie finden Sie unsere Stadt?
Student: Ich finde die Stadt sehr schön.
Teacher: Gut.
Teacher: Haben Sie noch eine Frage?
Student: Wie weit ist es?
Teacher: Nur dreihundert Meter.

2 Sample answers:
Teacher: Guten Tag. Kann ich Ihnen helfen?
Student: Ich suche einen Campingplatz in der Nähe.
Teacher: Ja, es gibt einen Campingplatz.
Teacher: Wie lange sind Sie hier?
Student: Ich bin zwei Wochen hier.
Teacher: Schön.
Teacher: Haben Sie eine Frage?
Student: Wie komme ich zum Campingplatz?
Teacher: Hier geradeaus bis zu der Brücke, dann gehen Sie nach links.
Teacher: Was machen Sie morgen?
Student: Morgen gehe ich wandern.
Teacher: Gut.
Teacher: Haben Sie noch eine Frage?
Student: Wo kann ich hier Essen kaufen?
Teacher: Es gibt einen Supermarkt neben dem Campingplatz.

41. Shops and shopping

1 Sample answer:
Ich sehe eine junge Frau. Sie hat braune Haare. Sie trägt ein weißes Hemd. Sie hat eine braune Handtasche. Sie ist in einem Geschäft. Sie sucht einen Pullover.

Sample answers to follow-on questions:
(a) Ich gehe nicht oft einkaufen. Ich finde es langweilig.
(b) Ich mag das Sportgeschäft. Es gibt dort tolle Sportschuhe.

2 Sample answer:
Auf dem Foto gibt es eine junge Frau in einem Buchladen. Sie hat blonde Haare und trägt eine Brille, die braun ist. Ihre Jacke ist hellbraun. Sie sieht ein Buch an, und ich denke, sie findet es interessant und wird es vielleicht kaufen.

Sample answers to follow-on questions:
(a) Ich kaufe nicht oft Bücher, weil ich meistens online lese.
(b) Ich habe letzte Woche einen neuen Pullover gekauft und auch einen Hut.

42. At the market

1 Sample answers:
Teacher: Guten Tag. Kann ich Ihnen helfen?
Student: Ich möchte eine Hose.
Teacher: Kein Problem.
Teacher: Welche Größe möchten Sie?
Student: Ich möchte eine kleine Größe, bitte.
Teacher: Natürlich.
Teacher: Und welche Farbe mögen Sie?
Student: Ich mag schwarz.
Teacher: Alles klar.
Teacher: Wie finden Sie das?
Student: Ja, das ist toll.
Teacher: Sehr gut.
Teacher: Haben Sie eine Frage?
Student: Was kostet das?
Teacher: Sieben Euro … Danke.

2 Sample answers:
Teacher: Guten Tag. Kann ich Ihnen helfen?
Student: Ich möchte bitte Blumen kaufen.
Teacher: Kein Problem.
Teacher: Für wen sind die Blumen?
Student: Sie sind ein Geschenk für meine Freundin.
Teacher: Schön.
Teacher: Haben Sie eine Frage?
Student: Welche Farben haben Sie?
Teacher: Rot, weiß, rosarot und gelb.
Teacher: Wie finden Sie diese Blumen?
Student: Ich finde sie ein bisschen zu klein.
Teacher: Alles klar.
Teacher: Haben Sie eine Frage?
Student: Haben Sie größere Blumen?
Teacher: Ja … Gerne …

43. Transport
1 Sample answer:
Ich gehe meistens zu Fuß zur Schule, weil es nicht sehr weit ist. Wenn es regnet, fahre ich manchmal mit dem Bus, oder meine Mutter fährt mich mit dem Auto. Das ist viel bequemer und auch schneller.
Ich denke, es ist gut, mit dem Rad zu fahren, denn es ist gesund und gut für die Umwelt. Reisen mit dem Flugzeug ist aber sehr schlecht für die Umwelt.
Gestern bin ich mit dem Bus in die Stadt gefahren, um in die Bibliothek zu gehen.
Später möchte ich ein Auto haben, aber ich weiß, dass Autos nicht umweltfreundlich sind.

2 Sample answer:
Public transport in my area is really bad because I live in a village in the countryside. There are few buses and we often have to use the car, as there is no alternative. Yesterday my brother drove me to school. It was raining hard and I couldn't go by bike.

44. Buying tickets for travel
1 (a) C (b) A (c) B (d) B (e) C
2 Sample answers:
Teacher: Guten Tag. Kann ich Ihnen helfen?
Student: Ich möchte nach München fahren.
Teacher: Sehr gut.
Teacher: Wann wollen Sie fahren?
Student: Ich will am Montag fahren.
Teacher: Mal sehen …
Teacher: Es gibt einen Zug um 11:00 Uhr und einen um 12:00 Uhr.
Student: Gibt es einen Zug am Nachmittag?
Teacher: Ja … es gibt Züge um 15:30 Uhr und um 18:00 Uhr.
Teacher: Mit welchem Zug wollen Sie fahren?
Student: Ich möchte um 15:30 Uhr abfahren.
Teacher: So … hier sind Ihre Fahrkarten.
Teacher: Haben Sie noch eine Frage?
Student: Wann kommt der Zug in München an?
Teacher: Ankunft in München um 20:00 Uhr.

45. Places of interest near me
1 Sample answer:
Es gibt vier junge Leute: zwei Mädchen und zwei Jungen. Sie sind vielleicht Freunde.
Ein Junge hat rote Haare und trägt einen blauen Pullover und eine dunkle Hose.
Sie sind in London. Ich denke, sie sind im Urlaub.
Das Wetter ist gut.
Sie gehen über eine Brücke und lachen. Sie sind glücklich.

Sample answers to follow-on questions:
(a) Ich gehe gern mit Freunden ins Kino.
(b) Es gibt ein Schloss in meiner Stadt.

2 Sample answer:
Ich wohne in der Nähe von York. Mein Dorf hat nicht viel Interessantes. Nicht weit von uns gibt es ein bekanntes Museum, das Bahnmuseum, wo man viele historische und moderne Züge sehen kann.
Auch in York kann man historische Gebäude sehen oder auf dem Markt einkaufen gehen. York ist sehr gut für Touristen, denn es gibt auch tolle Restaurants.
Letztes Jahr bin ich nach Durham gefahren. Das ist eine schöne alte Stadt mit viel Geschichte.
Später möchte ich nach Cambridge fahren, um die berühmte Universität zu besichtigen.

46. The environment
1 Sample answers:
Teacher: Guten Tag. Wie finden Sie die Umwelt hier in der Stadt?
Student: Ich denke, es gibt zu viele Autos in der Stadt. Die Luft ist schmutzig.
Teacher: Das ist ein Problem.
Teacher: Was ist für Sie das größte Problem?
Student: Das schlimmste Problem ist der Müll.
Teacher: Ich verstehe.
Teacher: Wie werden Sie in der Zukunft die Umwelt schützen?
Student: Können Sie die Frage wiederholen?
Teacher: Gerne …
Teacher: Wie werden Sie in der Zukunft die Umwelt schützen?
Student: Ich werde in der Stadt Müll sammeln.
Teacher: Gut.
Teacher: Haben Sie eine Frage?
Student: Und was machen Sie für die Umwelt?
Teacher: Ich fahre kein Auto.

2
1 Die **Stadt** ist nicht **sauber**.
2 **Verschmutzung** ist ein großes **Problem**.
3 Es gibt **Abfall** in dem **Park**.
4 Ich bin umweltfreundlich.
5 Wir recyceln Glas.
6 Ich kaufe oft recyceltes Papier.

47. Environmental problems
1 Read aloud and sample answers to follow-on questions:
(a) Es gibt zu viele Autos in meiner Stadt, und die Luft ist schmutzig.
(b) Ich recycle Papier und Glas, und ich fahre mit dem Bus, nicht mit dem Auto.

2 Sample answer:
Auf dem Foto gibt es einen Mann. Er ist auf dem Land und geht durch ein Feld. Er trägt eine Hose und ein T-Shirt. Das Foto ist in zwei Teilen.
Auf der rechten Seite ist die Welt schön. Der Himmel ist blau, und das Gras ist grün. Auf der linken Seite ist alles braun und trocken, weil die Welt zu warm ist. Es gibt kein Gras mehr. Das ist der Klimawandel.

Sample answers to follow-on questions:
(a) Das Hauptproblem ist der Klimawandel. Die Welt wird wärmer.
(b) Ich habe zu Hause Glas, Papier und Plastik recycelt und habe nicht zu viel Wasser benutzt.

48. The dangers of pollution
1 1 Wir **möchten** Energie **sparen**.
   2 Ich **dusche** mich jeden **Tag**.

3 Das **verbraucht** nicht so viel **Wasser**.
4 Zu Hause recycelt er Papier.
5 Ich will die Umwelt schützen.
6 Die Flüsse sind schmutzig.

2 Sample answer:
Es gibt drei junge Leute: einen Mann und zwei Frauen. Der Mann rechts hat kurze, schwarze Haare. Sie tragen alle grüne T-Shirts. Sie lächeln, aber konzentrieren sich.
Sie sind in einem Park oder vielleicht in einem Garten. Der Boden ist schmutzig, aber ich denke, das Wetter ist warm.
Sie sammeln Plastik, um der Umwelt zu helfen.

Sample answers to follow-on questions:
(a) Die Natur ist sehr ruhig.
(b) Ich habe Müll getrennt.

49. The natural world
1 Sample answers:
(a) I live in a village in the country.
(b) The fresh air is healthy.
(c) In my area there are lots of trees.
(d) Last weekend we went for a walk / hike in the wood(s) / forest.
(e) I like living here.

2 (a) sea
(b) airport
(c) concerts
(d) cycle paths
(e) safe

50. Individual actions for the environment
1 Sample answer:
Es gibt heute viele Probleme mit der Umwelt. Es gibt zum Beispiel schmutzige Luft, denn zu viele Leute fahren Auto.
Wir sollen alle etwas machen, um die Umwelt zu schützen. Wir haben nur eine Erde, auf der wir leben können.
In Zukunft werde ich nicht mit dem Flugzeug fliegen, weil das nicht umweltfreundlich ist.

2 Read aloud and sample answers to follow-on questions:
(a) Ich habe Angst, dass die Welt zu heiß wird, und dass es kein Wasser mehr geben wird.
(b) Ich habe Plastik, Glas und Papier recycelt und bin nicht mit dem Auto gefahren.

51. How to recycle
1 Sample answer (4 required):
Ich sehe vier Kinder.
Es gibt zwei Jungen und zwei Mädchen.
Sie sind in dem Garten zu Hause.
Das Wetter ist schön.
Sie recyceln Plastikflaschen.

2 Sample answer:
Ich interessiere mich für die Umwelt und will sie schützen. Deshalb trenne ich immer den Müll zu Hause und stecke Papier in den blauen Sack und Plastik in den gelben Sack. Es ist nicht schwierig, und alle sollen es machen / tun. Wenn man die Sachen trennt, kann man sie recyceln.

52. My school
1 Sample answer:
Ich sehe sechs Jugendliche.
Sie kommen in der Schule an. / Sie gehen in die Schule.
Alle haben eine Schultasche.
Es gibt auch zwei Autos.

2 Sample answer:
Es gibt fünf junge Leute: zwei Jungen und drei Mädchen. Sie sind außerhalb der Schule und tragen eine Schuluniform, die dunkelrot ist. Sie sind glücklich und sie laufen. Vielleicht ist der Schultag zu Ende. Das Schulgebäude ist im Hintergrund.

Sample answers to follow-on questions:
(a) Ich mag meine Schule. Das Gebäude ist ziemlich modern und die Klassenzimmer sind groß und hell.
(b) Gestern haben wir in der Englischstunde über Shakespeare gelernt.

53. School subjects
1 Sample answers:
Teacher: Guten Tag. Warum wollen Sie diese Schule besuchen?
Student: Mein bester Freund besucht diese Schule.
Teacher: Interessant.
Teacher: Was sind Ihre besten Fächer?
Student: Meine besten Fächer sind Mathe und Naturwissenschaften.
Teacher: Sehr gut.
Teacher: Haben Sie eine Frage?
Student: Was für Sport macht man hier?
Teacher: Wir spielen meistens Fußball und Basketball.
Teacher: Welche Hausaufgaben werden Sie heute Abend machen?
Student: Heute Abend werde ich Deutschhausaufgaben machen.
Teacher: Gut.
Teacher: Haben Sie noch eine Frage?
Student: Wie groß sind die Klassen?
Teacher: Alle Klassen sind klein.

2 (a) Malik (b) Jana (c) Malik (d) Jana (e) Robin (f) Robin

54. My teachers
1 Sample answer:
Dieses Jahr finde ich die meisten Lehrer und Lehrerinnen ziemlich gut, obwohl nicht alle fantastisch sind. Meine Deutschlehrerin ist vielleicht meine Lieblingslehrerin, weil sie nicht so streng ist. Wir wissen, dass sie das Beste für uns will, und deshalb ist sie sehr beliebt.
Sie ist ein gutes Beispiel. Andere Lehrer sind nicht so gut, weil sie manchmal böse sind und keine Zeit haben, uns mit Problemen zu helfen. Unser Mathelehrer kommt immer spät zum Unterricht und ist nicht gut organisiert.
Gestern hatten wir eine tolle Deutschstunde. Wir haben ein Video gesehen und dann über das Thema Umwelt diskutiert. Das hat wirklich Spaß gemacht, und wir haben viel gelernt.
Später möchte ich nicht Lehrer werden. Ich denke, diese Arbeit ist zu schwer, mit langen Arbeitszeiten, obwohl man lange Ferien hat. Als Lehrer wird man auch nicht gut bezahlt. Ich würde lieber einen Job mit Computern und Technologie haben.

2 Read aloud and sample answers to follow-on questions:
(a) Ich finde meine Lehrer meistens gut und freundlich.
(b) Ein guter Lehrer kann mit der Klasse kommunizieren.

55. The school day
1 Sample answer:
Dieses Jahr lerne ich dreimal in der Woche Deutsch: am Montag in der zweiten Stunde, am Mittwochnachmittag und am Freitag in der letzten Stunde.
Ich finde den Schultag lang und ich bin nach der Mittagspause müde. Ich denke, der Tag beginnt zu früh, weil ich mehr schlafen möchte.
Gestern in der Pause habe ich mit meinen Freundinnen gesprochen und habe Kuchen gegessen.

Morgen werde ich wie immer sechs Stunden haben. In der ersten Stunde habe ich Naturwissenschaften und in der letzten Stunde habe ich Musik.

2 (a) German (b) History (c) Music (d) English (e) Maths

56. School uniform
1 **Sample answer:**
Wenn ich in der Schule bin, muss ich eine Uniform tragen. Ich trage ein blaues Hemd und eine grüne Jacke. Für die Jungen ist es noch schlimmer, weil sie eine Krawatte tragen.
Ich denke, die Uniform kann praktisch sein, denn man muss nicht jeden Morgen denken, welche Kleidung man tragen soll. Auf der anderen Seite mag ich es nicht, dass wir alle dieselbe Kleidung tragen.
Gestern habe ich Fußball gespielt und habe schwarze Shorts getragen. Das sieht nicht schön aus, aber ist bequem.
Heute Abend werde ich wie immer meine Jeans tragen.

2 **Sample answers:**
  (a) Ich mag die Uniform nicht.
  (b) Wir tragen eine schwarze Jacke und ein weißes Hemd.
  (c) Die Jungen müssen eine graue Krawatte tragen.
  (d) Man darf nur schwarze Schuhe tragen.
  (e) Gestern habe ich rote Socken gekauft. / Gestern kaufte ich rote Socken.

57. School rules
1 **Sample answers:**
Teacher: Guten Tag. Wie finden Sie die Schulregeln?
Student: Ich finde die Schulregeln gut.
Teacher: Interessant.
Teacher: Welche Regel finden Sie gut?
Student: Es ist gut, dass Rauchen verboten ist.
Teacher: Ja, klar.
Teacher: Und welche Regel finden Sie nicht gut?
Student: Wir müssen in der Kantine essen.
Teacher: Alles klar.
Teacher: Wie finden Sie die Schuluniform?
Student: Die Schuluniform ist nicht modisch.
Teacher: Ich verstehe.
Teacher: Haben Sie eine Frage?
Student: Haben Sie andere Fragen?
Teacher: Nein, danke … das war alles.

2 **Sample answers:**
Teacher: Guten Tag. Warum sind Schulregeln wichtig?
Student: Schulregeln sind wichtig, denn sie machen die Schule sicherer.
Teacher: Interessant.
Teacher: Welche Regel ist die wichtigste?
Student: Ich denke, es ist nötig, dass Rauchen in der Schule verboten ist.
Teacher: Ja, klar.
Teacher: Haben Sie eine Frage?
Student: Werden Sie mit vielen Schülern sprechen?
Teacher: Ungefähr fünfzig.
Teacher: Welche Regel finden Sie nicht gut?
Student: Ich finde es schlecht, dass wir in der Pause die Schule nicht verlassen dürfen.
Teacher: Ich verstehe.
Teacher: Haben Sie noch eine Frage?
Student: Haben Sie andere Fragen?
Teacher: Nein, danke … das war alles.

58. School clubs
1 **Sample answer:**
Auf dem Foto gibt es fünf Mädchen.
Sie sind in dem Handballklub.
Sie spielen Handball.
Sie treiben Sport.

2 **Sample answers:**
Teacher: Guten Tag. Warum finden Sie Klubs wichtig?
Student: Ich finde Klubs wichtig, weil man etwas Neues machen kann.
Teacher: Ich verstehe.
Teacher: Und welche Klubs sollen wir haben?
Student: Wir brauchen Sportklubs, aber auch Klubs für Musik, Kunst und andere Interessen.
Teacher: Interessant.
Teacher: Haben Sie eine Frage?
Student: Wann fangen die neuen Klubs an?
Teacher: In drei Wochen.
Teacher: Was werden Sie heute nach der Schule machen?
Student: Ich werde heute zum Umweltklub gehen.
Teacher: Gut.
Teacher: Haben Sie noch eine Frage?
Student: Können wir einen Filmklub organisieren?
Teacher: Das ist eine gute Idee.

59. School trips
1 **Sample answers:**
  (a) I like school trips.
  (b) Sometimes we go to the coast.
  (c) It's fun because we are all together.
  (d) Last year we went / travelled.
  (e) My friend / girlfriend wants to go to Germany.

2 **Read aloud and sample answers to follow-on questions:**
  (a) Ich mag Schulreisen, denn das macht immer Spaß mit meinen Freunden.
  (b) Wir sind neulich auf das Land gefahren, um etwas über die Umwelt zu lernen.

60. Homework
1 **Sample answer:**
Ich verbringe zwei Stunden jeden Abend mit Hausaufgaben. Ich finde das langweilig. Dieses Jahr habe ich Prüfungen und ich muss viel lernen.
Hausaufgaben helfen uns, besser zu verstehen, was wir in der Schule lernen. Wir arbeiten aber oft zu viel, und das ist nicht gesund.
Heute Abend werde ich Mathehausaufgaben machen.

2 **Sample answer:**
In der Schule bin ich fleißig und ich versuche immer, gute Noten zu bekommen / kriegen. Ich mache viele Hausaufgaben, weil ich denke, dass es wichtig ist, die Verantwortung für sein eigenes Lernen zu übernehmen / akzeptieren. Gestern Abend habe ich drei Stunden mit Deutschhausaufgaben verbracht. Das war schwer / schwierig, aber ich glaube, ich verstehe das jetzt besser / dass ich das jetzt besser verstehe.

61. Stress at school
1 (a) (i) surroundings (ii) support (iii) conversation (iv) sleep (v) meals
  (b) B

2 **Read aloud and sample answers to follow-on questions:**
  (a) Ich finde die Schule sehr schwer. Es gibt zu viel zu tun.
  (b) Ich spreche mit Freunden oder mit meinen Lehrern.

62. Preparing for exams
1 Sample answers:
Teacher: Guten Tag. Wie lange arbeiten Sie jeden Abend?
Student: Ich arbeite zwei Stunden jeden Abend.
Teacher: Sehr gut.
Teacher: Und wo arbeiten Sie?
Student: Ich arbeite in meinem Schlafzimmer.
Teacher: Interessant.
Teacher: Wie oft machen Sie eine Pause?
Student: Ich mache jede Stunde eine Pause.
Teacher: Alles klar.
Teacher: Warum arbeiten Sie so fleißig?
Student: Ich möchte die Prüfungen bestehen.
Teacher: Gut.
Teacher: Haben Sie eine Frage?
Student: Wie findest du Prüfungen?
Teacher: Ich finde Prüfungen schwierig.

2
1. Man kann nicht **alles** in der **letzten** Minute **wiederholen**.
2. Ich habe **seit** vier Monaten **Nachhilfestunden** in **Biologie**.
3. Ich arbeite drei Stunden täglich.
4. Während ich lerne, höre ich keine Musik.
5. Ich will mich gut konzentrieren.
6. Ich hoffe, später an der Uni zu studieren.

63. My ideal school
1 Sample answer:
Es gibt acht Jungen und Mädchen.
Sie sind ziemlich jung.
Sie kommen aus der Schule.
Das Gebäude ist modern und weiß.

2
1. Alle **Schüler** finden das **Gebäude** sehr **altmodisch**.
2. Die **Lehrer** sind aber **hilfsbereit** und **kümmern** sich um uns.
3. Wir würden weniger Hausaufgaben bekommen.
4. Das wäre mein Traum.
5. Mein Lieblingsfach ist Englisch.
6. Ich hoffe auf gute Noten.

64. Plans for next year
1 Sample answer:
Dieses Jahr finde ich die Sportstunden in der Schule sehr gut, denn ich liebe Fußball und spiele in der Schulmannschaft.
Hausaufgaben und Prüfungen gefallen mir gar nicht, denn alles ist schwierig.
Nächstes Jahr will ich die Schule verlassen und Fußballspieler werden. Das ist mein Traum.

2 Sample answers:
Teacher: Guten Tag. Was möchten Sie in der Oberstufe lernen?
Student: Ich möchte Mathe und Naturwissenschaften lernen.
Teacher: Kein Problem.
Teacher: Was ist Ihr bestes Fach dieses Jahr?
Student: Mein bestes Fach ist Mathe.
Teacher: Interessant.
Teacher: Haben Sie eine Frage?
Student: Welche Noten brauche ich in den Prüfungen?
Teacher: Sie brauchen mindestens drei sehr gute Noten.
Teacher: Möchten Sie später auf die Uni gehen?
Student: Ja, ich möchte Naturwissenschaften studieren.
Teacher: Gut.
Teacher: Haben Sie noch eine Frage?
Student: Gibt es Schulreisen?
Teacher: Ja, wir machen viele Schulreisen und Schulausflüge.

65. Future studies
1 Sample answer:
Es gibt fünf Studenten.
Sie sind an der Uni.
Sie sitzen in einem Garten und reden.
Es gibt zwei Jungen und drei Mädchen.

2 Sample answer:
Ich sehe ein großes modernes Gebäude. Ich denke, das ist eine Uni, denn es gibt viele Studentinnen und Studenten. Im Vordergrund sind drei junge Leute: zwei junge Frauen und ein junger Mann. Sie haben Tablets mit.

Sample answers to follow-on questions:
(a) Ich möchte gern auf die Uni gehen. Ich will Englisch studieren.
(b) Ich plane, zuerst zu reisen, und dann will ich ein Studium machen.

66. Future career
1 Sample answer:
Ich bin freundlich und verstehe mich gut mit anderen Menschen.
Es ist wichtig für mich, mit vielen Leuten zu arbeiten und nicht allein in einem kleinen Büro.
Ich will auch genug Geld verdienen.
Ich möchte später in einem Modegeschäft arbeiten, wo es modische Kleidung und laute Musik gibt.

2 Read aloud and sample answers to follow-on questions:
(a) Ich will später Lehrerin werden.
(b) Ich habe jeden Tag zu Hause Müll recycelt.

67. Pros and cons of some jobs
1 Sample answer:
Meine Schwester arbeitet in einem Restaurant. Sie mag ihre Arbeit, weil sie nette Kollegen hat. Das Restaurant ist nicht weit von unserem Haus, also ist es einfach, zu Fuß zur Arbeit zu gehen.
Ich denke, es ist wichtig, dass man gut bezahlt wird, sonst wird man unglücklich, besonders wenn die Arbeit schwer ist. Freundliche Kollegen sind auch etwas Positives.
Ich habe bis jetzt keinen Job gehabt, weil es in meiner Stadt nicht viele Jobs für Jugendliche gibt.
In ein paar Jahren will ich im Bereich Informatik arbeiten.

2 Sample answers:
Teacher: Guten Tag. Welche Fächer mögen Sie in der Schule?
Student: Ich mag Kunst und Englisch.
Teacher: Interessant.
Teacher: Und welche Interessen haben Sie?
Student: Meine Hobbys sind Musik und Lesen.
Teacher: Gut.
Teacher: Welche Arbeit wollen Sie später machen?
Student: Ich will in einer Bibliothek arbeiten.
Teacher: Alles klar.
Teacher: Was finden Sie gut an dieser Arbeit?
Student: Es ist ruhig und es gibt viele Bücher.
Teacher: Gut.
Teacher: Haben Sie eine Frage?
Student: Wie finden Sie Ihre Arbeit?
Teacher: Ich finde meine Arbeit sehr interessant.

68. My dream job
1 Sample answers (only 4 are required):
Es gibt einen Lehrer und eine Lehrerin.
Ich sehe sieben kleine Kinder.
Sie sind glücklich.
Die Frau hat lange Haare.
Es gibt Bilder an der Wand.
Der Boden ist blau.
Sie sind in der Schule.
Sie sind in einem Klassenzimmer.

2 Read aloud and sample answers to follow-on questions:
   (a) Mein Traumberuf ist Lehrer.
   (b) Ich denke, das Studium macht Spaß.

69. Gap year
1 Sample answer:
Es gibt einen jungen Mann. Er hat kurze Haare und trägt einen blauen Pullover und eine schwarze Hose. Er hat einen Koffer.
Ich denke, er ist am Bahnhof oder am Flughafen.
Er ist vielleicht auf dem Weg nach Amerika oder Afrika.

Sample answers to follow-on questions:
(a) Ich finde Reisen toll.
(b) Ich will nach Amerika reisen.

2 Questions and sample answers:
1 Was willst du im nächsten Schuljahr machen?
   Ich will nächstes Jahr in die Oberstufe gehen, um Kunst, Englisch und Mathe zu lernen. Dann werde ich die Schule verlassen.
2 Möchtest du auf die Uni gehen? Warum oder warum nicht?
   Ich möchte nicht direkt auf die Uni gehen, sondern will ein Jahr reisen, bevor ich ein Studium mache.
3 Welche Pläne hast du für die Zukunft?
   Ich werde vielleicht nach Afrika reisen und in einer Schule für kleine Kinder helfen.
4 Welche Arbeit möchtest du später machen? Warum?
   Später möchte ich Mathelehrer werden und in einer Großstadt arbeiten.
5 Hast du schon einen Job gehabt?
   Ja, ich habe letztes Jahr als Kellner in einem Café gearbeitet, um Geld zu verdienen. Ich spare das Geld, damit ich später reisen kann.

70. Equality and helping others
1 Read aloud and sample answers to follow-on questions:
   (a) Meine Stadt ist klein und ruhig.
   (b) Diskriminierung ist schlecht.
2 Sample answer:
I live in Vienna, the capital city of Austria and a famous centre for music, art and culture. The New Year concert is popular worldwide. People in the city come from different countries, therefore the culture is very interesting. My mother works with refugees, who have left their homeland because of war.

71. Holiday activities
1 Sample answer:
In den Ferien fahren wir manchmal nach Berlin, um unsere Familie zu sehen. Mit dem Flugzeug reisen ist teuer, und wir fliegen nicht oft.
Ich möchte ein anderes Land besuchen, weil das Wetter dort besser ist. Aber Flugzeuge sind schlecht für die Umwelt.
Nächsten Sommer bleibe ich zu Hause und gehe mit Freunden aus.

2 Sample answer:
Das Wetter ist sehr schön, warm und sonnig. Das Meer ist blau, und viele Leute schwimmen. Die Leute sind im Urlaub. Die meisten Leute liegen in der Sonne. Ich denke, das ist vielleicht in Südeuropa. Die Gegend sieht schön aus.

Sample answers to follow-on questions:
(a) Ich liebe einen Strandurlaub, wenn das Wetter schön ist.
(b) Letztes Jahr war ich bei meiner Familie in London.

72. Camping
1 Sample answer:
Es gibt sechs junge Leute, zwei Jungen und vier Mädchen, und eine Frau.
Sie zelten auf einem Campingplatz.
Sie haben ein Zelt.
Sie machen ein Feuer.
2 (a) excited (b) fun (c) forest (d) hiking (e) cold

73. Holiday accommodation
1 1 Wir sind in einer **Ferienwohnung** am **Meer**.
   2 Unsere Tante **übernachtet** in einem **kleinen** Hotel.
   3 Hinter dem **Haus** gab es einen **winzigen** Garten.
   4 Ich mag die Sommerferien.
   5 Ich finde Zelten sehr unbequem.
   6 Wir waren letztes Jahr auf dem Land.
2 Read aloud and sample answers to follow-on questions:
   (a) Ich verbringe gern Zeit mit Freunden, wenn ich keine Schule habe.
   (b) Letztes Jahr habe ich im Sommer einen Kunstkurs besucht.

74. Other holiday accommodation
1 Read aloud and sample answers to follow-on questions:
   (a) Ich fahre manchmal nach London.
   (b) Ich mag Reisen, aber es ist teuer.

2 Read aloud and sample answers to follow-on questions:
   (a) In meiner Gegend gibt es einen schönen Wald und ein altes Kunstmuseum.
   (b) Ich bin letztes Jahr nach London gefahren und habe ein Fußballspiel gesehen.

75. Making a complaint
1 Sample answer:
Das Restaurant ist in meiner Stadt in der Nähe von dem Park und nicht weit von meinem Haus.
Meiner Meinung nach ist das Restaurant sehr klein und hat viele Tische, aber das Essen ist immer gut.
Ich will bald ins Restaurant gehen. Ich werde nächste Woche mit meinem Freund dort essen.

2 Sample answers:
Teacher: Guten Tag. Kann ich Ihnen helfen?
Student: Mein Zimmer ist kalt und schmutzig.
Teacher: Das ist nicht so schön.
Teacher: Was ist Ihre Zimmernummer?
Student: Ich habe Zimmer Nummer 200.
Teacher: Danke.
Teacher: Haben Sie eine Frage?
Student: Kann ich ein anderes Zimmer haben?
Teacher: Ja, das machen wir.
Teacher: Wann werden Sie heute Morgen aus dem Hotel gehen?
Student: Ich gehe um 10:00 Uhr aus dem Hotel.
Teacher: Gut.
Teacher: Haben Sie noch eine Frage?
Student: Wann wird das Zimmer fertig sein?
Teacher: Gegen 13:00 Uhr.

76. Pros and cons of travelling

1 Sample answer:
Auf dem Foto sehe ich ein Mädchen und einen Jungen. Sie sehen glücklich aus und lächeln. Das Mädchen trägt einen grauen Pulli und hat braune mittellange Haare, und ihr Freund trägt ein rosarotes Hemd.
Sie sitzen in einem Bus. Sie fahren vielleicht in die Stadt. Es gibt viele andere Leute im Bus.

Listen to the recording

Sample answers to follow-on questions:
(a) Ich fahre jeden Tag mit dem Bus zur Schule. Das ist praktisch und ziemlich schnell.
(b) Ich bin letztes Jahr nach Amerika geflogen.

2 Sample answer:
Ich fahre meistens mit dem Bus zur Schule. Das ist nicht sehr bequem, aber es macht Spaß, denn ich bin mit meinen Freundinnen zusammen.
Wenn man öffentliche Verkehrsmittel benutzt, ist das besser für die Umwelt, denn es gibt nicht so viele Autos.
Ich will im Sommer mit dem Zug nach London fahren.

77. Plans for next summer

1 Sample answer:
Als ich ein Kind war, haben wir die Sommerferien im Ausland verbracht, wo das Wetter wärmer ist und man in der Sonne liegen oder im Meer schwimmen kann. Jetzt haben wir nicht so viel Geld, und ein Urlaub im Ausland ist teuer.
Ich denke, es gibt auch viele Vorteile, wenn man zu Hause bleibt. Erstens kann man jeden Tag seine Freunde:innen sehen und viel Spaß zusammen haben. Zweitens ist es billiger, und man hat mehr Geld für andere Dinge, wie zum Beispiel im Restaurant zu essen, Fußballspiele zu sehen oder Ausflüge in der Gegend zu machen. Vor einigen Jahren sind wir nach Berlin gefahren. Die Großstadt war wunderschön, und es gab so viel zu sehen und zu tun.
Diesen Sommer werde ich einen Job finden und mein eigenes Geld verdienen. Das freut mich sehr, weil ich ein Auto kaufen will und Geld sparen muss.

2 (i) B (ii) B (iii) C

78. Past holidays

1 Sample answers:
(a) Das Hotel war bequem und modern.
(b) Es gab einen schönen Strand.
(c) Die Leute waren sehr freundlich.
(d) Ich habe Geschenke für meine Freunde und Familie gekauft.
(e) Das Wetter war gut, und es war jeden Tag warm.

2 Sample answer:
Letztes Jahr sind wir nach Österreich in Urlaub gefahren. Meine Großeltern wohnen dort in den Bergen, also brauchen wir kein Hotel. Wir sind eine Woche geblieben, und das Wetter war die ganze Zeit gut. Ich bin in dem See schwimmen gegangen. Am letzten Tag haben wir ein traditionelles Mittagessen gegessen.

79. Holiday problems

1 Sample answer:
Letzten Sommer waren wir zwei Wochen in Deutschland. Wir haben gezeltet, und das Wetter war gut.
Der Campingplatz war klein und schmutzig. Es gab kein heißes Wasser. Das war schlecht.
Nächstes Jahr will ich nicht zelten. Ich werde in einem Hotel wohnen und ein Badezimmer haben.

2
1 **Letztes** Jahr war ich in einem **Skigebiet** in **Österreich**.
2 Die **Unterkunft** in einer **Hütte** in den **Bergen** war schmutzig.
3 Die Zugreise hat lange gedauert.
4 Das Wetter war jeden Tag schlecht.
5 Das Frühstück hat uns nicht geschmeckt.
6 Die Umgebung hat einen großen Eindruck gemacht.

80. Lost property

1 Sample answers:
Teacher: Guten Tag. Kann ich Ihnen helfen?
Student: Ich habe mein Handy verloren.
Teacher: Ich verstehe.
Teacher: Können Sie es beschreiben?
Student: Es ist rot und neu.
Teacher: Gut.
Teacher: Um wie viel Uhr sind Sie angekommen?
Student: Ich bin um 7:00 Uhr angekommen.
Teacher: Danke.
Teacher: Wie lange bleiben Sie in Deutschland?
Student: Ich bleibe eine Woche.
Teacher: Schön.
Teacher: Haben Sie eine Frage?
Student: Haben Sie mein Handy?
Teacher: Ich glaube schon … Moment, bitte.

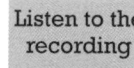

Listen to the recording

2 Sample answer:
Letzte Woche am Dienstag bin ich mit dem Zug von Köln nach München gefahren. Leider, weil ich sehr müde war, habe ich mein Handy in dem Zug gelassen / vergessen. Am nächsten Morgen bin ich zum Bahnhof zurückgegangen. Ich hatte Glück, weil jemand mein Handy gefunden hat und es ins Büro gebracht hat.

81. Places to visit

1 Read aloud and sample answers to follow-on questions:
(a) Meine Stadt ist klein und ruhig.
(b) Im Sommer gehe ich gern zum Strand.

2 Sample answer:
I live in Munich in South Germany. It is a big city with beautiful buildings. It is situated near the mountains, where there is beautiful countryside. Therefore, there are always many tourists. My friend works as a guide and organises tours in the old part of the city / in the old town. As a child, I often visited the famous Botanical Garden.

82. Holiday jobs

1 (a) C (b) C (c) B
2 (a) nervous (b) fourteen (c) helpful (d) a restaurant
(e) vocabulary

83. Buying gifts and souvenirs

1 Sample answers:
Teacher: Guten Tag. Kann ich Ihnen helfen?
Student: Ich möchte ein Geschenk für meinen Freund kaufen.
Teacher: Kein Problem.
Teacher: So … wie viel Geld haben Sie?
Student: Ich habe fünfzehn Euro.
Teacher: Alles klar.
Teacher: So … wie finden Sie dieses Geschenk?
Student: Ja … das ist schön.
Teacher: OK.
Teacher: Gefällt es Ihnen?
Student: Ich nehme das, danke.
Teacher: Sehr gut.
Teacher: Haben Sie eine Frage?
Student: Was kostet das?
Teacher: Also … zehn Euro.

2 Sample answer:
Eine junge Frau steht vor einem Geschäft. Ich denke, sie sieht Postkarten an. Sie ist vielleicht im Urlaub, weil sie Sommerkleidung und eine Sonnenbrille trägt. Sie hat lange braune Haare. Im Hintergrund gibt es Autos und ein Motorrad.

Sample answers to follow-on questions:
(a) Ich kaufe ein T-Shirt oder eine Sonnenbrille.
(b) Letzte Woche habe ich ein Buch für meinen Bruder zum Geburtstag gekauft.

84. Weather
1 Sample answer:
Es gibt einen Mann und eine Frau.
Sie haben ein Kind.
Der Hund ist schwarz und weiß.
Sie sind im Park.

2 (a) rain (b) foggy (c) snow (d) closed

85. Tourism and the environment
1 Sample answers:
(a) Ich fahre mit dem Zug nach Berlin.
(b) Im Sommer gibt es viele Touristen.
(c) Jedes Jahr ist das Wetter wärmer.
(d) Flugzeuge sind sehr schlecht für die Umwelt.
(e) Im August habe ich einen guten Urlaub in Österreich gehabt. / Im August hatte ich gute Ferien in Österreich.

2 Sample answer:
Ich habe Angst, dass wir die Welt zerstören, in der wir leben. Heute wollen viele Touristen in den Ferien ins Ausland fliegen, obwohl sie wissen, wie schlecht das für die Umwelt ist. Klimawandel ist das größte Problem, aber niemand macht / tut etwas, um die Situation zu verbessern. Wir sind alle verantwortlich.

86. Practice for Paper 1: Speaking
1 Read aloud and sample answers to follow-on questions:
(a) Meine Stadt ist ziemlich schmutzig.
(b) Ich komme gern zu Fuß zur Schule.

2 Sample answers:
Teacher: Guten Tag. Kann ich Ihnen helfen?
Student: Ich möchte drei Karten, bitte.
Teacher: Kein Problem.
Teacher: Um wie viel Uhr wollen Sie schwimmen?
Student: Ich will um 11:00 Uhr schwimmen.
Teacher: Schön.
Teacher: Wie lange wollen Sie bleiben?
Student: Ich will eine Stunde bleiben.
Teacher: Alles klar.
Teacher: Wie wollen Sie bezahlen?
Student: Ich habe meine Karte.
Teacher: Gerne.
Teacher: Haben Sie noch eine Frage?
Student: Gibt es hier ein Café?
Teacher: Ja. Es gibt ein kleines Café.

3 Sample answers:
Picture 1
Es gibt ein modernes Klassenzimmer. Die Fenster sind groß. Ich sehe eine junge Lehrerin und sieben Schüler in dem Zimmer. Es gibt drei Mädchen und vier Jungen. Sie tragen keine Uniform. Sie lesen und schreiben. Ich denke, das ist eine Englischstunde.

Picture 2
Ich sehe fünf Schüler – es gibt Mädchen und Jungen. Sie spielen Basketball draußen in der Nähe der Schule. Das Wetter ist ziemlich gut, und sie tragen T-Shirts. Es ist vielleicht die Pause oder die Mittagspause. Die Schule ist modern und hat große Fenster.

Sample answers to follow-on questions:
Picture 1
(a) Meine Schule ist gut and sehr modern.
(b) Meine Lieblingslehrerin ist freundlich und nicht langweilig.

Picture 2
(a) Wir haben dreimal die Woche Sport.
(b) Mein Lieblingsfach ist Englisch.

Broader conversations:
Sample questions and answers:
(Past tense)
1 Was hast du gestern in der Schule gemacht?
Gestern habe ich Mathe gelernt.
In der Pause habe ich gegessen und habe mit meinen Freunden gesprochen.
2 Hast du dieses Jahr gute Arbeiten in der Schule geschrieben?
Meine Arbeiten in Deutsch und Englisch waren gut, aber in den Naturwissenschaften war ich ganz schwach.
3 Hast du dieses Schuljahr eine Schulreise gemacht?
Wir sind nach Manchester gefahren und haben ein Spiel im Stadion gesehen. Das war toll.

(Future tense)
4 Was wirst du im nächsten Schuljahr machen?
Nächstes Jahr möchte ich Fremdsprachen und Mathe lernen. Das sind meine Lieblingsfächer.
5 Möchtest du später auf die Uni gehen?
Ich möchte auf die Uni gehen, vielleicht in Durham oder London. Ich will Deutsch und Französisch studieren.
6 Welche Arbeit willst du später haben?
Ich will bei einer großen Firma, zum Beispiel bei einer Bank arbeiten, und ich möchte einige Jahre in Europa arbeiten.

87. Practice for Paper 1: Speaking
1 Read aloud and sample answers to follow-on questions:
(a) Ich gehe morgens gern laufen.
(b) Ich mag Teamsport mit Freunden und spiele oft Fußball.

2 Sample answers:
Teacher: Guten Tag. Kann ich Ihnen helfen?
Student: Ich suche eine Apotheke.
Teacher: Kein Problem.
Teacher: Die Apotheke liegt an der Hauptstraße.
Student: Wie weit ist das?
Teacher: Nicht sehr weit. Dreihundert Meter entfernt.
Teacher: Wie lange bleiben Sie in Österreich?
Student: Ich bleibe acht Tage.
Teacher: Schön.
Teacher: Was werden Sie heute machen?
Student: Heute werde ich das Schloss besuchen.
Teacher: Viel Spaß!
Teacher: Haben Sie noch eine Frage?
Student: Wo kann ich hier Essen kaufen?
Teacher: Es gibt einen Supermarkt gegenüber der Apotheke.

3 Sample answers:
Picture 1
Es gibt vier Mädchen. Sie gehen in dem Park zusammen spazieren. Alles ist grün und es gibt große Bäume. Das Wetter ist sonnig. Jedes Mädchen hat ein Handy und spricht mit jemandem. Es ist komisch, denn sie sprechen nicht miteinander.

Picture 2
Es gibt vier Jugendliche: zwei Jungen und zwei Mädchen. Ich denke, sie sind in der Bibliothek in der Schule, denn es gibt viele

Bücher. Vielleicht machen sie Schularbeit oder Hausaufgaben zusammen. Sie benutzen Tablets, um bei der Arbeit zu helfen.

Sample answers to follow-on questions:
Picture 1
(a) Mein Handy ist absolut wichtig für mein Leben.
(b) Ich habe Infos für meine Hausaufgaben im Internet gefunden.

Picture 2
(a) Wir benutzen jeden Tag Computer in dem Unterricht.
(b) Ich habe mit meiner Oma über Skype gesprochen.

Broader conversations:

Sample questions and answers:
(Past tense)

1 Was hast du gestern im Internet gemacht?
Ich habe auf einer Modewebseite eine neue Hose gekauft. Dann habe ich eine E-Mail geschickt, weil meine Freundin in Amerika Geburtstag hatte.
2 Hast du ein Problem mit den sozialen Medien gehabt?
Ich habe keine Probleme mit den sozialen Medien gehabt, aber ich weiß, dass es manchmal Cyberkriminalität gibt.
3 Hast du schon online eingekauft?
Ja. Ich kaufe oft online, denn es ist oft billiger als in einem Geschäft. Ich habe gestern ein Buch bei Amazon gekauft.
4 Hast du neulich ein Computerspiel gespielt?
Computerspiele finde ich nicht interessant. Ich habe neulich Filme heruntergeladen. Das finde ich besser als Videospiele.

(Future tense)
5 Wie wirst du heute Abend dein Handy benutzen?
Ich werde mit Freunden chatten und ich werde Fotos auf Instagram hochladen.
6 Was möchtest du nächste Woche online kaufen?
Ich möchte nächste Woche eine neue Jacke und eine Hose online kaufen.
7 Wann wirst du ein neues Handy bekommen?
Ich hoffe, meine Eltern werden mir ein neues Handy zum Geburtstag kaufen. Das wird das beste Geschenk sein!
8 Welchen Film würdest du gern herunterladen?
Ich würde sehr gern den neuen Film Vanya mit Andrew Scott sehen, aber ich muss warten, bis der Film online ist, dann werde ich ihn herunterladen.

88. Practice for Paper 2: Listening
1 (a) C (b) A (c) B (d) C
2 1 Ich **suche** ein **Geschenk** für meine Schwester.
   2 Was **kostet** die rote **Bluse**?
   3 Welche **Größe** ist das **lila** Kleid?
   4 Der Hut ist modisch.
   5 Ich mag diese Farbe nicht.
   6 Der schwarze Pullover gefällt mir.

89. Practice for Paper 2: Listening
1 (a) Lara
       Advantage: her colleagues / nice colleagues
       Disadvantage: the working hours / long hours
   (b) Arda
       Advantage: (new) projects
       Disadvantage: boss never happy / content / demanding boss
2 1 Dieses **Jahr** ist **Biologie** mein bestes **Fach**.
   2 Mein **Mathelehrer** ist **gewöhnlich** ziemlich **ungeduldig**.
   3 Ich würde lieber Naturwissenschaften lernen.
   4 Nächstes Jahr gehe ich in die Oberstufe.
   5 Da kann ich meine Fächer wählen.
   6 Ich versuche, gute Noten zu bekommen.

90. Practice for Paper 3: Reading
1 (a) industry (b) night life (c) on Sundays (d) handbags
2 (a) I am healthy.
   (b) I eat fruit and vegetables every day.
   (c) Once a week I go to the gym.
   (d) Yesterday I did a dance class.
   (e) I am happier, when / if I stay / keep active.

91. Practice for Paper 3: Reading
1 (a) (i) it's suffering (ii) forests are destroyed / animal species are disappearing (iii) carrying on as if everything is OK (iv) changing our lifestyles
   (b) B

2 **Sample answer:**
When school is over / finished, I would like to go to university to study. My favourite subject is history, because I'm interested in the events of the past. I look forward to leaving my hometown, because life here can be rather boring. I hope to meet lots of new people.

92. Practice for Paper 4: Writing
1 **Sample answer:**
Meine Schule ist sehr alt, aber nicht groß. Die Schule sieht nicht sehr schön aus, aber die Klassenzimmer sind warm und bequem. Ich bin glücklich in meiner Schule, denn ich habe viele Freunde und nette Lehrer.
Nächstes Jahr bleibe ich in der Schule. Ich will Englisch, Musik und Deutsch lernen.

2 **Sample answer:**
Ich versuche immer, gesund zu essen und genug zu schlafen. Jeden Tag esse ich Gemüse und Obst und ich trinke viel Wasser. Ich denke, ich bin sehr aktiv.
Ich bin sehr sportlich und liebe Fußball und Tennis. Ich finde Sport sehr positiv, weil ich mit Freunden spiele, und das macht Spaß. Letzte Woche bin ich zweimal schwimmen gegangen, weil das Wetter so schön war. Ich bin auch mit dem Rad in die Schule gefahren. Das ist schneller, als zu Fuß zu gehen.
In Zukunft werde ich Kurse in einem Fitnesszentrum besuchen.

93. Practice for Paper 4: Writing
1 **Sample answer:**
Ich versuche immer, gesund zu essen und genug zu schlafen. Jeden Tag esse ich Gemüse und Obst und ich trinke viel Wasser. Ich denke, ich bin sehr aktiv.
Ich bin sehr sportlich und liebe Fußball und Tennis. Ich finde Sport sehr positiv, weil ich mit Freunden spiele, und das macht Spaß. Letzte Woche bin ich zweimal schwimmen gegangen, weil das Wetter so schön war. Ich bin auch mit dem Rad in die Schule gefahren. Das ist schneller, als zu Fuß zu gehen.
In Zukunft werde ich Mitglied in einem Fitnesszentrum werden.

2 **Sample answer:**
Ich benutze jeden Tag mein Handy, um mit Freunden in Kontakt zu bleiben. Ich finde es auch nützlich, um Musik zu hören und Videos zu sehen.
Ich finde diese schnelle Kommunikation toll, weil es unser Leben viel einfacher macht. Heute kann man viel machen, was früher nicht möglich war.
Das Internet kann nützlich sein, wenn man für Hausaufgaben Informationen braucht, oder etwas online kaufen will. Die negative Seite ist, dass es Gefahren gibt. Cyberkriminalität ist schlimm, und man darf keine Daten mit fremden Leuten teilen.
Ich benutze soziale Netzwerke nicht oft. Ich finde Facebook altmodisch. Instagram und Snapchat sind besser, weil es meistens junge Leute in diesen Netzwerken gibt. Mit Instagram sehe ich, was meine Freunde machen und ich habe gestern Fotos hochgeladen.
Später werde ich vielleicht zu Hause arbeiten können und nicht jeden Tag ins Büro fahren müssen.

94. Gender and plurals
1 (a) das (b) der (c) die (d) es (e) das (f) die (g) der (h) das
2 (a) die (b) das (c) das (d) der (e) der (f) die
3 (a) pl (b) sg (c) pl (d) sg / pl (e) pl (f) sg (g) sg (h) pl (i) sg (j) sg / pl

95. Indefinite articles and possessives
1. (a) ein (b) eine (c) ein (d) ein (e) eine (f) ein (g) eine (h) ein (i) ein (j) ein
2. (a) kein (b) kein (c) keine (d) kein (e) keine
3. (a) meine Schwester (b) deine Familie (c) seine Frau (d) ihr Freund (e) unsere Stadt (f) meine Hausaufgaben (g) seine Jacke (h) ihre Party (i) deine Kleidung (j) mein Glas

96. Nominative and accusative cases
1. (a) Der (b) Das / den (c) Der / das (d) Die / die (e) Die / den (f) Die / das (g) Der / die (h) Die
2. (a) einen / eine (b) ein (c) einen (d) Ein (e) einen (f) einen
3. (a) Meine / meinen (b) dein (c) Mein / seine (d) Ihr (e) unser (f) Meine

97. Other cases and prepositions
1. (a) der Lehrerin (b) dem Haus (c) seiner Mutter (d) meinem Vater (e) ihren Freunden (f) meinen Eltern
2. (a) abroad / overseas (b) on / at the coast (c) in the country(side) (d) at our house (e) above all (f) on the contrary
3. (a) des Mädchens (b) der Stadt (c) des Wetters (d) der Sommerferien (e) der Ärzte
4. (a) The girl's brother is quite sporty.
   (b) In the middle of the town is a market.
   (c) In spite of the weather we are going camping.
   (d) During the summer holidays I play basketball.
   (e) The doctors' work is very hard.

98. Prepositions with the accusative or dative
1. (a) neben dem Fluss (b) in die Stadt (c) in dem Garten (d) in dem Meer (e) auf dem Tisch (f) unter dem Baum (g) an der Wand (h) unter das Bett (i) hinter dem Fitnesszentrum (j) vor den Computer (k) zwischen dem Kino und der Bibliothek (l) in das Haus
2. (a) die (b) das (c) den (d) die
3. (a) We are looking forward to the holidays.
   (b) My sister and I talk about the problem.
   (c) I'm waiting for the next train.
   (d) The pupils are thinking about the future.

99. *Dieser, jener* and *jeder*
1. (a) Diese (b) jeder (c) diesen (d) diese (e) Jede (f) Dieser (g) dieses (h) Jener (i) diesem (j) jenem
2. (a) Welchen (b) welchem (c) diesem (d) Diese (e) dieses (f) dieses (g) Jede (h) Jeder (i) Jede (j) jedem (k) Jedes (l) jedes
3. (a) jedes (b) diese (c) diesen (d) jedes (e) jeden

100. Adjective endings
1. (a) schwarze (b) neuen (c) weißen (d) braunen (e) bekannte
2. (a) kleiner (b) ältere (c) interessantes (d) gesundes (e) kleine
3. (a) schwarzen (b) frisches (c) freundliche (d) schönes

101. Comparative and superlative adjectives
1. (a) interessanter (b) intelligenter (c) schneller (d) kleiner
2. (a) modernste (b) schwerste (c) langsamste (d) teuerste
3. (a) schöner / am schönsten (b) fleißiger / am fleißigsten (c) schneller / am schnellsten
4. (a) My father is taller than me / I am.
   (b) What is the highest mountain in Switzerland called?
   (c) What sort of films do you like watching the most?

102. Personal pronouns
1. (a) du (b) uns (c) ihr (d) mir (e) Ihnen (f) dich (g) sie (h) ihm (i) sie (j) dir
2. (a) euch (b) uns (c) mir (d) ihm (e) dir (f) ihr

103. Word order 1
1. (a) Nächstes Jahr fahren wir in die Schweiz.
   (b) Jeden Morgen geht mein Bruder im Park laufen.
   (c) In der Schule lerne ich am liebsten Englisch.
   (d) In den Ferien spielen meine Freunde Fußball.
2. (a) Letzte Woche hat mein Freund eine Party gehabt.
   (b) Plötzlich ist die Katze aus dem Fenster gesprungen.
   (c) Wir sind wegen des Wetters spät in Berlin angekommen.
3. (a) Er wird morgen Golf spielen.
   (b) Wann wirst du einkaufen gehen?
   (c) Nächstes Jahr werde ich die Schule verlassen.
4. (a) Ich muss zuerst meine Hausaufgaben machen.
   (b) Meine Schwester will nach London fahren.
   (c) Bald können wir endlich mehr Freizeit haben.

104. Conjunctions
1. (a) Wir bleiben diesen Sommer zu Hause, weil Reisen sehr teuer ist.
   (b) Ich will nach der Schule studieren, weil ich Arzt werden will.
   (c) Er geht auf dem Land wandern, weil das Wetter schön ist.
   (d) Mein Bruder geht zu jedem Fußballspiel, weil er ein großer Fan ist.
   (e) Wir sollen die Umwelt besser schützen, weil es nur eine Welt gibt.
2. (a) Es war sehr spät, als ich nach Hause gekommen bin.
   (b) Als ich nach Hause gekommen bin, war es sehr spät.
   (c) Bevor er zur Arbeit geht, isst er das Frühstück.
   (d) Die Lehrerin hilft uns, damit wir besser verstehen.
   (e) Wir wollten ausgehen, da ich Geburtstag hatte.
3. (a) It was very late when I got home.
   (b) When I got home, it was very late.
   (c) Before he goes to work, he has breakfast.
   (d) The teacher helps us, so that we understand better.
   (e) We wanted to go out, as it was my birthday.

105. Word order 2
1. (a) Wir fahren dieses Jahr in den Urlaub, um die Sonne zu genießen.
   (b) Ich werde nach London fahren, um eine Arbeitsstelle zu suchen.
   (c) Er fährt auf dem Land Rad, um an der frischen Luft zu sein.
2. (a) Ich hoffe, nächstes Jahr ein Auslandsjahr zu machen.
   (b) Wir versuchen, gesünder zu leben.
   (c) Mein Freund beginnt, mehr Sport zu treiben.
3. (a) der (b) das (c) die (d) den (e) die

106. The present tense
1. (a) wohne (b) spielen (c) gehst (d) kauft (e) übernachten (f) macht (g) kocht (h) Liebst (i) schicken (j) Besuchst (k) arbeitet (l) beginnt
2. (a) fährst (b) fahre (c) lesen (d) liest (e) spricht (f) gibt (g) schläft (h) trifft (i) trägt (j) hilft

107. Reflexive and separable verbs
1. (a) iii (b) ii (c) i (d) vi (e) iv (f) v
2. (a) uns (b) mich (c) sich (d) sich (e) uns (f) dich
3. (a) kommt … an (b) rufe … an (c) kommen … zurück (d) lade … herunter (e) gehen … aus
4. (a) zurückgekommen (b) angerufen (c) hochgeladen (d) angekommen (e) ferngesehen
5. (a) Ich werde morgen in der Schweiz ankommen.
   (b) Später wird er Musikvideos im Internet ansehen.
   (c) Meine Eltern werden die Lichter ausmachen.

108. Irregular verb tables 1
1. (a) isst (b) fährt (c) gibt (d) hast (e) hilft (f) läufst
2. Both tiers:
   (a) mochte (b) musste (c) hatten (d) konnte (e) hatten
   Higher tier:
   (a) begann (b) blieb (c) aßen (d) fuhr (e) gab
3. (a) bin / gegangen (b) hast / gegessen (c) sind / gefahren

109. Irregular verb tables 2
1. (a) nehme (b) sieht (c) spricht (d) trägst (e) trifft (f) vergisst
2. Both tiers:
 (a) wollte (b) war (c) sollte (d) waren (e) wollten

 Higher tier:
 (a) nahmen (b) rief (c) schrieben (d) schwamm (e) saßen
3. (a) bin / geschwommen (b) hast / genommen (c) haben / gesprochen (d) hat / gewusst

110. Using irregular verbs in different tenses
1. (a) singen (b) vergisst (c) sehen (d) mag (e) fährt (f) habe
2. (a) beginnt (b) schreibt (c) spricht (d) trägst (e) trinken
3. (a) Das Konzert hat spät begonnen.
 (b) Was hat er in der Pause gegessen?
 (c) Ich bin zu Fuß zur Schule gegangen.
 (d) Wir haben dir ein Geschenk gebracht.
 (e) Ich habe einen neuen Krimi gelesen.
 (f) Wir haben unseren Freunden geholfen.
 (g) Ich bin jeden Morgen am Strand gelaufen.
 (h) Mein Eltern sind spät nach hause gekommen.
 (i) Er hat viel Kaffee getrunken.
4. Both tiers:
 (a) hatte (b) konnten (c) musste

 Higher tier:
 (a) rief (b) sprachen (c) fand

111. *Sein* and *haben*
1. (a) Hast (b) hat (c) habe (d) haben (e) Habt (f) ist (g) sind (h) Bist (i) bin (j) Sind
2. (a) hatten (b) hatte (c) hatten (d) hatte (e) hatten (f) war (g) waren (h) war (i) Waren (j) warst
3. (a) ist / gewesen (b) Hast / gehabt (c) hat / gehabt (d) bist / gewesen (e) haben / gehabt (f) sind / gewesen

112. Modal verbs in the present tense
1. (a) will (b) sollen (c) magst (d) darf (e) muss (f) können
2. (a) My brother wants to go to university.
 (b) We should protect the environment.
 (c) Which shirt do you like?
 (d) You're not allowed to smoke here.
 (e) I have to / must learn these words by tomorrow.
 (f) When can we visit you?
3. (a) konnten (b) wolltest (c) mochte (d) durfte (e) sollte (f) musste (g) durften (h) sollten (i) konnte (j) wollte (k) mochten

113. The perfect tense with *haben*
1. (a) habe / gespielt (b) Hat / gekauft (c) haben / geschickt (d) haben / gewartet (e) habe / gearbeitet (f) hat / gelernt
2. (a) gelesen (b) gegessen (c) getrunken (d) gesprochen (e) geholfen (f) geschrieben (g) getroffen (h) gegeben

114. The perfect tense with *sein*
1. (a) bin (b) bist (c) sind (d) sind (e) ist (f) ist (g) sind (h) bin (i) ist
2. (a) Bist du nach Berlin gefahren?
 (b) Wir sind spät gestern Abend angekommen.
 (c) Wie ist der Unfall passiert / geschehen?
 (d) Sie sind krank gewesen.
 (e) Sie ist sportlicher geworden.

115. The imperfect tense
1. (a) spielte (b) lernten (c) kämpften (d) kochte (e) malte (f) kaufte
2. (a) war (b) lief (c) kam (d) blieb (e) konnten (f) aßen (g) schwammen (h) ging (i) gab (j) fuhr (k) Hatten (l) wussten

116. The future tense
1. (a) wirst (b) werde (c) wird (d) werden (e) werden
2. (a) Mein Freund wird im Oktober auf die Uni gehen.
 (b) Ich denke, ich werde Tierärztin sein.
 (c) Wir werden nächstes Jahr eine Party haben.
 (d) Es wird in der Zukunft nicht genug Wasser geben.
 (e) Flugzeuge werden unsere Welt weiter zerstören.
3. (a) Next September, I'm going into the Sixth form.
 (b) This evening, we want to eat with my grandparents.
 (c) In the future, I definitely will not get married.
4. (a) Später möchte ich mit Tieren arbeiten.
 (b) Ich hoffe, Schauspieler zu sein.
 (c) Nächste Woche will ich neue Kleidung kaufen.

117. The conditional
1. (a) Ich würde Geschichte studieren.
 (b) Mein Bruder würde eine Lehre machen.
 (c) Unsere Lehrerin würde nicht zufrieden sein.
 (d) Was würden sie machen?
 (e) Vielleicht würde ich die Schule verlassen.
2. (a) What would he do if he were / was rich?
 (b) I would book an expensive holiday on an island.
 (c) If he could, my brother would live with his girlfriend.
 (d) If I was head, there would be no more homework.

118. Paper 1: Speaking (Foundation)
1. Read aloud and sample answers to follow-on questions:
 (a) Meine Stadt ist klein und ruhig.
 (b) Ich gehe gern mit meinen Freunden einkaufen.

2. Sample answers:
Teacher: Guten Tag. Kann ich Ihnen helfen?
Student: Ich möchte einen Tisch für zwei Personen.
Teacher: Kein Problem.
Teacher: Und was möchten Sie trinken?
Student: Wir möchten einen Kaffee und einen Tee.
Teacher: In Ordnung.
Teacher: Was möchten Sie essen?
Student: Wir wollen Kuchen essen.
Teacher: Alles klar.
Teacher: Wie finden Sie unsere Stadt?
Student: Ich finde die Stadt sehr schön.
Teacher: Gut.
Teacher: Haben Sie eine Frage?
Student: Was kostet das?
Teacher: Alles zusammen 21 Euro.

3. Sample answers:
Picture 1
Es gibt eine Familie mit zwei Eltern und drei Kindern. Die Kinder sind Mädchen. Zwei sind Jugendliche und das andere ist ziemlich jung. Es ist am Morgen. Sie sitzen in der Küche zu Hause und essen das Frühstück. Ich sehe Brot, ein Glas und Tee auf dem Tisch. Die Familie ist glücklich.

Picture 2
Es gibt zwei Kinder. Sie sind draußen und spielen mit einem Ball. Das Mädchen hat lange blonde Haare und sitzt in einem Rollstuhl. Der Junge trägt eine dunkelblaue Jacke und einen grauen Hut. Ich denke, es ist Herbst oder Winter und das Wetter ist kalt.

Sample answers to follow-on questions:
Picture 1
(a) Ich gehe gern mit meiner Familie ins Kino.
(b) Zum Frühstück esse ich Brot mit Butter und Käse.

Picture 2
(a) Ich gehe gern mit Freunden tanzen oder einkaufen.
(b) Ich spiele gern draußen jeden Tag Fußball und Tennis.

Broader conversation
1 Sag mir etwas über eine gute Freundin oder einen guten Freund.
   Eine gute Freundin von mir heißt Maura. Sie ist groß und sportlich. Sie hat blonde Haare und blaue Augen.
2 Was hast du letztes Wochenende mit Familie oder Freunden gemacht?
   Ich bin letzten Samstag mit Freunden ins Kino gegangen. Wir haben einen Science-Fiction-Film gesehen.
3 Mit wem hast du deinen Geburtstag gefeiert?
   Ich habe eine Party mit der Familie gehabt und dann gingen meine Freunde und ich am Abend aus.
4 Was wirst du mit Freunden in den Schulferien machen?
   Wir werden schwimmen gehen und Tennis spielen.
5 Was wirst du am Wochenende mit Familie oder Freunden machen?
   Ich werde meine Großeltern sehen, und wir werden zusammen essen.

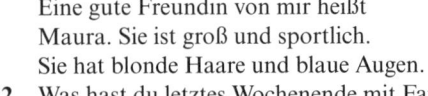
Listen to the recording

119. Paper 2: Listening (Foundation)
1 (a) B (b) A (c) C
2 A, C, E
3 (a) car (b) on foot (c) lights
4 A, C, F
5 (a) C (b) A (c) C (d) B
6 (a) families coming to Germany from abroad
   (b) for a better life (c) gave a concert
7 (a) B (b) C (c) B
8 (a) keep in touch (b) possible (c) week (d) dangerous
   (e) cheaper
9 A, D, E
10 (a) A (b) B (c) B (d) C
11 (a) (i) Science museum (ii) not interested in science at school
   (iii) learning about the natural world
   (b) (i) the many dark pictures (ii) doing her own painting / the (gallery) shop / buying postcards
12 1 Ich **mag** Obst und **Gemüse**.
   2 Ich bin **Torwart** in der **Mannschaft**.
   3 **Bananen** sind gut für die **Gesundheit**.
   4 Man soll genug Wasser trinken.
   5 Junge Leute sind gestresst.
   6 Freizeit spielt eine wichtige Rolle.

122. Paper 3: Reading (Foundation)
1 (a) Yusuf (b) Jonas (c) Anna (d) Jonas (e) Yusuf (f) Anna
2 A, C, F
3 (a) (i) A (ii) C (iii) B (iv) C
   (b) B – food
4 (a) the family is / lives together (b) many families in the world don't have that chance
5 A, D, F
6 (a) practical (b) necessary (c) outside
7 (a) (i) C (ii) B (iii) A (iv) B
   (b) A
8 (a) (i) every day (ii) pictures (iii) news
   (b) A
   (c) B
   (d) (i) it will take people's jobs (ii) it will give us more free time
9 (a) not interested in health / knows it is important to be active OR is on handball team OR trains twice a week
   (b) used to smoke / does a dance course
   (c) had an unhealthy diet OR was often ill / is a vegan OR eats mainly fruit and vegetables OR has more energy / zest for life

10 (a) My best friend is sporty and funny.
   (b) I get on well with him.
   (c) We have fun together because we have a lot in common.
   (d) Last Saturday we ate in town.
   (e) After that, we went to the football match.

127. Paper 4: Writing (Foundation)
1 **Sample answer:**
Es gibt fünf junge Leute.
Sie sind draußen.
Sie benutzen Handys.
Die Mädchen haben lange braune Haare.

2(a) **Sample answer:**
Das Kino ist an der Hauptstraße in der Nähe von dem Restaurant. Man kann mit dem Bus fahren. Es ist einfach.
Ich finde das Kino schön und modern. Die Plätze sind bequem, aber die Karten sind zu teuer.
Nächste Woche werde ich am Samstag mit Freunden einen Film sehen. Wir wollen Wonka sehen.

2(b) **Sample answer:**
Ich gehe gerne einkaufen und gehe am Wochenende mit meiner Schwester in die Stadt. Mein Lieblingsgeschäft heißt New Look, denn die Kleider sind nicht sehr teuer.
Das Einkaufszentrum ist modern, und ich finde die Geschäfte sehr gut.
Nächsten Samstag will ich Schuhe kaufen. Ich will rote Schuhe für eine Party haben.

3(a) **Sample answer:**
Meine Schule ist groß und sehr historisch. Wir haben alte Klassenzimmer, wo es im Winter zu kalt ist. Die Lehrer*innen sind gut und meistens freundlich.
Mein Lieblingsfach ist Mathe, weil ich es einfach finde. Der Lehrer ist auch gut. Dieses Jahr mag ich Deutsch nicht, denn die Lehrerin ist nicht sehr freundlich.
Gestern hatte ich eine tolle Sportstunde. Wir haben Handball gespielt, und das hat viel Spaß gemacht.
Nächstes Jahr werde ich diese Schule verlassen und auf eine andere Schule gehen. Ich will Mathe, Physik und Englisch lernen.

3(b) **Sample answer:**
Ich mache alles mit meinen Freundinnen und Freunden. Wir arbeiten zusammen, denn wir machen oft nach der Schule Hausaufgaben in einer Gruppe, und wir spielen zusammen, wenn wir Sport machen, oder wir gehen samstags ins Kino.
Freunde sind sehr wichtig für mich, weil ich glücklicher bin, wenn ich sie sehe. Sie helfen auch, wenn ich ein Problem habe.
Letzte Woche haben wir einen sehr lustigen Film gesehen, der Wonka heißt. Das hat Spaß gemacht und wir haben alle Eis gegessen.
Am Sonntag wollen wir zum Strand fahren, wenn das Wetter gut ist.

4 **Sample answers:**
   (a) Ich mag das warme Wetter / Ich liebe warmes Wetter.
   (b) Im / In dem Sommer gibt es viele Besucher hier.
   (c) Wir fahren in den Ferien / im Urlaub nicht ins Ausland.
   (d) Heute will ich mit Freunden*innen Tennis spielen.
   (e) Letzte Woche habe ich eine Bootsfahrt / eine Fahrt mit dem Boot gemacht.

129. Paper 1: Speaking (Higher)
1 **Read aloud and sample answers to follow-on questions:**
   (a) Ich spiele gern Tennis und ich schwimme.
   (b) Ich mag Fastfood, aber es ist ungesund.

Listen to the recording

156

Gestern hatte ich eine tolle Sportstunde. Wir haben Handball gespielt, und das hat viel Spaß gemacht.
Nächstes Jahr werde ich diese Schule verlassen und auf eine andere Schule gehen. Ich will Mathe, Physik und Englisch lernen.

1(b) Sample answer:
Ich mache alles mit meinen Freundinnen und Freunden. Wir arbeiten zusammen, denn wir machen oft nach der Schule Hausaufgaben in einer Gruppe und spielen zusammen, wenn wir Sport treiben oder samstags ins Kino gehen.
Freunde sind sehr wichtig für mich, weil ich glücklicher bin, wenn ich sie sehe. Sie helfen auch, wenn ich ein Problem habe.
Neulich haben wir einen sehr lustigen Film gesehen, der Wonka heißt. Das hat Spaß gemacht und wir haben alle Eis gegessen.
Am Sonntag wollen wir zum Strand fahren, wenn das Wetter gut ist.

2(a) Sample answer:
Ich wohne in einer Großstadt in Nordengland, wo die Umwelt nicht so sauber ist. Inzwischen gibt es hier keine Industrie mehr, aber der Verkehr in der Stadt verursacht andere Probleme für die Gesundheit der Einwohner. Die Luftverschmutzung sieht man überall in der Gegend, weil es ganz klar zu viele Autos gibt. Einerseits wohne ich gern hier, weil es viel zu tun gibt und die Stadt voller Leben ist. Wir haben Kinos, Restaurants, tolle Geschäfte und Theater. Andererseits sieht die Stadt schmutzig aus, weil es oft viel Müll gibt.
Ich mache alles, was ich kann, um die Umwelt zu schützen. Neulich habe ich jeden Tag zu Hause den Müll getrennt und recycelt. Ich habe mehr nachhaltige oder recycelte Produkte gekauft. Ich habe auch letztes Wochenende mit einer Gruppe Schulfreunde Müll im Park gesammelt.
In der Zukunft werde ich bestimmt ein Elektroauto kaufen, denn das ist umweltfreundlicher als ein normales Auto.

2(b) Sample answer:
Die Technologie ist total wichtig für das moderne Leben und ich weiß nicht, was wir ohne Handys und Computer machen würden. Ich benutze mein Handy den ganzen Tag lang, entweder um mit Familie in Kontakt zu bleiben oder um Informationen im Internet zu suchen. Das Internet ist unglaublich nützlich und einfach zu benutzen. Dort kann man alles herausfinden, ohne in die Bibliothek gehen zu müssen. Man soll aber nicht vergessen, dass es auch im Internet falsche Information und falsche Nachrichten geben kann, und das ist bestimmt ein großer Nachteil.
Neulich habe ich ein Geburtstagsgeschenk für meine Freundin online bestellt. Ich wollte ihr Blumen schenken und habe eine Firma gefunden, mit der man nicht nur Blumen, sondern auch Geburtstagskarten verschicken kann. Das war sehr praktisch.
Heute Abend werde ich eine Webseite benutzen, um einen Campingplatz in der Schweiz zu finden. Meine Freunde und ich möchten im Sommer eine Woche in den Bergen zelten.

3 Sample answer:
Ich fahre nicht oft in den Urlaub, aber ich liebe reisen / Reisen. Im Moment habe ich eine Arbeit / einen Job / eine Arbeitsstelle und ich spare, um Fahrkarten zu kaufen. In zwei Jahren werde ich genug Geld haben. Es ist mein Traum, in der Zukunft nach Amerika zu fliegen und die Kultur dort zu erleben.

2 Sample answers:
Teacher: Guten Tag. Warum wollen Sie diese Arbeit?
Student: Ich mag Mode und ich finde das Geschäft sehr cool.
Teacher: Interessant.
Teacher: Was für eine Person sind Sie?
Student: Ich bin fleißig und freundlich.
Teacher: Sehr gut.
Teacher: Wann möchten Sie mit der Arbeit anfangen?
Student: Ich möchte nächste Woche anfangen.
Teacher: Wunderbar.
Teacher: Haben Sie eine Frage?
Student: Wie sind die Arbeitszeiten?
Teacher: Von 9:00 Uhr bis 16:00 Uhr. Also sieben Stunden.
Teacher: Haben Sie noch eine Frage?
Student: Was bezahlen Sie?
Teacher: Elf Euro pro Stunde.

3 Sample answers:
Picture 1
Auf dem Foto gibt es eine Mutter, die vielleicht mit ihrer Tochter zusammen ist. Ich denke, sie sind Touristen im Urlaub. Sie sind auf der Straße in einer Altstadt, und es gibt schöne historische Gebäude. Sie sehen sehr glücklich aus. Die Mutter trägt einen blauen Pullover und hat eine rote Tasche. Sie haben beide schwarze Haare. Das Wetter sieht gut aus, und es ist Sommer.

Picture 2
Zwei Kinder spielen in dem Schnee im Garten. Sie sind glücklich und haben viel Spaß. Es ist ein schöner Tag, die Sonne scheint und der Himmel ist blau, aber es sieht sehr kalt aus. Die Kinder tragen Winterkleider. Man sieht auch einen Berg und große Bäume auf dem Foto.

Follow-on questions and sample answers:
Picture 1
(a) Ich treibe gern Sport und ich gehe schwimmen.
(b) Ich habe mit Freunden gezeltet.

Picture 2
(a) Ich gehe gern laufen und ich mag Radfahren.
(b) Ich bin im Schnee wandern gegangen.

Broader conversation: sample questions and answers:
1 Sag mir, was du letzte Woche in deiner Gegend gemacht hast.
Ich habe in dem Park Tennis gespielt, denn das Wetter war gut und ich mag Tennis.

2 Bist du schon in ein anderes Land gefahren?
Ich bin einmal in die Schweiz gefahren. Es war sehr schön.
3 Was hast du in den letzten Ferien mit Freunden und Freundinnen gemacht?
Ich habe oft meine Freunde getroffen, um Sport zu treiben, und wir sind auch schwimmen und ins Kino gegangen.
4 Welche Aktivitäten wirst du in den Ferien in deiner Gegend machen?
Ich werde in den Sommerferien einen Tenniskurs im Fitnesszentrum machen. Das wird Spaß machen, und ich werde dann besser spielen.
5 Was für Pläne hast du für die nächsten Ferien?
Ich möchte mit meinen Freunden zelten gehen, wenn meine Eltern ja sagen.
6 Welche Region möchtest du besuchen?
Ich würde gern nach Afrika fliegen. Es ist ein schöner Kontinent, und das Wetter ist viel besser als in England.

130. Paper 2: Listening (Higher)
1 (a) B (b) C (c) B
2 (a) keep in touch (b) possible (c) week (d) dangerous (e) cheaper
3 A, D, E
4 (a) B (b) A (c) B (d) C
5 (a) (any one of:) she seems healthy / happy / not stressed
  (b) to have time for everything
  (c) (any one of:) exercise / fun / quiet
6 (a) gardens (b) beach (c) quieter
7 (a) advantage: he could be a vet / disadvantage: loneliness
  (b) advantage: fun student life / disadvantage: expensive
  (c) advantage: better job / career opportunities / disadvantage: pressure to achieve
8 (a) C (b) A (c) C (d) B (e) B (f) B
9 (a) B, D, E
  (b) (i) it's a mixture of genres (ii) world famous actors (iii) it's complicated OR improbable / unlikely / unrealistic (iv) whether it's brilliant OR whether it's crazy
10 1 Ich **verstehe** mich gut mit meiner **Mutter**, weil sie **geduldig** ist.
    2 Mein **Verhältnis** zu meinem Bruder ist schlecht, denn er ist **faul** und **egoistisch**.
    3 Man soll Zeit mit anderen verbringen.
    4 Mit Freunden habe ich viel gemeinsam.
    5 Ich kann mit ihnen über alles sprechen.
    6 Wir treiben oft zusammen Sport.

133. Paper 3: Reading (Higher)
1 (a) practical (b) necessary (c) outside
2 (a) (i) C (ii) B (iii) A (iv) B
  (b) A
3 (a) (i) every day (ii) pictures (iii) news
  (b) (i) A (ii) B
  (c) (i) it will take people's jobs (ii) it will become more important / it will give us more free time
4 (a) (i) (any one of:) to escape religious differences / war / danger (ii) they have lost everything (iii) (any one of:) give language practice / talk to them / play with the children
  (b) B
5 (a) B, E, F
  (b) (i) to see family / has relatives there (ii) beautiful / perfect climate / good for water sports (iii) water sports / diving
  (c) B
6 (a) B, D
  (b) (i) no limit / as many as they want (ii) 8 days before the class (iii) pay for the year in advance
7 (a) (i) B (ii) A (iii) A
  (b) (i) she never wears designer clothes (ii) combining clothes to look cool / not spending much money
8 (a) involve everyone in improving the environment / set an example for other towns
  (b) leave the car at home 3 days a week / walk or use the bus 3 times a week
  (c) clean up the town AND improve the appearance of the town
9 Sample answer:
At home we usually eat healthily / a healthy diet, but sometimes we cook / make chips. That is my brother's favourite meal. I try to do exercise regularly. I either play sport with friends or go swimming. Yesterday, I went swimming in the sea because I was stressed by schoolwork. There is a lot of pressure because of exams.

138. Paper 4: Writing (Higher)
1(a) Sample answer:
Meine Schule ist groß, und die Gebäude sind sehr historisch. Wir haben alte Klassenzimmer, wo es im Winter zu kalt ist. Die Lehrer*innen sind gut und meistens freundlich.
Mein Lieblingsfach ist Mathe, weil ich es einfach finde und immer gute Noten bekomme. Dieses Jahr mag ich Deutsch nicht, denn die Lehrerin ist sehr streng.